A SHOT
RANG OUT

BOOKS BY JON L. BREEN

Novels

Listen for the Click (UK title Vicar's Roses)
The Gathering Place
Triple Crown
Touch of the Past
Loose Lips
Hot Air
Eye of God
Probable Claus

Short Story Collections

Hair of the Sleuthhound
The Drowning Icecube and Other Stories
Kill the Umpire: The Calls of Ed Gorgon

Reference Works

What About Murder?
Novel Verdicts: A Guide to Courtroom Fiction
What About Murder? 1981-1991

Anthologies edited

Murder California Style (with John Ball for SoCal MWA)
American Murders (with Rita A. Breen)
Sleuths of the Century (with Ed Gorman)
Mystery: The Best of 2001
Mystery: The Best of 2002

Essay collections edited

Murder Off the Rack (with Martin H. Greenberg)
Synod of Sleuths (with Martin H. Greenberg)

A SHOT RANG OUT

Selected Mystery Criticism

by

Jon L. Breen

Surinam Turtle Press

ISBN 13: 978-1-60543-168-0

ISBN 10: 1-60543-168-0

Cover Art: Gavin L. O'Keefe
Preparation: Jon L. Breen and Fender Tucker

Surinam Turtle Press #10

For Ed Gorman

Table of Contents

INTRODUCTION

This is a book of opinions from nearly forty years as a writer and reviewer of mystery and detective fiction. Beginning as a contributor to the early mystery fanzines, Allen J. Hubin's *The Armchair Detective* and Lianne Carlin's *Mystery Reader's Newsletter*, continuing with *Library Journal* in the unlikely role of true-crime specialist, in the early 1970s, I became a review columnist for *Wilson Library Bulletin* and in late 1976 was asked by Frederic Dannay (the editing half of the EQ team) to take over the "Jury Box" column in *Ellery Queen's Mystery Magazine* for the ailing John Dickson Carr. My first column appeared in the January 1977 issue.

In the early 1980s, my novel writing career was beginning to take off, and two reference books for Scarecrow Press were taking up quite a bit of my reading time. *What About Murder: A Guide to Books About Mystery and Detective Fiction* (1981) and *Novel Verdicts: A Guide to Courtroom Fiction* (1984) both won Edgar awards in the biographical/critical category and subsequently would be followed by (respectively) a book-length supplement and a second edition. I took a hiatus from the deadlines of regular reviewing, relinquishing the columns in *WLB* and *EQMM* to two excellent replacements, Kathleen L. Maio and Allen J. Hubin respectively. Even in the mid-'80s, I continued to do some reviewing, for a rather unlikely market: *Los Angeles Federal Savings Quarterly*. Later in the decade, when Al Hubin made the decision to move on, I returned to "The Jury Box," which I have occupied ever since.

In the first decade of the 21st Century, I began to contribute occasional essays and reviews to *The Weekly Standard*, a Washington-based opinion journal. (I don't share their neoconservative world view, so it's a good thing I wasn't asked to write about politics.) I've also done occasional reviews and essays, plus a column of additions to "What About Murder?" for *Mystery Scene*.

Generally, I can choose what I write about, and I select those books I expect to enjoy. But I don't share the view of some mystery critics who only write about what they can praise. If I commit to reading a book, I will write about it, and to be taken seriously, a reviewer can't find everything in the garden lovely. Even in writing a short review, I try to say something interesting about the book, and usually I highlight some good points even if my overall assessment is unfavorable. I'm doing my job as much for the reader who thinks, "He didn't like it that much, but I probably will," as for the one who shares my tastes.

While a lot of my interest is focused on the early history and Golden Age period of detective fiction, the present volume (as suggested by editor Richard A. Lupoff) was conceived as a consideration of the genre post-Anthony Boucher, the greatest mystery reviewer of the 20th Century. Thus, I have confined myself mostly to writers who have been active in the decades since 1970, around the time I started reviewing and shortly after Boucher's death in 1968. A few articles include historical topics, but arguably all have some relevance to more recent times. Several of the writers considered did most of their work in Boucher's time but remained active after his death. I have deliberately not included much about writers of legal thrillers and courtroom fiction, since they are extensively covered in the two editions of *Novel Verdicts*.

This collection is divided into four sections.

First, fifteen essays about single authors. They are not advanced as the most important crime fiction writers of the period (though some of them certainly are) but are simply ones I've been asked to write about at length. All are previously published (date and source noted at the beginning) and were written with different purposes, sometimes as a pure career assessment, other times a review of a biography, and often as a review of a current book that spins off into an overview. While I have not revised these, I have added a note at the end of some of them, either bringing them up to date or explaining how my opinion may have changed or developed since the piece was written.

Second, shorter assessments of a hundred writers, usually quoting from my published reviews in "The Jury Box" or elsewhere. They were chosen because I had something to say about them, not necessarily because they are the most important or even the ones I like the most.

Third, topical articles that discuss history, trends, subgenres, writing advice, and personal hobby horses, again including some afterthoughts and updating.

Fourth, a pair of recent pieces harking back to my early days as a true-crime reviewer, both concerning real-life mysteries that fiction writers find especially fascinating.

In the few cases that the essays diverge from the published versions, they revert to my original copy. I have arranged both the fifteen longer author pieces and the section of one hundred shorter summaries alphabetically, and I have listed authors considered at any length in the topical essays after the essay's title in the table of contents. Since this is a critical guide rather than a bibliographic reference, there is no biographical information on the authors discussed, apart from some of the single-author pieces. Also I have not attempted to list publishers and publication dates of all the books reviewed, this information being easily available elsewhere. However, all the essays reprinted and columns quoted are dated, and dates are given for books discussed whose publication antedated the appearance of the review.

In both my fiction and my critical writing, I have had the (apparently) unusual experience of consistently good luck with editors. At the risk of leaving someone out, I must acknowledge those who encouraged, facilitated, and often improved my work: Arthur Plotnik at *Wilson Library Bulletin*; Gary Kuris at Scarecrow Press and *WLB*; Frederic Dannay, Eleanor Sullivan, and Janet Hutchings at *EQMM*; Alex N. Campbell, Jr., at *Los Angeles Federal Savings Quarterly*; Ed Gorman and Kate Stine at *Mystery Scene*; Joseph Bottum and Philip Terzian at *The Weekly Standard*; Martin H. Greenberg and John Helfers at Tekno-Books; and of course the founders of the present feast, Richard A. Lupoff of Surinam Turtle Press and Fender Tucker of its parent company Ramble House. Finally, I salute my wife of 38 years and in-house editor Rita Breen, who read most of this stuff before it left the house and saved me from silliness, self-indulgence, lack of clarity, and lax proofreading.

Jon Breen
August 2008

SECTION ONE

AUTHOR STUDIES

MICHAEL CONNELLY

Mystery Scene, issue #75, 2002

Some novelists stake out an immediate claim on the bestseller lists but are routinely panned or ignored by critics. Others are lauded for the quality of their work but sell barely enough copies to keep getting published. A lucky few have it both ways, connecting with readers and critics alike. The prime crime-writing overachiever to emerge in the 1990s was Michael Connelly, a self-effacing journalist-turned-novelist who seemingly planned his career as carefully as he plans one of his thrillers.

Born in Philadelphia and educated in Florida, Connelly became a police reporter to gather knowledge for his fiction and moved to Southern California (and a job with the Los Angeles *Times*) to soak up the milieu that inspired Raymond Chandler. In 1993, the same year he shared a Pulitzer Prize with other *Times* staffers, he won an Edgar award for his first novel, *The Black Echo* (1992), and became a full-time novelist.

Though no innovator, Connelly masterfully exploits established patterns, approaches, and devices. *The Black Echo*, for example, rings fresh changes on the old tunnel robbery ploy (which goes back to Doyle's "The Red-Headed League" and beyond) and a time-honored whodunit surprise associated with one of the classics of detective fiction—to say which one would give too much away. *The Black Ice* (1993) gives an old chestnut from the days of R. Austin Freeman's Dr. Thorndyke fresh life through the use of an exceedingly clever dental clue.

Connelly is the perfect crime writer for 2002, so good a fit with current fashions that it is easy to overlook his embodiment of longer standing and more central genre traditions. First, the ingredients that find favor in the contemporary market:

A Macho-Sensitive Loner Hero. Maverick L.A. cop Harry (short for Hieronymus) Bosch, protagonist of eight of Connelly's eleven novels to date, is a good guy and a dedicated policeman but projects an aura of barely contained violence. He is a Vietnam veteran, whose background as a "tunnel rat" helps him to the solution in *The Black Echo*. When first met, he has been demoted from the prestigious Robbery-Homicide division to Hollywood homicide after shooting to death a suspected serial killer who was reaching under a pillow not for a gun but for his toupee. Bosch's loner tendencies, facilitated by having a partner who moonlights in real estate, let Connelly draw on both private eye and police procedural conventions. In the tradition of James Lee Burke's Dave Robichaux and Robert B. Parker's Spenser, Bosch's combination of toughness and vulnerability make him attractive to both male and female readers.

Lots of Pages. Though the under-200-page length common twenty or more years ago remains ideal for most mystery plots, the current market demands longer books. This goal can be achieved by greater complexity, increased detail and depth of characterization, or (all too often) pure padding. In Connelly's books, generally just under 400 pages, no detail or action goes undescribed, but there is seldom a sense of padding. A recent inquirer to Connelly's website would like his books stretched to Tom Clancy-like length, but Connelly declines for the right reasons.

A Dash of Soap Opera. While you can read the cases of Sherlock Holmes, Nero Wolfe, or Hercule Poirot in any order, the current market likes story lines that run from book to book. While their intellectual but unemotional investment in their cases usually allowed the above mentioned characters to emerge unscathed and unchanged, today's central character is expected to develop from book to book and to experience great personal anguish in each entry. In one of several ways he departed from his model Chandler (whose Philip Marlowe was usually more observer than involved character), Connelly piles the miseries on Bosch and gives him an extensive back story. In an example of Connelly's painstaking planning, the first novel refers to past events that will be explored in detail later: the Dollmaker serial killer in *The Concrete Blonde* (1994) and the murder of Bosch's mother in *The Last Coyote* (1995).

A Pinch of Situation Comedy. One way to fill those obligatory extra pages is to introduce a large cast of continuing characters. Less skilled writers will drag these secondary figures in for no good reason other than to fulfill the regular reader's expectations, but Connelly's usually have some necessary function in the story. They can also be unpredictable: Deputy Chief Irvin Irving of Internal Affairs, early in the series a Ming the Merciless comic antagonist with evil minions named Lewis and Clarke, later becomes a Bosch ally.

A Sense of Authenticity. Crime fiction has always sought at least an illusion of reality, but today's readers expect ever more copious, accurate, and often unpleasant detail of how things are done in real life. The demand for heightened realism is best satisfied by the police procedural category, which removes one layer of unreality: the cops are involved with the crime by professional necessity, not happenstance. Realism, though, is a tricky thing. A good detective novel has a strong, intriguing, and essentially artificial plot that would never unfold so neatly in real life. In a classical detective novel (by Agatha Christie, Dorothy L. Sayers, or John Dickson Carr) or a traditional private-eye novel (by Chandler, Dashiell Hammett, or Ross Macdonald), no one cares that the plot is unlikely as long as the characters act in a credible manner. In a procedural, with its extra fillip of reality, the puzzle can be so surrounded by the trappings of real life that the artificial situation becomes believable. Connelly, surely one of the most tireless researchers in crime fiction, introduces some police, legal, and forensic details, such as the medfly in a victim's stomach in *The Black Ice* or *The Black Echo*'s account of a suicide who changed his pants after shooting himself to avoid his body being found soiled, that sound too bizarre and outlandish not be true. Cop jokes, such as calling senior-citizen volunteers in police stations the "Nod Squad," also ring true.

Cynicism about Authority. As surely as Joe Friday, played by Jack Webb in the old radio/TV series *Dragnet*, Harry Bosch is a heroic policeman, just the kind of man we would want to have protecting us. Unlike Friday, a perfect cop surrounded by other perfect cops, Bosch lives in a world where all cops are not good guys and anyone might be bent. He must struggle not only against crime and corruption but also against petty departmental bureaucracy.

An Appeal to the Highbrows. Connelly invites serious literary consideration by his expressive style, his thematic concerns, and his love of symbols, beginning with Bosch's own name, chosen by his prostitute mother because the nightmare landscapes of the 16th-century Dutch painter reminded her of contemporary L.A. The lone coyote Bosch watches from his precarious hillside home in the early books symbolizes his own status as an endangered species in the police department. Birds are symbols in *Void Moon* (2000) (the hummingbirds who die in Leo Renfro's pool) and *A Darkness More Than Night* (2001) (the owls in artist Bosch's paintings). In an extreme example of Connelly's Dickensian way with character names, the FBI agent who becomes Bosch's investigative and romantic partner in *The Black Echo* is named Eleanor Wish. When Eleanor, now a professional gambler and clearly bad

news, comes back into his life in *Trunk Music* (1997), Bosch re-
sumes their affair and even marries her. That decision epitomizes a
self-destructive determination to live (sometimes literally) on the
edge: when Bosch's stilt house overlooking a canyon is con-
demned after an earthquake, he continues to live in it surrepti-
tiously and, after it is demolished, insists on rebuilding in the same
dangerous spot.

A Vivid Locale. Connelly's use of his L.A. background, well-
trod as it has been by Chandler and other writers, is wonderful.
Los Angeles landmarks are used in creative ways: the funicular of
the title as a murder scene in *Angels Flight* (1999); Mulholland
Drive, overlooking the Hollywood Bowl and Dodger Stadium, in
Trunk Music. Connelly also does a fine job with Las Vegas, particularly enjoying the contrast between its attempt to be a family
destination and its unsavory roots in organized crime, in *The Poet*
(1996) and *Void Moon.*

These elements spell success, but the attribute that most en-
dears Connelly to mystery traditionalists is one less honored in the
current market. Along with the action set pieces and patches of
psychological angst, Connelly is a stealth classicist, valuing clues
and misdirection in his best works like a reincarnated practitioner
from the Golden Age of Detection, generally dated between World
Wars. It's arguable that Connelly, with his ornate plots, verbal
clues, and delivery of a final twist after the mystery appears to be
resolved, has more in common with Ellery Queen than Raymond
Chandler.

In three of his novels, Connelly leaves the Bosch saga to feature other characters. Two of these are among the strongest demonstrations of his classical tendencies, while the third is his most
uncharacteristic novel to date.

The Poet switches from third person to first and introduces
Denver journalist Jack McEvoy, who doesn't believe his cop twin
brother Sean, haunted by a Black Dahliaesque murder, could have
committed suicide. McEvoy has much in common with Bosch:
he's a loner, an assertive smoker, driven, obsessive, and haunted
by a family tragedy; though otherwise literate, he is given to saying "me and so-and-so" in the nominative case. With passages
from Poe as his calling card, the serial killer called the Poet seems
to belong more to 1930s novels by Queen, Christie, S.S. Van Dine,
or Philip MacDonald than the sort usually met in contemporary
crime fiction. The clues to the Poet's identity are so broad that
only the extreme unlikelihood of the solution, along with the sus-

picion that Connelly may be repeating a surprise from an earlier book, makes the reader put them aside.

Blood Work (1998), another elaborate and scrupulously clued puzzle, introduces ex-FBI agent Terry McCaleb, recipient of a heart transplant who is asked to investigate the murder of his donor, a seemingly mundane crime that turns out to be part of a grand pattern.

Void Moon is a departure in a couple of respects: a crook procedural instead of a cop procedural, it features a woman as focal character, parolee and dissatisfied Porsche salesperson Cassie Black. Leo Renfro, a superstitious crook who believes in *feng shui* and astrology along with less systematic forms of superstition, sets up a job for her in Las Vegas, at the Cleopatra Casino that previously spelled disaster. The title refers to astrological bad news that takes place when the moon is moving between planets. There is some surprise in the conclusion but more pure suspense and less puzzle than earlier Connelly works.

A Darkness More Than Night involves Bosch and McCaleb as virtually co-equal central characters. (Jack McEvoy also returns but in a secondary role.) This is the Connelly novel most concerned with art, a frequent reference point in all of his work. It also deals most directly with the paintings of Hieronymus Bosch. While Harry Bosch is serving as lead investigator at the prosecution table in the trial of a film director accused of murdering an actress, the ostensibly retired McCaleb looks at a crime-scene tape as a favor to a friend and winds up suspecting Bosch of serial murder. The novel points up the differing attitudes toward violence of the two characters as well as the difficulties of a law enforcement professional remaining neutral and in control.

The latest Connelly novel, *City of Bones* (Little, Brown), concerns the discovery in a remote part of the Hollywood Hills of the bones of a much-abused child. Harry Bosch takes on tracing the possible suspects in the twenty-year-old murder. The usual Connelly hallmarks are here: symbolism (hit rather hard) of the bones representing a city's buried secrets; Los Angeles landmarks like the LaBrea Tar Pits and the unfinished Venice canals; illustrations of how departmental politics can affect an investigation; and a whodunit puzzle, less abundantly clued than usual, that will keep readers guessing to the end. Bosch's often invisible partner, Jerry Edgar, a divorced father viscerally affected by the finding of the bones, makes his most extended appearance in the series. Though initially Bosch seems a more laid-back figure than in previous books, he goes through the requisite emotional trauma and leaves the reader in doubt about his future.

If you have to pick one or two books to represent Connelly, the best may be *The Concrete Blonde* (some first-rate courtroom action along with one of his strongest plots) and *Angels Flight* (one of the great L.A. mysteries). The weakest (though still better than most of the competition) are *The Last Coyote* (over-complicated with an excess of falling action at the end) and *Trunk Music* (the return of Eleanor Wish is very hard to take and probably should have been resisted). But this is my advice to the discerning crime fiction reader: read all of Connelly and read him in order. You might even read him in one sustained gulp. Few writers can stand up to that, but for this article I devoured eight Connellys in a row without feeling stuffed.

Postscript 2008: Connelly has continued to turn out very good books in the years since this piece appeared, the best of them probably The Lincoln Lawyer, *about L.A. defender Mickey Haller. I wrote in a* Weekly Standard *review (December 12, 2005): "Back in the day of Perry Mason, fictional trials usually focused on saving the unjustly accused. In recent years, in part because dubious verdicts in high-profile cases have remolded public attitudes, the opposite situation has been increasingly common: the criminal is known, and the problem is how to make the case. But how can you have a get-the-scumbag trial novel when your hero is the defense lawyer? Constantly intriguing and surprising the reader, Connelly answers the question in brilliant fashion."*

LOREN D. ESTLEMAN

(review of *Nicotine Kiss*, Forge, 2006; *Little Black Dress*, Forge, 2005; *The Undertaker's Wife*, Forge, 2005)

The Weekly Standard, July 3, 10, 2006

Loren D. Estleman wrote most of his first novel in longhand during sessions of an Elizabethan poetry class at Eastern Michigan University. Some of that poetry must have sunk in subliminally, because he has become one of the great stylists in contemporary fiction, one of the few popular writers—Raymond Chandler was another—worth reading strictly for the beauty of their prose, their loving manipulation of language. The closest present-day comparison working similar ground may be Robert B. Parker, but Estleman is far superior in ambition and achievement. At least three barriers serve to deny (or delay) the serious literary reputation Estleman deserves: he is prolific; he is versatile; and he writes in popular genres.

That first book, *The Oklahoma Punk* (1976, reprinted as *Red Highway*), an unoriginal case study of a Prohibition-era bank robber, offers a first glimpse of preoccupations that would mark the 23-year-old author's future work: historical detail, western background, shifting in time (from 1933 to 1922 and back), and frequent film allusions. The name of the very first character introduced, special agent William Farnum, resonates with old movie buffs. Throughout his career, Estleman, who acknowledges the influences on his first novel of Elmore Leonard, Edward Anderson, and W.R. Burnett, has paid direct or indirect homage to the authors who have gone before, while probing the edges of the fiction, film, and legend they have created.

Estleman the literary chameleon can adopt whatever style suits his subject matter. While it's questionable that rewriting two Victorian horror classics as Sherlock Holmes novels was a project worth doing, *Sherlock Holmes Versus Dracula; or, The Adventure of the Sanguinary Count* (1978) and *Dr. Jekyll and Mr. Holmes* (1979) capture the Conan Doyle/Dr. Watson prose style as perfectly as any of the hordes of pastiche writers.

Most of Estleman's output of more than fifty novels can be grouped into four categories: the cases of private investigator Amos Walker, the saga of hired killer Peter Macklin, a series on the 20th-Century history of Detroit, and Westerns. Three of these product lines are represented in new books appearing within the last twelve months.

Walker, who first appeared in *Motor City Blue* (1980), is an old-fashioned loner private eye in a rapidly changing world. The first-person narrative approximates the style and voice of Chandler's Philip Marlowe as successfully as any of that simile master's imitators, while observing Detroit as acutely as Chandler captured Los Angeles. The sense of chronological displacement is stronger than ever in *Nicotine Kiss*. In a post-9/11 world of Homeland Security, e-Bay, and Harry Potter, Walker scatters allusions to Perry Como, Clifton Webb, radio quizzes, and movie cowboys. Defining his role, Walker seems to be channeling Carroll John Daly's pioneering 1920s private eye Race Williams, who described himself as a halfway house between the cops and the crooks: "Chaos and order, black and white, the rock and the hard place. I'd built my business square between them. That makes me the only police force some people can turn to when they have a complaint. It's a definite niche."

In his latest case, Walker adheres to the private-eye code as surely as Dashiell Hammett's Sam Spade. Jeff Starzek, a smuggler of cigarettes and other contraband across the U.S./Canadian border, has gone missing. Though Walker neither knew him well nor liked him much, it was Starzek who delivered him to the hospital when he was shot outside a Michigan bar on the first day of deer season. Though hobbling around on a cane after a lengthy hospital stay, Walker takes the case, working out a satisfyingly twisty plot involving counterfeiting and murder.

The requisite mystery and hard action are present, but the quotable narrative and dialogue are the main attractions. Walker on babies: "I'd never paid them that much attention. They can't answer questions and don't hit very hard." On the continuing challenge to law enforcement: "The only sure way to stop a crime is to make it legal." On the Detroit winter: "…[T]he first snow of November is still there in April, covered by layers like lasagna, each dyed a different color by the soot and oxidized iron that has bled into it in varying amounts." A Homeland Security agent on an important distinction: "Islamics pray to Allah. Islamists only get on their knees to blow an arms dealer." A doctor who has just admonished Walker for straining his bad leg to the edge of amputation isn't surprised the shamus doesn't have insurance: "From what I've seen, you couldn't get a group rate with the bullfighters' union. What are you, a crash dummy for Smith and Wesson?" Walker replies, "Only on the side. The rest of the time I'm a detective." Doctor: "I thought detectives were stealthy." Walker: "I didn't say I was any good at it."

Little Black Dress features Peter Macklin, introduced as a killer for hire in *Kill Zone* (1984) and returned to four times since. From the beginning, Macklin has had domestic troubles, including an understandably alcoholic wife and a drug-taking son who wants to follow in his dad's hit-man footsteps. Now he has another wife, has given up assassination for hire, and is trying to escape the remnants of his bloody past, but you just know he won't bring it off. For me, the Macklin saga, a multi-volume soap opera in which crooks off each other (or try to) like the principals in a Roadrunner cartoon, is the least rewarding part of Estleman's oeuvre. Still, *Little Black Dress* has its benefits: a terrific final line and some pointed satire on a jerk bestselling author who, enamored of the big bookstore chains, grouses about his present book-signing venue: "I don't like independents. They all smell like old magazines and they treat me like an idiot because I'm not starving".

There is no new title in Estleman's multi-volume history of 20th-Century Detroit, but the books are worth seeking out. *Jitterbug* (1998) gives a vivid sense of the World War II home front, with the Ford plant converted to defense uses, a migration of southern blacks and poor whites creating racial tensions, and a throat-slitting serial killer disguised as a soldier (and in his own twisted mind a patriot) who takes his victims' ration books and leaves the trademark message KILROY WAS HERE. *Edsel* (1995), narrated by former newspaperman Connie Minor, now in advertising and assigned the top-secret job of promoting the titular car line, includes some great 1950s advertising history, including Winston's introduction of the filter-tip cigarette and the marketing success of Ivory Soap "because the careless way it was milled caused it to float in the bathtub." A Ford executive admits, "The first car we ever made was the best. It climbed mountains and crossed deserts on a teaspoonful of gas and any kid with a pair of pliers could fix anything that went wrong with it. It's all been downhill since the Model T. We just add lights and horns and whistles so people won't notice." Unlike his fellow writer of 20th-Century historicals Max Allan Collins, Estleman rarely includes a note separating fact from fiction, and *Edsel* could use one—I wondered how many of his Ford executives were real people.

The inevitable fading of the Western in contemporary culture—from film, TV, the bookshelves—may cause us to neglect
some our best American writing. Some of Estleman's Westerns
are fairly traditional. *Sudden Country* (1991), which transplants
Robert Louis Stevenson's *Treasure Island* to the Texas Panhandle,
includes the following classic shoot-'em-up dialogue: " 'Why did
you kill Peckler?'/'Son of a bitch cheated at cards.'/'You weren't
playing cards.'/'I recollected suddenlike.' "
      His more recent works in the genre, though they include gun-
fights and colorful historical personages, are far more unusual and
represent the pinnacle of his achievement as a novelist. Recognizing that many frontiersmen were better educated than today's college graduates, Estleman writes eloquent dialogue for his western-
ers, abjuring semi-literate cowboy dialect. He goes beyond the
ranchers, cattle rustlers, and lawmen to feature people in other
walks of life, while displaying a James M. Cain-like interest in
how things work in particular jobs and industries.
      The Rocky Mountain Moving Picture Association (1999) is a
tribute to the pre-World War I pioneers who fought the Edison
monopoly and invented movies as we know them. Its protagonist,
wannabe writer Dmitri Pulski, takes the name Tom Boston in tribute to Jack London and leaves the family ice business, though not
before it is delineated as vividly and knowledgably as the movie
business, circa 1913. *The Master Executioner* (2001) follows me-
ticulous, scientific hangman Oscar Stone from the Civil War to
1897, describing his work in rich and nonjudgmental detail. It's
remarkable that a novel on this subject should take no strong position for or against capital punishment.
      The similarly structured *The Undertaker's Wife* illuminates
19th-Century mortuary practices. We first meet the famous restorer
of corpses Richard Connable late in his career, near the turn of the
20th Century. Elihu Warrick, "the well-known Chicago speculator,
railroad investor, and meatpacking magnate," has committed suicide while en route from to New York on the Michigan Central.
Connable, though semi-retired at least in the mind of his wife
Lucy, is summoned from Buffalo to Cleveland to prepare the deceased for an open-casket funeral, while concealing the bullet
wound in Warrick's head lest the fact of his suicide cause a share-
holder's panic. The action flashes back to Civil War-era Monroe,
Michigan, where Lucy is first attracted to Richard because of his
remarkable job reconstructing the ravaged face of her twin brother,
a Union infantryman killed in an explosion. Their personal and

professional story continues in San Francisco and several other points along the way, including Hays City, Kansas, where the colorful sheriff, Wild Bill Hickok, sends Connable considerable business. With the violence mostly off-stage, the emphasis is on the characters. Neither a traditional Western nor a mystery nor even a crime story, *The Undertaker's Wife* is more than anything a study of marriage.

Estleman's *Writing the Popular Novel* (2004), which can be recommended for its insights and entertainment value even to those who never intend to write a word for publication, reveals much about his outlook and methods. Though a language purist who spends a whole chapter called "Gears and Pulleys" on English mechanics, he is enough of a maverick to defend the use of *contact* as a verb on the reasonable ground that no single word does the same job. In excerpts from a journal he kept while writing *Bloody Season* (1988), a novel of the OK Corral gunfight closely based on the historical record, he describes the process of making a credible fictional character from an extremely contradictory historical personage, Wyatt Earp. How could the same man have both Earp's positive attributes (solid friendships, devotion to duty, fidelity to second wife) and his negative ones (desertion of first wife, arrests for horse thievery and a confidence game)? At first believing Earp was essentially a gambler, Estleman finally decided the key that explained the complex Earp was something he constantly reiterated to interviewers: he was a businessman.

For all the admiring reviews and steady sales his books have received, a great popular writer may be passing under the radar. When it was suggested his writing manual should have "a subtitle promising lessons on how to write a best-selling novel," Estleman had to point out a hitch: "I explained that since I'd never written a best-selling novel, I wouldn't know where to begin. This confession surprised some editors, who assumed that because my name had been around since man learned to walk upright, I must have cracked the venerated *New York Times* list many times. My sales have always been respectable, although not spectacular...." Given that Estleman is as outstanding and as accessible a writer as any regular inhabitant of the lists, indeed vastly better than most, one can only wonder why everyone isn't reading him.

JACK FINNEY

They're Here...Invasion of the Body Snatchers: A Tribute,
edited by Kevin McCarthy and Ed Gorman (Berkley, 1999)

Milwaukee-born Walter Braden Finney (1911-1995), professionally known as Jack, was one of the best and most successful writers of popular fiction in the second half of the twentieth century. That may sound like hyperbole—certainly many writers have written more bestsellers and made their names more familiar to the public—but it's an easy statement to defend.

Consider this: each of Finney's four novels of the fifties was serialized in a high-paying slick magazine; each of them was bought for motion picture adaptation; each of them was actually filmed successfully; and at least one of the films is considered a classic of its genre. His fifth novel, written with a particular star in mind, was adapted to film with that star in place. A later novel, though never filmed at least partly because of the expense that would be required to do it justice, has become a beloved modern classic.

Does this record of success mean Finney had a rare affinity with the popular taste of his times? Yes. Does it mean he wrote his books with one eye on the possibility of a screen adaptation? Yes, he readily admitted it. Does it mean he was a hack who pandered to his audience, adjusting his viewpoint to coincide with theirs? No. Does it mean he hit on a workable formula and repeated it from book to book? Anything but. Does it mean he wrote screen treatments and published them disguised as novels? Decidedly not. Few writers could have it both ways, attaining outstanding commercial success while being true to a consistent artistic vision, as completely as Jack Finney.

Finney might be likened to Earl Derr Biggers, a popular writer of earlier in the century who also had a sensibility uncannily attuned to what the public wanted and the ability to deliver it in a natural, uncontrived way. Unlike Biggers, who is best remembered for his creation of detective Charlie Chan, Finney almost never returned to the same cast of characters. He did, however, have a recurring theme that turned up even in the most unexpected corners of his work: that American life is gradually, sometimes subtly, sometimes dramatically, changing for the worse; that only a few years ago, times were simpler but richer; people were more innocent, more optimistic, more joyful; lives had more purpose and were more fully lived; things were just, well, better all around, not just when *we* were younger but when the country and the world were younger. Finney's protagonists are afflicted with a sweet but painful nostalgia, a longing for a time or a place or a mood other than their own. (Continuing for a moment the comparison with Biggers, consider the nostalgic view conveyed in *The House Without a Key* of Honolulu, now [in 1925] ruined by tourism and commercialism but a paradise in the relatively recent 1880s.)

While Finney's two most famous works are undoubtedly *The Body Snatchers* (1955), thanks to the two successful film versions, and *Time and Again* (1970), for the richness of his time-travel plot, he produced in his half-century career a wide variety of crime, fantasy, mainstream, and science fiction in which he often returned to his familiar theme of wistful nostalgia but, in subject matter and approach, almost never repeated himself.

Finney's first published story, "The Widow's Walk," appeared in *Ellery Queen's Mystery Magazine* for July 1947. According to the introduction by editor Queen (Frederic Dannay), "Mr. Finney is thirty-five years old, married, has no children, and lives in Manhattan. At present he is a copywriter in the advertising agency of Dancer-Fitzgerald-Sample—he has been writing advertising copy for the past twelve years. The *EQMM* Annual Contest spurred him to writing fiction, almost the only writing he has done outside of his work since he finished college in 1934....[N]ow he is tilting his typewriter at the windmill of radio. His first attempt at radio ratiocination is, in his own words, 'quite a bloody script—two killings in less than fifteen minutes' (which is certainly par for the course)." I'm not sure how much radio writing Finney actually did—probably not very much, since it didn't take him long to establish himself in the far more lucrative slick magazine market.

In a concluding note, EQ credits "The Widow's Walk," a domestic crime short story of the type later dramatized on Alfred Hitchcock's TV program, with "two of the most important elements in a detective story": a clue and fair play to the reader. The story is the first-person account of a young woman named Annie contemplating the murder of her invalid mother-in-law. Its wickedly clever surprise twist makes it a classic of the type, and editor Queen's claim of fair play is borne out.

Finney appeared only twice more in *EQMM*. In introducing a November 1951 reprint of the 1948 *Collier's* story "It Wouldn't

Be Fair," EQ describes the story as a parody of classical detective fiction. Again the main character is named Annie, but quite a different Annie. The mystery-obsessed girlfriend of New York cop Charley, she "often solves cases a full forty-eight pages before Perry Mason" and her disdain for the intelligence of real-life police puts a crimp in their romance. While showing its author a knowledgeable devotee of the kind of pure detective fiction he seldom ventured to write, the story also demonstrates the qualities Queen's introduction claims for Finney's fiction: "Jack Finney has developed a slick, sophisticated, streamlined style; his dialogue is bright; his situations are genuinely amusing; his characters combine warmth and gaiety—and who can resist those qualities these cold and gloomy days?"

Finney's continuing theme of longing for a world outside one's present reality is manifest in both stories: the first Annie's for her happy pre-mother-in-law married life, the second Annie's for the comforting (and *fair*) world of classical detective fiction. For one Annie, a reasonable compromise solution presents itself; for the other, there is only despair.

Finney's third and last *EQMM* appearance is "The Other Arrow," a January 1956 reprint of a 1952 story written with F.M. Barratt and originally published in *Collier's* as "Diagnosis Completed." Described as a medical mystery in the Dr. Thorndyke/Dr. Coffee mode, it also includes a Queenian dying message from the murder victim, a pharmacist's diabetic wife. The relationship of retiring Dr. Lerner and his young replacement Dr. Knapp is in the great tradition of medical fiction and drama. Dr. Lerner's old-fashioned view of general medical practice, complete with house calls, even more remote now than at the time the story was first published, carries the theme of longing for a better time.

The fact that *EQMM* never published a second Finney original is accounted for by his remarkable record of success selling to the major American slick magazines. Between 1947 and 1962, he contributed (by my quick count) 53 short stories and three serialized novels to those slicks indexed in *Reader's Guide to Periodical Literature*. Initially *Collier's* was his major market; after that publication's mid-fifties demise, he became a regular first in *Good Housekeeping* and finally in *McCall's*, with scattered contributions to *Ladies' Home Journal*, *Cosmopolitan*, and *Saturday Evening Post*. At least one of his later stories, "Hey, Look at Me!", would appear in *Playboy*, equally well-paying but not indexed by the conservative *Reader's Guide*. While his *genre* stories—crime, fantasy, and science fiction—often had a later life, his unreprinted works of general fiction—with tantalizing titles like "Breakfast in Bed" (*Collier's* 5-15-48), "My Cigarette Loves Your Cigarette" (*Collier's*, 9-30-50), and "Husband at Home" (*LHJ* 4-51)— illustrate the impermanence of most magazine fiction.

In Finney's most famous short stories, the s.f. and fantasy tales collected in *The Third Level* (Rinehart, 1957) and *I Love Galesburg in the Springtime* (Simon and Schuster, 1963), the nostalgia for a past better and happier than the present is usually conveyed through time travel situations that foreshadow his definitive treatment of that device in *Time and Again*. In the first volume's title story, the 1950s narrator happens upon a third level of Grand Central Station where the year is 1894—unable to buy a ticket to idyllic Galesburg, Illinois, with his odd-looking new-style money, he returns to the present and ends the story searching for the third level and failing to find it. The final twist is a tribute to Finney's storytelling savvy and a note especially appropriate to the fifties. (How ironic that the period Finney's heroes so often want to escape from is the one that many of today's nostalgics would like to go back to!)

Finney continues his romanticization of Galesburg, where he had attended Knox College, at greater length in the title tale of the second volume of short stories. Beginning with a businessman telling the reporter narrator about his decision *not* to build a factory in Galesburg following his encounter with a ghost streetcar, the story concerns the efforts of the past city to resist encroachments of the present.

Brilliant as he is in the short story form, Finney may be even better as a novelist. As Marcia Muller writes in *1001 Midnights* (Arbor, 1986), Finney "has the unusual ability to create edge-of-the-chair tension and sustain it throughout a long narrative." This knack is well demonstrated in his first novel, *Five Against the House*, serialized in *Good Housekeeping* in 1953, and published in book form by Doubleday the following year.

Nineteen-year-old narrator Al Mercer, like his creator at an earlier time, is a small-college student in Illinois. Beginning on one boring rainy day, he joins three at-loose-ends fraternity brothers to plot a crime. At first, it is to be a Brinks truck robbery, but after an embarrassing encounter with the police while following such a truck, they decide instead to return to Reno, where they had all worked the previous summer, to knock over Harold's Club.

They are helped in their planning by Al's waitress girlfriend Tina Greyleg.

Five Against the House is a big caper novel, but it's an amateur caper, generally more interesting (to this reader at least) than a professional one. Most of the conspirators, especially Al and Tina, are presented sympathetically. Al offers Tina this rather strained rationalization for the robbery:

'I think gambling is wrong. People have learned that everywhere, and gambling's been outlawed nearly everywhere in all civilizations. Now, just because a handful of men in the state of Nevada make it technically legal, doesn't make it right. Hell, gambling's *wrong* and you know it. A few people profit, giving nothing and doing nothing in exchange. And I think everyone concerned is harmed by it....

'So I say they're fair prey....I feel I'm honest, and wouldn't steal. But to me this isn't stealing; by any standard I respect, that money doesn't belong to Harold's Club, and I'll take it if I can, and it will never bother my conscience for a moment.'

Finney's technique, repeated in later caper novels, is to hint at the group's method but withhold details until the crime itself is carried out. The author's nostalgic bent is displayed in an imprecation to value the ordinary, as when the Reno conspirators are crossing the country imprisoned in a trailer and value their rare nighttime forays outside, as well as the turns at the wheel that permit them to see ordinary things with fresh eyes.

While a big caper novel about knocking over a gambling casino sounds like pure fiction noir, Finney's slick-paper style somewhat lightens the mood. As in most of his later books, the view of sexuality is very restrained by contemporary standards, reflecting (in common with most of his happy endings) a fifties movie sensibility. But one of the darkest moments in Finney's work comes when a policeman offers the boys a harrowing description of the future he sees for them in prison.

Finney's second novel, *The Body Snatchers*, was serialized in *Collier's* (November 26 through December 24, 1954) and published in expanded form as a Dell paperback original in 1955. In many ways, the novel is closely followed in Don Siegel's 1956 film *Invasion of the Body Snatchers*. In fact, quite a bit of Finney's dialogue was transferred directly into Daniel Mainwaring's script, and of course the central situation is unchanged. But in some very important ways the two versions differ. Both are classics, but not necessarily for the same reasons.

The Body Snatchers includes the familiar Finney paean to small-town America and old-fashioned doctoring, the latter in the person of Santa Mira general practitioner Miles Bennell, a character even more given to kidding and wisecracks on the page than as played on the screen by Kevin McCarthy. Miles is asked by old girlfriend, now fellow divorcee, Becky Driscoll to look into her cousin Wilma's claims that her beloved Uncle Ira is not really her uncle, though no change in his manner, appearance, or memory is apparent. Miles finds similar cases are epidemic in the little town. Gradually the truth is revealed: extraterrestrials have come to earth in the form of giant seedpods and taken over the bodies of the townspeople, turning them into emotionless automatons whose mimicking of human memory, appearance, and mannerisms is not quite good enough to fool sensitive friends and relatives.

While the film is rightly credited with reflecting the anti-Communist paranoia of the fifties, the novel's mood is different. It is more a cerebral science-fictional mystery, the greater space afforded by print allowing for speculation and theorizing about the problem at hand that the film has no time for. When a partially-formed pod creature is found in the basement of Miles's writer friend Jack Belicec, there is more consideration and discussion of what the phenomenon means and what to do about it. When psychiatrist Mannie Kaufman (Dan in the film) presents his theory of mass hysteria, he offers several historical cases to support his claim.

Some of the most striking scenes in the book are not in the film at all. When Miles and Becky are trapped in his office, with pods waiting to replicate them when they fall asleep, he concocts an ingenious way to misdirect the pods through the use of his two office skeletons. A particularly chilling scene finds Miles and Becky visiting the public library to research newspaper references to the giant seed pods, only to find that the beloved town librarian Miss Wyandotte is among those who have been snatched. One astonishing passage offers a harsh snapshot of American race relations, as Miles compares the changes in the snatched townspeople to an unexpected view of a black shoeshine man's bitter reality.

Introducing the 1976 Gregg Press reprint of *The Body Snatchers*, Richard Gid Powers describes Miles Bennell and other Finney heroes as "inner-directed individuals in an increasingly other-directed world...[whose] adventures could be used as classroom illustrations of Tocqueville's theory about the plight of the free individual in mass democracy." He goes on to sum up the achievement of Finney's novel as "a raw and direct mass-market version of the despair over cultural dehumanization that fills T. S. Eliot's 'Wasteland' and William Faulkner's *The Sound and the Fury.* Finney adroitly uses the classic science fiction situation of an invasion from outer space to symbolize the annihilation of the free personality in contemporary society."

Finney's third novel and second paperback original, *The House of Numbers* (Dell, 1957), was the expanded version of a magazine short story (*Cosmopolitan*, July 1956). The first-person narrator this time is 26-year-old Benjamin Harrison Jarvis, who finds himself in the surprising position of assisting his brother Arnie's escape from San Quentin. Thus, it's the second of the author's three big caper novels and like the other two is based on in-depth research into its background. As Marcia Muller writes in *1001 Midnights*, "Finney knows San Quentin, although his view of it is colored by his association with then-warden Harley O. Teets, a humanitarian administrator to whom the book is dedicated. (In fact, the dialogue of the fictional warden reads a lot like a public relations release.)"

The third of the big caper books, *Assault on a Queen* (Simon and Schuster, 1959), was serialized in the *Saturday Evening Post* (August 22 through September 26, 1959) as "U-19's Last Kill." It begins with a third-person prologue in which Frank Lauffnauer, formerly a German submarine crewman in World War I, rediscovers his old ship sunk off Fire Island. But most of the story is told by a typical Finney narrator, 26-year-old network publicist Hugh Brittain, whose pervasive dissatisfaction with his empty life leads him to quit his job and join some other Navy veterans in an elaborate crime: refurbishing the old submarine and using it to rob the Queen Mary. Once again, Finney's amateur criminals try to show they aren't really evil people by offering justification for an *almost* victimless crime. Vic DeRossier, the old Navy buddy who is trying to bring Hugh into the caper, likens the caper to knocking over a house party of the very rich:

'...[E]very last person there is either out-and-out wealthy, very well off, or making a slug of money. Every one of them, Hugh, or they wouldn't be there. Would you take a few hundred dollars from each of them, if you could? It'd be illegal, all right; a crime, and yet—every single one of them could easily afford it. It'd mean no more to them than losing fifty cents to you....To you, though, it would make all the difference in the world; you'd be closer to rich, to having the kind of life you want than you ever will be otherwise.'

As the conspirators, including of course one beautiful woman, take on the job of getting the submarine back in working order, Finney drives home his customary theme in a passage that may also explain the rarity of sports references in his nostalgic reveries: "There is an enormous loss we all of us suffer, growing up—we stop playing. The things adults call play very seldom are. With hardly an exception they're competitions, even hunting or fishing, even golf, all alone. Rarely ever again do we experience pure play, doing something for its own sake completely, utterly absorbed and lost in it, nothing else mattering."

The main character of *Good Neighbor Sam* (Simon and Schuster, 1963) was created with Jack Lemmon in mind. In case anyone missed the envisioned casting, the jacket copy unsubtly compares Finney's comic novel to *Some Like it Hot* and *The Apartment*. Sam Bissell is a 29-year-old copywriter for the San Francisco advertising firm of Burke & Hare. He is married to Minerva (Min), a 25-year-old brunette who, in the manner of Finney heroines, thinks she is too heavy but really isn't. Their sexy neighbor Janet needs a husband in order to inherit her grandfather's fortune. Since her divorce is pending, her lawyer argues she is still married under strict interpretation of the will, though the other legatees could argue she was not married according to the *spirit* of the will. When Janet's cousins come to visit, Jack (his wife ever understanding) is pressed into service as the neighbor's husband. Finney handles the farcical events to follow with a flawless comic touch and along the way presents some pointed satire on his former profession of advertising, having much fun with campaigns on behalf of Nesfresh eggs and a nostrum called "BELS for the belly." One slogan on behalf of a client's product is wisely rejected at the source: "SCIENTIFIC TESTS PROVE! THE ONLY CIGARETTE THAT PRODUCES BENIGN TUMORS!"

Good Neighbor Sam is pure comedy and the first Finney book that can't be easily pigeonholed in the crime, fantasy, or s.f. genres. However, a comic turn by an inept private eye and the con game aspect of the plot *almost* nudge it into the crime fiction category.

Finney continued in a farcical vein in *The Woodrow Wilson Dime* (Simon and Schuster, 1968), expanded from the short story "The Coin Collector," originally published in *Saturday Evening Post* (January 30, 1960) as "The Other Wife" and included in Finney's second collection, *I Love Galesburg in the Springtime*. The hero is another advertising copywriter, New Yorker Ben Bennell (note the surname), whose discovery of the titular coin allows him to cross over into a recognizable but somewhat altered parallel universe.

His next novel, the illustrated *Time and Again* (Simon and Schuster, 1970), is Finney's finest achievement. Narrator Simon Morley, an advertising illustrator, is recruited by a top-secret government project created to test Einstein's theory of time. The evocation of Einstein means the events of the novel, outrageous as they may seem, can arguably be classified as science fiction rather than pure fantasy. As project director Dr. Danziger, a Harvard theoretical physicist, explains it,

> '...[W]e're mistaken in our conception of what the past, present and future really are. We think the past is gone, the future hasn't yet happened, and that only the present exists. Because the present is all we can see....[W]e're like people in a boat without oars drifting along a winding river. Around us we see only the present. We can't see the past, back in the bends and curves behind us. But it's there....[A] man ought to be able to step out of that boat onto the shore. And walk back to one of the bends behind us.'

The means to achieve this turning backward in time consists of finding a place unaltered since the period you want to visit and surrounding yourself with objects and information from that time. Thus, Si Morley is set up in an apartment in the Dakota, an old New York apartment building on the edge of Central Park, where he steeps himself in New York of the 1880s, reading contemporary newspapers and magazines; using furniture and household appliances, growing whiskers and wearing clothes appropriate to the period; determinedly thinking himself into the targeted place and time. And eventually, he carries his camera and sketch pad into the wonderland of New York in 1882.

In this novel, Finney's rare ability to describe rooms and their contents, street scenes in all their detail achieves its ultimate application. Period photographs and drawings are reproduced to help the process, but the magic of the writing does most of the work. A passage describing a walk along Fifth Avenue captures the scene and the time-traveler's sense of wonder:

> The cross streets slipped by—Forty-ninth, Forty-eighth, Forty-seventh, Forty-sixth—all strange unfamiliar identical streets of uninterrupted row after row of high-stooped brownstones precisely like blocks still existing on the West Side. As we'd moved down toward the thick of the city, the street became more and more alive. There they were now, moving along the walks, crossing the street—the people. And I looked out at them, at first with awe, then with delight; at the bearded, cane-swinging men in tall shiny silk hats, fur caps like mine, high-crowned derbies like the man's across the aisle, and—younger men—in very shallow low-crowned derbies. Almost all of them wore ankle-length great coats or topcoats, half the men seemed to wear pince-nez glasses, and when the older men, the silk-hatted men, passed an acquaintance, each touched his hat brim in salute with the head of his cane. The women were wearing head scarfs or hats ribbon-tied under the chin; wearing short, tight-waisted cutaway winter coats, or capes or brooch-pinned shawls; some carried muffs and some wore gloves; all wore button shoes darting out from and disappearing under long skirts.
>
> There—well, there they *were*, the people of the stiff old woodcuts, only...these moved. The swaying coats and dresses there on the walks and crossing the streets before and behind us were of new-dyed cloth—maroon, bottle-green, blue, strong brown, unfaded blacks—and I saw the shimmer of light and shadow in the appearing and disappearing long folds. And the leather and rubber they walked in pressed into and marked the slush of the street crossings; and their breaths puffed out into the winter air, momentarily visible. And through the trembling, rattling glass panes of the bus we heard their living voices, and heard a girl laugh aloud. Looking out at their winter-flushed faces, I felt like shouting for joy. (ellipses are Finney's)

The inventive and eventful plot carries Si, along with his last-century girlfriend Julia, back to the present and back again to the past. In an afterword to the novel headed "A Footnote," Finney writes of one dramatic sequence,

Occasionally my efforts at accuracy became compulsive, as in my account of the World Building fire and events just preceding it, in which I became obsessed with getting times of day and exact details of changing weather during the fire, and names of tenants and even the room numbers...correct or close to it. I even tell myself that my fictional solution to the mystery of that forgotten fire's origins blends so well with the known facts that it might have been accepted as truth at the time. This kind of research becomes time-wasting foolishness, but fun.

And following some crediting of the illustrations, Finney concludes his footnote on a characteristic note: "The photographs and sketches represent the time pretty well, I think, even though they couldn't all be strictly of the eighteen-eighties. Before 1900 things didn't change so fast as now—one more reason why Si so wisely decided to stay back there."

Half of Finney's writing life remained after *Time and Again*, but he would be considerably less prolific. He would produce four more books at widening intervals in the quarter century remaining to him. All have their attractions, but they are inevitably somewhat anti-climactic after his masterpiece.

Marion's Wall (Simon and Schuster, 1973) returns to the young-married suburban ambiance of *Good Neighbor Sam*. Thirty-year-old narrator Nick Cheyney, an employee of Crown Zellerbach, and wife Jan are peeling wallpaper in their new apartment in an old San Francisco house when they unearth a 1926 message from a former tenant: silent film actress Marion Marsh, once the lover of Nick's father when he lived in the same building. A public TV viewing of Marion's silent film appearance causes the ghost of the actress, who died in a roaring-twenties car crash when her film career had only just begun, to materialize. She inhabits the body of Jan to attempt a movie comeback, and later Nick is himself possessed by the shade of Rudolph Valentino. The novel is a valentine (no pun intended) to silent movies and movie collectors—for Nick, a prime MacGuffin is the lost reels of Erich Von Stroheim's famous film *Greed*. The novel depicts an earlier era for film buffs, a pre-video period when viewing was often tied to one-shot TV showings and the only chance to own a film was to buy comparatively expensive eight-millimeter prints from a Blackhawk catalog. (When the novel was reprinted along with *The*

Woodrow Wilson Dime and *The Night People* in the 1987 omnibus *Three by Finney*, the action was misguidedly updated to 1985, making total nonsense of the chronology and the film collecting references.)

The Night People (Doubleday, 1977) also involves Northern California suburbanites. Lew Joliffe, an apartment-dwelling San Francisco lawyer, is a transplanted midwesterner nostalgic for snow. At night, he takes solitary walks and does odd things (like lying down in the lanes of a freeway or acting out pitching on a Little League mound) without the knowledge of his girlfriend, Jo Dunne. With Harry and Shirley Levy—he's another lawyer attracted to daredevil stunts and generally harmless pranks—Lew and Jo form the titular Night People, whose final stunt, involving scaling the super-structure of the Golden Gate bridge, is a lulu. For some reason, though, these characters, four slow-rising yuppies who need to get a life, are less endearing than the author's usual. It may be that Finney's decision (otherwise unprecedented in the novels) to write in the third person damaged the kind of tenuous reader identification needed to render his central characters likeable.

By this time, Finney was taking more and more time between books. His penultimate work, *Forgotten News: The Crime of the Century and Other Lost Stories* (Doubleday, 1983), is his only nonfiction book, a volume that had its roots in the research for *Time and Again*. Beginning with an appreciation of the woodcut illustrations in *Frank Leslie's Weekly*, Finney goes on to recount at length the 1857 murder case of dentist Harvey Burdell, culminating in the trial of Emma Cunningham for the crime, and slightly more briefly the sinking of the steamship *Central America* in the same year. As in most of his fiction, Finney employs first person, describing the way he did his research and his reactions to what he found in the 1857 files of the New York *Times* and *Leslie's*. The book is extensively illustrated in a style similar to *Time and Again*.

From Time to Time (Simon and Schuster, 1995) makes Simon Morley a series character, the only one in Finney's canon. Morley, who stayed in New York of the 1880s at the end of *Time and Again*, now visits 1912 in an effort to prevent World War I. The *Titanic* is also involved in the plot. In reviewing the novel in *EQMM* (September 1995), I remarked, "The sequel isn't quite up to the original—the contrivances that set the story in motion are somewhat strained, and the plot seems an excuse for the musings on time and social history—but Finney's unique touch disarms criticism. Like its predecessor, the novel makes an effective use of period photographs and drawings. The glimpse into the life of vaudeville performers, though only slightly related to the story, is especially memorable."

Why has Finney the writer been so much less well-known than the books and stories he wrote? For one thing, he was somewhat reclusive, rarely giving interviews and never (at least to my knowledge) appearing at fan conventions. While not quite a popular fiction equivalent of Thomas Pynchon or J.D. Salinger, he clearly believed the work should speak for itself. Secondly, he had a disdain for being pigeonholed in a genre. His attempt to reach a wider slick-magazine readership with adaptations of science fictional concepts developed over the years in the pulps and digests did not endear him to the s.f. community, who often disdain such efforts. And accomplished as he was in the crime fiction field, he effectively left it after *Assault on a Queen* to produce works that often drew on several popular genres—romance, fantasy, mystery, science fiction, comedy—at once. Such mixing of categories, now routine in the works of bestselling writers like Stephen King and Dean Koontz, was far less common in the sixties and seventies and certainly militated against brand-name identification.

One supposes all of this mattered little to Finney, who apparently made enough money to write what he wanted to and take as much time as he needed to do it. Any writer offered the chance to make a financial killing *and* write a couple of modern classics along the way would probably take it, even if (maybe, in Finney's case, *especially* if) relative personal anonymity was part of the package.

NICOLAS FREELING

The Weekly Standard November 17, 2003

The mystery writer Nicolas Freeling made a dreadful commercial decision—and a dubious artistic one—when he killed off his popular detective, Amsterdam police inspector Piet Van der Valk. But is that the complete explanation for why one of the most gifted and original writers of crime fiction has been so forgotten by critics? Even the obituaries after his death this summer at age seventy-six were the kind that finds it more surprising that the man had still been alive than that he had just died.

Freeling produced challenging and distinctive crime fiction for forty years. But after nods to his early mysteries starring Van der Valk—a Mystery Writers of America Edgar, a French *Grand prix de littérature policière*, and some recognition from the Crime Writers Association of Great Britain—the awards givers turned their backs. MWA's Grand Master and CWA's Diamond Dagger for lifetime achievement were denied him. Of several lists of the hundred greatest crime novels, only H.R.F. Keating's *Crime & Mystery: The 100 Best Books* (1987) found room for him—and that grudgingly. There is no Freeling companion, no book-length biography, and no critical study. A mystery bookseller told me sales of Freeling's books come about as frequently as leap years.

Few would have predicted such a fate in the 1960s. While working as a cook in an Amsterdam restaurant, the English-born Freeling was accused of stealing food and briefly jailed. Encountering the Dutch criminal justice system, he was interrogated by a detective who would become the model for Van der Valk. From his first appearance in *Love in Amsterdam* (1962) to his demise in *Auprés de ma Blonde* (1972), the Dutch policeman's cases eventually filled eleven books.

Freeling was contemptuous of typical mystery fiction, and his books often involve non-standard detective-story plotting. But they are not anti-detective stories: The problems the author sets, the detective solves. He wrote what is now called the "literary thriller"—although that has become a nearly meaningless term these days, since it became its own commercial category. Not surprisingly, given his earlier career, Freeling is among the most food-obsessed of mystery writers (although he stops short of including recipes, which Rex Stout did in the Nero Wolfe novel *Too*

Many Cooks). In his emphasis on setting the scene, attention to domestic detail, and favoring of verbal conflict and plot movement over explicit violence and physical action, Freeling has more in common with the cozy writers than most in the police-procedural school. His prose can be annoyingly eccentric at times, but more often evocative and eloquent.

Like the admitted model, Georges Simenon's Maigret, Freeling's Van der Valk takes an unconventional approach to police work, exhibits lone-wolf tendencies, is happily married, and is more interested in character than forensics. Van der Valk's blunt speaking style, along with a seeming contempt for Dutch Calvinist values of conformity, respectability, civility, and order, have hurt his police career, but he is valued for his ability to crack unusual cases, especially those that exploit his linguistic ability and understanding of various European cultures. The Dutch sleuth's cases, whydunits as much as whodunits, often explore his relationship with the criminal, played out in a series of encounters that resemble social chats more than cat and mouse.

For a big-city policeman, Van der Valk is well traveled: Belgium, France, Austria, Germany, Spain, Ireland. Freeling, who lived most of his life on the continent, had a sharp eye for the quirks and oddities of the various nationalities, and he was really more a European writer than a British one. (Most of his rare sports allusions, for example, are to bicycle racing—something you couldn't get the British to follow even if you offered them free beer.)

The Van der Valk novels avoid any set formula. Julian Symons, who celebrated serious studies of criminal psychology, preferred *Criminal Conversation* (1966), in which Van der Valk investigates a doctor suspected of murdering a blackmailer. Keating and the CWA judges gave their nod to *Question of Loyalty* (1964; British title *Gun Before Butter*), tracing the double life of a murder victim involved in the smuggling of butter from Holland into Belgium. In both these books, Van der Valk takes the stage at the end to explain the crime from the criminal's viewpoint. American readers, including the Edgar judges, preferred the heightened suspense and physical action (including the theft of a helicopter from a skiing competition and the serious wounding that would change the course of Van der Valk's career) of *The King of the Rainy Country* (1966). Puzzle-novel traditionalists Jacques Barzun and Wendell Hertig Taylor appreciated *Strike Out Where Not Applica-*

ble (1967), with a wider range of suspects and the classic situation of a murder victim apparently kicked by a horse.

My own favorite is *Double Barrel* (1965), about Van der Valk's undercover investigation of a rash of anonymous letters in a northeast Holland boomtown. He pays repeated friendly visits to the chief suspect, a supposed Jewish refugee. That the man is actually a notorious Nazi is so clearly foreshadowed, few readers will be surprised, but Van der Valk's ethical pondering over whether to turn him in is deftly handled. *The Lovely Ladies* (1971; British title *Over the High Side*) has an ending more pretentious than profound and may be the worst of the Van der Valks. But even this book is memorable for his sexual encounter with a suspect (unconvincing) and the scene where he confesses, wisely or not, to his wife Arlette (painfully believable).

In the early 1970s, British television extended Van der Valk's fame beyond the printed page, but Freeling couldn't stand prosperity. In *Auprés de ma Blonde*, he struck down Van der Valk much more irrevocably than Conan Doyle disposed of Sherlock Holmes. Now working in the Hague and contemplating retirement to a cottage in France, Van der Valk goes for a walk and is shot from a passing car before the novel's half-way point. Arlette, who ultimately solves and avenges her husband's murder, would briefly star in her own series of mystery novels. In *The Widow* (1979), now remarried and living in Strasbourg, Arlette opens an advice service, becoming a combination mobile Dear Abby and private eye, but she can't carry a book as her husband did, and the English sociologist Arthur Davidson is not engaging in the supportive-spouse role. After one more novel, Freeling wisely abandoned the series. Van der Valk himself would return for a final bow in *Sand Castles* (1989), a case before his death rather than a resurrection.

Symons believed that Freeling "lost his way as a writer" when he killed Van der Valk. Certainly Freeling's next attempt to create a detective—Henri Castang, a French policeman—was never as vivid or interesting a character, nor was Castang's wife, former Czech gymnast Vera, a match for Arlette. First appearing in *A Dressing of Diamond* (1974) Castang ended his career (in retirement rather than death) in *A Dwarf Kingdom* (1996).

But some of Freeling's best work came in three late books without any of his continuing characters. *A City Solitary* (1985) and *One More River* (1998) concern expatriate English novelists who resemble their creator. In the former, Walter Forrestier, subject of a home-invasion robbery, is reluctant to help the police and winds up collaborating with the criminal. *One More River* is ostensibly a novel left behind by the late John Charles, who receives threats to his life from an unknown source. The author's-notebook format allows for tangents, artful disorganization, and shifts between first and third person. *Some Day Tomorrow* (2000), also calculatedly random and discursive, continues Freeling's exegesis on the Dutch national character, along with learned digressions on literary, biological, medical, geographical, social, and culinary topics, through the story of a retired Dutch botanist suspected of killing a teenage girl.

How can we account for Freeling's estrangement from the crime fiction establishment? H.R.F. Keating is repelled by his sense of superiority, finding him "infuriatingly knowing," with passages of untranslated French and obscure allusions. It's true that Freeling's literary, artistic, musical, and cinematic references are sometimes arcane, but not all readers are bothered by such authorial showboating. Dorothy L. Sayers had the same habit—to the point of having her two main characters propose marriage to each other in Latin.

Freeling's published attitudes to the field, both in his novels and critical writing, may have boiled more blood than his show of erudition. He heaped disdain on such characters as Father Brown, Nero Wolfe, Hercule Poirot, and Perry Mason, and he was more scathing in his dismissal of bread-and-butter mystery fiction than any major figure since Raymond Chandler. Freeling viewed himself as a savior of the form, one who would bring quality of style, theme, and social commentary to a debased genre.

In *Criminal Convictions: Errant Essays on Perpetrators of Literary License* (1994), Freeling argues for the extension of crime fiction into the literary mainstream, believing virtually all great fiction is crime fiction. Of the eight writers he discusses, four are generally considered outside the genre (Stendhal, Dickens, Conrad, Kipling) and four within (Doyle, Chandler, Sayers, Simenon). For the latter group, his approval is only partial. He likes Sherlock Holmes but blames the sleuth's success for the later emergence of racist vigilantes like Bulldog Drummond. *Gaudy Night* is virtually the only Sayers novel he deems successful. Even Maigret is admired only for his earliest cases. In discussing Chandler (and finding only his first four novels praiseworthy), he dismisses Dashiell Hammett as a poor writer. Along the way, Freeling manages swipes at Anthony Berkeley, Erle Stanley Gardner, and Margery Allingham, while faintly praising Ross Macdonald.

Then there is the matter of Freeling's political views, which some critics, especially of the Castang novels, have found intrusive. His left-liberal European socialist perspective, including a fuzzy view of crime and punishment, may grate on conservative readers. In *The Lovely Ladies*, Freeling summarizes his ambivalent views on the police: "A policeman has a good trade put to poor use, like a painter commanded to put a coat of glossy enamel over rusty corrugated iron, shrugging, and doing as he is told." He assumes that police generally are corrupt, brutal, and incompetent; that capital punishment is barbaric and prisons an abomination. He compares crime with art in a passage from *Criminal Convictions* unlikely to cheer victims and prosecutors: "Crime is the expression of longing and losing, and what else is our poetry, our music? We seek and do not find; upon this harsh condition we build our frustrations, our self-hatreds. The nature of crime is also the nature of art."

But it isn't that simple, even to Freeling. His politics are arguably separable from the human truths explored in the novels. Freeling is rarely simplistic or overtly didactic, and most of his cultural observations and character insights are beyond politics. That his villains are not purely evil but rather formed by society and environment is not merely a political statement but a recognition that shades of gray make for better fiction, even in popular genres.

Some of his most sweeping statements of European leftist views come from the mouth of Walter Forrestier in *A City Solitary*. But, in light of the way the novel ends, can we assume Freeling really believes all the views he gives Walter? The novel could be read as showing up the barrenness of the left in its seeming denial of evil. Sometimes Freeling, more independent thinker than ideologue, comes across more centrist than leftist. In *A City Solitary* he writes: "the only difference between left- and right-wing governments was that the left did slightly sillier things, but with slightly better intentions."

If his crime and punishment views are troublesome, Freeling's family values should delight social conservatives. The Van der Valk and Castang series especially present a continuing tribute to marriage. Husband and wife relationships are at the heart of his work—he depicts good marriages and bad, and in the bad ones, the husband is generally at fault. Often his protagonists' wives seem better than they deserve. In his critical writing, he celebrates Cissy Chandler as a key to her husband Raymond's success. In

One More River, novelist John Charles considers the marriage of Samuel Pepys. Mrs. Pepys "is a sweet woman, true, good, honest." In Pepys's diary passages after she discovers his infidelity, "There are few pages, I think, in which naked suffering is so baldly set down. 'Poor wretch,' he says, of both women. He realizes that he loves both, and is in hideous torment. He is too honest to say it of himself." Eventually Charles comes to realize how he drove away his own wife and in the last entries in his notebook wants her back.

Whatever one thinks of his politics (global or literary), his social views, or his artistic pretensions, Freeling's work will outlive most of his contemporaries. Rewarding even when most annoying, Freeling deserves a serious revival.

WILLIAM CAMPBELL GAULT

Mystery Scene, Winter 2008

The $50 first prize in a 1936 newspaper short story contest launched Milwaukee native William Campbell Gault (1910-1995) on a professional writing career that would span nearly sixty years. Among the most original and critically acclaimed mid-20th-Century mystery writers, Gault combined storytelling knack with strong social consciousness.

By the time his first novel appeared, Gault had served a long apprenticeship in the pulp magazines, beginning with sports stories before branching out into mysteries. The action of the Edgar-winning *Don't Cry for Me* (1952) takes place around Christmas 1950 in Southern California. First-person hero Pete Worden is the playboy black sheep of a wealthy family, a former USC quarterback whose relationship with intellectual beauty Ellen Gallegher is a typical male-female pairing in Gault's world. When Pete decks one of suave gangster Nick Arnold's more dangerous party guests, the thoughtful host provides Pete with a bodyguard, an offbeat character who left the Communist Party because you have to change your mind too much. The angry guest turns up dead in Pete's apartment with a steak knife in his throat, making Pete the major suspect. Apart from the murder investigation, Pete has a major ethical conflict: will he or won't he accept a job offer from Arnold?

The book has a bittersweet quality, conveying the loneliness of the holiday season for the unattached and harshly satirizing the commercialized Christmas celebration that goes on while Americans are cold and dying in Korea. The finishing confrontation between Pete and a surprising but believable killer is matched by an unexpected but appropriate ending to the romantic story. Gault's local color and pervasive literary references sometimes seem extraneous rather than organic, and the social commentary would be better integrated with the story in later books. Still, *Don't Cry for Me* remains a remarkable debut.

Through the early '50s, Gault produced detective novels without continuing characters, each in a fresh, vividly realized background. Later he would opine that his non-series books represented his best work. In *The Bloody Bokhara* (1952), the only Gault novel set in Milwaukee, a rare Persian rug is sought by a cast of colorful characters, including a beautiful, enigmatic woman who falls in love with the rug-dealer hero. The novel is much more original than most with *Maltese Falcon*-like plots.

The Canvas Coffin (1953) is one of the finest boxing mysteries ever written. The narrator, middleweight champion Luke Pilgrim, has a typical Gaultian relationship (rough but literate jock and artistic, sophisticated woman) with a Chicago commercial artist. Gault's well chosen details capture L.A. of the '50s: the seal tank outside a restaurant on Pacific Coast Highway, TV coverage of wrestling, the blue bakery windmill, tacky Lincoln Blvd., pervasive used car lots. The question of who will win the upcoming title fight piques the reader's curiosity as much as who committed the murder, though the brutal fight scene will win few fans for boxing. Another good non-series sports mystery, *Fair Prey* (1956), written under the pseudonym Will Duke, follows its main character's adventures on the pro golf tour.

Run, Killer, Run (1954), a rare third-person Gault novel, illuminates his political stance: Republican, socially concerned, anti-McCarthyite, a consistent voice for non-simplistic morality. While the finish is exciting, the padding (usually the lead character's repetitive introspection) renders it one of the author's weakest efforts of the decade.

Gault's best-known series hero makes his debut in *Ring Around Rosa* (1956). Beverly Hills private eye Brock (the Rock) Callahan, who had three years in the wartime OSS before playing guard for the Los Angeles Rams, is the son of a San Diego policeman killed in the line of duty. He knows all the LAPD's Rams fans but gradually finds himself losing his cop friends. Brock's doubts about his abilities as an investigator will assail him periodically throughout the series. In a variation on Chandler's *Farewell, My Lovely*, boxer Juan Miro (a little client, in contrast to Chandler's massive Moose Malloy) wants Callahan to find his missing fiancée, the nightclub stripper Rosa. Brock meets interior decorator Jan Bonnet, launching a prickly but strong relationship that will continue throughout the series. The novel ends satisfactorily with one of private eye fiction's standard least-suspected-person solutions, well executed with genuine clues.

Day of the Ram (1956), opening at a Rams/Bears game and concerning the murder of promising Ram quarterback Johnny Quirk, ranks with *The Canvas Coffin* and *Fair Prey* as one of Gault's best adult sports stories. *The Convertible Hearse* (1957) has the most appropriate possible background for a '50s L.A. mystery: the machinations of the used-car business. *Come Die With Me* (1959) concerns the murder of a jockey and allows Brock to vent his negative feelings about horse racing, a sports background not presented as extensively as football, boxing, and golf in earlier books. In *Vein of Violence* (1962), about the murder of a silent picture actress, Brock says of an old movie star's TV comeback, "He had been a star in a medium run by fools and now he was trying to get a new start in a medium run by thieves."

County Kill (1962), one of the best in the series, is the first to employ as a locale San Valdesto, a fictionalized version of Santa Barbara, where Gault lived in the last few decades of his life. The novel features one of the most memorable of Gault's many strong female characters: Mexican bar proprietor Juanita Rico, who altruistically if illegally practices British-style drug addict maintenance to keep the Anglo pushers from getting rich and thus prevent the creation of new addicts.

Gault's other '50s private eye, Joe Puma, shares many superficial characteristics with Brock Callahan: a big guy, more confident about his muscle than his intellect, operating out of Beverly Hills. But while the reader knows Brock will always do the right thing, Joe threatens to spin out of control. For all his talk about honesty, surrounded by temptations he moralistically resists, he seems to protest too much. He is obsessed with the idea of marrying a rich woman. One senses Joe has his price, albeit a high one. Where Brock values male bonding and is an integral part of the old-player network, Joe is a man who much prefers the company of women and has contempt for the immaturity of perpetual jocks.

Though Joe Puma appeared third-person in at least one early magazine story ("And Murder Makes Four," *Detective Tales*, March 1951) and in *Shakedown* (1953; written as Roney Scott), his series proper begins with *End of a Call Girl* (1958). Asked by a madam to find a missing prostitute, Joe gets $100 a day and expenses, the girls the same price but no expenses. In a strong windup to a satisfactorily complicated plot, Puma confronts an interesting killer. A homophobia typical of the times is shared by *all* the straight characters, who use the kind of words for gays that a Gault character would surely abhor if applied to ethnic groups.

At one point in *Night Lady* (1958), set in a professional wrestling background, Joe has a fight with a "policeman," the wrestler charged with keeping in line any colleagues who seek to climb the ladder by legitimately beating people. The description of the fight shows Joe can be a ruthless bastard in a way foreign to Brock Cal-

lahan. Becoming increasingly twisted in *The Wayward Widow*
(1959), Puma loses his girl at the end to a Neapolitan and calls him
a "lousy wop," shocking conduct indeed for a Gault hero. *Sweet
Wild Wench* (1959), a book-length version of the non-Puma magazine novelette "But the Prophet Died" (*Dell Mystery Novels*, January 1955), finds Joe investigating the Children of Proton, whose
religion is based on electricity and the atomic structure. Of the
crazy cults that turn up in Southern California private-eye fiction,
this is one of the more interesting because of the more extensive
description of its theology.

Through most of the '50s, Gault continued to write short stories for the mystery digests, the pulps having virtually disappeared. The Joe Puma stories, usually of novelette length and as
fully plotted as the novels, would be collected with some early
non-series work in the posthumous collection *Marksman and
Other Stories* (2002).

After his final Puma and Callahan books of the '60s, *The
Hundred-Dollar Girl* (1961) and *Dead Hero* (1963) respectively,
Gault left the mystery for nearly twenty years, concentrating on
his sports juveniles. With that market weakening in the late '70s,
he reentered the field with a new series of cases for Brock Callahan novels, now married to Jan and living in San Valdesto.

While the new books lacked the snap and energy of Gault's
'50s peak, their characterization, social observation, and underlying humanity were notable. In *The CANA Diversion* (1980), Jan
goes to jail for demonstrating against the building of a nuclear
power plant in San Valdesto, and Ellen Puma, a previously unsus-
pected wife of Joe, asks Brock to find her missing husband.
Brock's police contact calls Puma "a real shady operator," and
Brock counters that he's "no angel, I'll grant you, but I've known
a dozen cops who were worse!" When the murdered Joe Puma
proves to have been severely bent, Brock makes up an alternate
scenario to keep the truth from Ellen and their law-school-bound
son.

The Dead Seed (1985) introduces an unusual twist on the religious cult: its leader is working in cahoots with a deprogrammer to
soak rich parents. The courtroom climax attempts a statement
about legal justice vs. vigilante justice. *Death in Donegal Bay*
(1984) has an interesting villain in Cyrus Reed Allingham, a
moral-majority supporter whose castle refuge includes a mined
moat.

In his last years, Gault contributed columns to *Mystery Scene* and letters to *Mystery and Detective Monthly,* was elected president of Private Eye Writers of America and given its lifetime achievement award, and saw two final novels published, both with appreciative introductions by Bill Pronzini: the last Callahan case, *Dead Pigeon* (1992), and the non-mystery Hollywood novel *Man Alive* (1995), written in 1957 and admiringly rejected for commercial reasons by his publishers.

Gault was one of the strongest voices in genre fiction for ethical behavior and racial and political tolerance. His voice was so distinctive, few fans would fail to recognize it in a blind test. Artificial distinctions of genre aside, he was a *serious* writer, as concerned with social issues and non-simplistic morality as with telling a fast-moving story. Quite a few writers could plot, pace, and people a mystery as well as Gault, but not many could reach a reader as deeply on a gut level.

CHESTER HIMES

(review of *Chester Himes: A Life* by James Sallis, Walker, 2001)

The Weekly Standard, May 28, 2001

In 1926, a distracted teenage busboy in Cleveland's Wade Park Manor Hotel opened an elevator door, stepped through without looking, and fell forty feet. A half century later, a world-famous American novelist living in Spain, by the roadside instructing his wife on how to change a tire, backed his wheelchair into a ditch. The two accidents, comic in description if horrific in reality, illuminate both the character of Chester Himes, who didn't always consider the potential consequences of his actions, and the worldview of a writer who titled his second volume of autobiography *My Life of Absurdity*. Both comic violence and unprovoked mishaps are frequent in Himes's fiction.

Chester Himes (1909-1984) is unquestionably a major African American writer. But in a typical irony, the author of ambitious mainstream novels for prestigious firms like Doubleday and Knopf is best remembered for a series of mysteries, launched for a quick buck and initially published as paperback originals. Increased speed of production and freedom to cast off the constraints of "serious literature" gave Himes the opportunity to be himself, to explore through dark humor and satire the themes that had preoccupied his more calculated autobiographical and "protest" fiction.

The Harlem detective team of Coffin Ed Johnson and Grave Digger Jones, tough cops and dedicated family men, first appeared in *For Love of Imabelle* (1957), written at the invitation of Marcel Duhamel, editor of the French publisher Gallimard's crime fiction imprint *La Série Noire*. Seven more complete novels followed, ending with *Blind Man with a Pistol* (1969), plus the unfinished *Plan B* (1993), in which Coffin Ed injures himself walking into an open manhole, a piece of slapstick reminiscent of some of Himes's own misfortunes.

Now, in *Chester Himes: A Life*, James Sallis has produced a superior new account of Himes's life and work. It is eloquently written and includes a wide range of well-chosen quotations and analogies to other literature. (One can only wish the quality of the text were matched in the primary bibliography, which lists without original publication dates reprint editions used by Sallis, and the spotty index that made rechecking points for this article difficult.)

Growing up a black male in early-20th Century America wasn't the most promising of starts, though in some ways Himes had it better than most. He was born in Jefferson City, Missouri, the youngest of three brothers. His parents were well-educated, middle class, and in their differing ways ambitious. But they were also unhappy, torn by conflict over how to deal with their minority status: his light-skinned mother was the more militant, resenting white people and regarding her more accommodating husband as an Uncle Tom with a "slave mentality." While many African Americans of the time managed to lead productive and relatively happy lives with a tolerable level of frustration, those of less docile temperament found second-class citizenship (a cliché but a true one) infuriating and emasculating. Himes's life as much as his fiction reflects how built-in disadvantages combined with unaccountable chance can shape a person's actions and outlook.

Himes was a complex individual. Though charming, well mannered, handsome, articulate, and funny, he was also difficult, deeply angry, bitter, and given to violent bursts of temper. Serious and hardworking in his writing career, he was often irresponsible in his personal life.

Himes's brother Joseph was blinded in a freak accident in 1923, an incident for which Chester felt unreasonable guilt. Following his own hotel accident, in which he suffered serious back injuries, and an unsuccessful student career at Ohio State University, Himes served a term for armed robbery in the Ohio State Penitentiary from 1928 until his parole in 1936. While in prison, he began selling short stories to Negro periodicals, and in 1934 he became a contributor to *Esquire*, first identified by his prisoner number, 59623. Following the standard advice, Himes wrote what he knew, mostly about criminals and prisoners but not always about African Americans—that Himes was black was not revealed to *Esquire* readers until 1936.

Though Himes later would claim he knew little about mystery fiction before he began writing it, he had read Dashiell Hammett and colleagues in *Black Mask* and other pulp magazines while in prison. Indeed the team of Coffin Ed and Grave Digger had precursors in the early story "He Knew," published in *Abbott's Weekly and Illustrated News* in 1933 and apparently never reprinted. (It is not included in *The Collected Stories of Chester Himes* [1991], which the publisher's blurb contends "includes all of Himes's surviving stories.") As described in Stephen F. Milliken's *Chester Himes: A Critical Appraisal* (1976), "He Knew," with its ironic O. Henry-ish twist, sounds like a natural for anthologization in lieu of a Coffin Ed/Grave Digger short story.

Though prison was clearly a turning point in Himes's life, Sallis notes that only six pages out of 743 in two volumes of minutia-crowded but selectively reticent memoirs are about his incarceration. *The Quality of Hurt* (1972) and *My Life of Absurdity* (1976) often gloss over important and interesting matters to fill in details that mean little to readers. For insights, Sallis turns to his subject's autobiographical novels, while recognizing the dangers of basing biography on fiction. (For one difference, the protagonist of Himes's prison novel *Cast the First Stone* [1952] was white.)

Married shortly after his release, Himes held many jobs in the years that followed, most, apart from a stint with the Federal Writers Project in Ohio, menial ones. Even after he became a published novelist, when Himes sought other employment to make ends meet, the best "day jobs" open to him were as a janitor or servant. As late as 1955, after returning briefly from Europe, he worked as a porter at an Automat in New York.

When Himes and his wife migrated to California in 1941, he found a society more malignantly racist than the one he had left in the Midwest. On the verge of employment as a script reader at Warner Brothers, he was rejected because Jack Warner didn't "want no niggers on this lot."

Himes's West Coast experience resulted in *If He Hollers, Let Him Go* (1945), an uncomfortably realistic depiction of a proud black man's lot in wartime Los Angeles. Its psychological insights and the detailed depiction of the shipyards background recall the work of James M. Cain. According to Sallis, it was originally conceived as a mystery novel "in which whites were being killed apparently at random all about L.A."

The controversial book, which seemed on the brink of bestsellerdom until it was apparently torpedoed from within Doubleday, considered aspects of black American life that were rarely openly discussed, including social strata based on skin color, black anti-Semitism, and the complex and dangerous mutual attraction of black men and white women.

Himes the compulsive truth-teller is aptly compared by Melvin Van Peebles to the Flemish painter Brueghel the Elder who "called it like he saw it....[s]o unflinchingly in fact that doctors today, 400 years later, have been able to identify medieval maladies from studying the characters he painted, diseases of which people weren't then aware. Chester saw America unflinchingly, too...." However, as Himes's friend Henry Moon told him, "Everything you say here is true, but these aren't things that white people want to hear about. Things like this need to be kept quiet, between colored people." (Quotes are from Sallis.)

If He Hollers, Let Him Go's tragic central figure Bob Jones represents an irony of the past century's racial strife: that, for all their determination to rediscover pre-slavery cultural roots, African Americans have much more in common with other Americans than with Africans. Jones believes in America and its ideals, desperately wants to embrace the American dream, but finds himself constantly blocked from full citizenship. While not even whites have complete control over their lives, Jones believes, Negroes have none at all. It falls to his light-skinned girlfriend to make the case for accommodation. Himes is fair enough (and maybe personally conflicted enough) to write her an eloquent defense.

Himes's political views are hard to pin down, because his commitment to unvarnished truth was greater than his ability to follow any particular ideology. He wrote in *The Quality of Hurt*, as quoted by Sallis, "Reactionaries hate the truth and the world's rulers fear it; but it embarrasses the liberals, perhaps because they can't do anything about it."

The Communist Party attracted many black writers and artists (including Richard Wright, Ralph Ellison, Paul Robeson, and Langston Hughes) by talking a good game against racism, but Himes soon realized how little real concern the Party had for blacks. Himes satirized the Party in his second novel *Lonely Crusade* (1947), and later would make the doubtful claim that a conspiracy of Communists destroyed his literary career in the United States.

While *Lonely Crusade* was excoriated by the Communist press, the reviews from mainstream media, as quoted by Sallis, were not nearly as hard on Himes's book as he remembered. Still, the novel had the problem (or the virtue) of offending not only the extreme left wing but nearly everyone on the political and racial spectrum. Himes's desire to credit a conspiracy is understandable: in a single morning, two department store book signings and an appearance with influential radio personality Mary Margaret McBride were canceled.

Some European Communists continued to celebrate Himes after the Party in America had turned on him. But he remained firmly anti-Communist. In a 1970 German radio interview, transcribed in Michel Fabre and Robert Skinner's *Conversations with Chester Himes* (1995), Himes stated that the Party had used the civil rights struggle for its own ends but had done nothing to help blacks. In the same interview, Himes, for all his bitterness toward white people and his growing conviction that blacks could not achieve real equality without violence, pronounced integration preferable to segregation in addressing problems between the races.

In 1953, stung by the failure of his books to achieve due recognition in the United States and divorced from his first wife, Himes left his home country. Like most of the expatriated black American artists—Wright, Robeson, Sidney Bechet, James Baldwin, Josephine Baker—Himes found refuge not in Africa but in Europe, a culture in many ways similar to that of the United States but perceived as less racist.

In the changing world of the middle 1960s, either because Himes had found his true niche in crime fiction or because his downbeat vision of American society had become more palatable, success came at last. Living in Spain with his second wife, he was able to enjoy relative financial stability and due recognition from the literary world, sadly accompanied by steadily failing health and continued anger and bitterness, until the end of his life in 1984.

Detective fiction is about making sense of things, and Himes's life and work often seem to be about how little sense can be made of anything. Thus, one might expect Himes to produce anti-detective fiction, that aggravating form in which problems are posed but solutions withheld, using the trappings of the mystery to subvert it. Only *Blind Man With a Pistol* fits that description. In the last two chapters, the title character, who has no connection with the rest of the story, goes on his shooting rampage, and the Harlem detective team are seen using their expensive weapons to shoot rats. The novel's mysteries, including who committed the murders and the identity of the shadowy rackets boss Mr. Big, are never solved. But the other novels in the series are genuine detective stories.

Himes the crime fiction writer is most often celebrated for his vivid descriptions of Harlem, his offbeat characters and their colorful dialogue, his depiction of violence-as-everyday-life, and his pungent observations about race relations. But his plotting skill is often overlooked or denigrated. Sallis makes the odd claim that,

"In the Harlem novels...Himes largely rejected plot, adopting the simplest gimmicks (what mystery folk call a MacGuffin)...as frameworks on which to hang vivid scenes and confrontations among outlandish characters."

A MacGuffin is the object that sets the plot in motion, the thing all the characters in the story are after. Examples from director Alfred Hitchcock, who is credited with inventing the term, include the secret plans in *The 39 Steps* and the uranium ore in *Notorious*. Hammett's *Maltese Falcon* is another archetype. MacGuffins are plentiful in Himes's work—a trunk full of fool's gold in *For Love of Imabelle*, a hidden bundle of numbers winnings in *The Big Gold Dream* (1960), an envelope of campaign funds in *All Shot Up* (1960), a cotton bale full of money in *Cotton Comes to Harlem* (1965), a string of eels containing heroin in *The Heat's On* (1966), a Gladstone bag with payment for a rejuvenation potion in *Blind Man With a Pistol*. But he hardly rejected plot, respecting the mystery genre, observing many of its conventions, and meeting its requirements of misdirection and surprise. Even the outline of the unfinished *Plan B*, an over-the-top apocalyptic vision of race war in the United States that is more satirical thriller than detective novel, described some solid sleuthing by the Harlem cop team, leading up to the shocking conclusion in which the two old friends choose up sides and Grave Digger shoots and kills Coffin Ed.

All of Himes's crime fiction makes rewarding reading. Purely as a detective story, *The Real Cool Killers* (1959), the multi-twist affair chosen to represent Himes in the Library of America's American Noir volumes, is probably the best. Comprising crime, detection, solution, and (in a tense hostage situation) genuine suspense, the novel develops the two Harlem sleuths as unique and sympathetic characters, including Coffin Ed's relationship with his daughter. Justice is done, if indirectly; and, in contrast to the last books in the series, the ending is upbeat, positive, even sentimental. Most important to the mystery lover, Himes is as determined as Agatha Christie to divert the reader's attention from the real killer.

Himes needs to be evaluated in at least three contexts: as an African-American writer, as a practitioner of crime fiction, and as a figure in the wider world of American letters. The first two are easy. Himes's stature as an important black novelist, alongside contemporaries Wright and Ellison, seems secure. Though a few black mystery writers preceded him, Himes was the first who could stand with the best in the genre regardless of race, and it was he who paved the way for contemporaries like Walter Mosley, Gary Phillips, Gar Anthony Haywood, and Paula L. Woods.

The third context is more problematic. American literature of the Twentieth Century is so obsessed with race and ethnicity, it's difficult to say whether black skin was more a help or a hindrance to literary reputation. In a color-blind America, Himes's early books might have achieved greater recognition for their style and narrative power, but in such a society they would have had no reason to exist. Himes had the mixed blessing of being ahead of his time, a whistle-blower revealing the truth he saw before the literary world of any color was ready to hear it.

Postscript 2008: This was my first author study for The Weekly Standard *and was shortened and edited considerably for publication. I have restored most of my original text, which may not read quite as smoothly but adds some points I wanted to make. Editor Joseph Bottum revised the second to last paragraph to point out none of Himes's books was as famous as Wright's* Native Son *or in a class with "the absolute classic of black American fiction, Ralph Ellison's* Invisible Man," *points I have no quarrel with.*

EDWARD D. HOCH

Mystery Scene, Spring 2008

Edward D. Hoch (February 22, 1930-January 17, 2008) was born, died, and lived his entire life in Rochester, New York. Obituaries and tributes focused on his amazing record of between 900 and a thousand published stories, including contributions to every issue of *Ellery Queen's Mystery Magazine* from May 1973 to the present; on his stature as an Edgar winner, past President and Grand Master of Mystery Writers of America; and on his personal qualities: a perpetually cheerful disposition, unchallenged integrity, and generosity of time and advice to fans and other writers. He and his wife of fifty years Patricia brightened every mystery event they attended. No one in the field was more universally loved and respected than Ed Hoch.

But lost in all of this may have been Hoch's significance as a writer. He practiced the increasingly lost art of the classical detective short story better than all but a handful of writers in the history of the genre. For some of us, as long as Ed Hoch was at work, the Golden Age never really ended. Many of his stories were novels in miniature, fully cast and plotted whodunits solved by the interpretation of fairly placed clues, often involving impossible crimes and seemingly supernatural elements that would be dispelled in the final summing-up. He was especially good at conveying exotic locales, most of which he had not visited but brought to life through extensive research. Like one of his literary models, G.K. Chesterton, he could introduce serious religious, moral, and ethical themes without obtruding on the forward pace of the story. His spare style was adaptable to any purpose, and he had a mastery of story structure from the very beginning of his career.

Hoch's first story, "Village of the Dead," appeared in the otherwise unremarkable December 1955 issue of *Famous Detective Stories*, one of the last surviving mystery pulps. Its editor, Robert A.W. "Doc" Lowndes, years later would buy the first story of Stephen King. Hoch's breakthrough culminated years of knocking on the door. He wrote in the 1989 *MWA Annual*, "[I]n my late teens and early twenties I tried a great many different forms: mysteries, westerns, science fiction, fantasy, and even mainstream fiction. I submitted stories to *The New Yorker* and literary essays to *The Saturday Review*." But detective fiction was his natural home.

He joined MWA in 1949, attending his first meeting in 1950. One of the last links to the organization's formative years, he took special pride in being the first (and probably only) MWA President who started as an affiliate member.

"Village of the Dead" introduced Hoch's first series character, Simon Ark, who claimed to be 2000 years old and on a quest for Satan. Though the detective was quasi-supernatural, his cases would always be solved by rational means. The plot foreshadowed in some ways the Jonestown massacre: why did the inhabitants of a whole village walk off a cliff in an apparent mass suicide? In that 1989 article, Hoch commented that he wanted his readers to learn something as well as being entertained, "and so I started filling my stories with all sorts of odd facts and historical trivia....In the first Ark story...the reader learned more about the Fourth Century cult of the Circumcellions than most people care to know. In other stories, readers learned about...methods of execution in ancient Rome, and even about the Seventeenth Century practice of damasking—concealing the pages of banned books into wallpaper by overprinting a heavy design of bright colors." This educational impulse continued throughout his career.

When I began reading and collecting mystery magazines at age twelve in summer 1956, I scorned the surviving pulps, though I periodically had a look at them on the newsstands. I knew their contributors were generally less distinguished than those of the best digests: *Ellery Queen's Mystery Magazine, The Saint Detective Magazine,* and *Manhunt.* An obscure Simon Ark story in one of the lesser digests, "Blood in the Stands" (*Terror Detective Story Magazine,* February 1957), turned me into a Hoch fan, for its baseball background and a puzzle plot, with clues in plain sight, that delivered the same kind of satisfaction as the stories of Ellery Queen. Now I bought every Ark-featured magazine I saw, including used issues of the pulps when I could find them. Sometime in the late 1950s or early 1960s, I wrote a letter to Frederic Dannay expressing the wish that Simon Ark stories would appear in *EQMM.* Unlikely as that may have seemed to both of us at the time, many years later, in the issue of October 1978, it actually happened with "The Treasure of Jack the Ripper."

In 2000, I noted to Ed that I'd never been able to track down the uncollected Simon Ark story "The Wolves of Werclaw" (*Famous Detective,* October 1956). To my astonishment, he sent me a pristine copy of the magazine, writing, "[when] magazines were a quarter and my future as a writer was still uncertain, I sometimes plunked down five bucks and bought twenty copies. With the coming of Xerox machines in the early '60s I cut way back on my purchases."

Hoch finally cracked his most desired market, *EQMM*, in the December 1962 issue with a story about his second major series character, Captain Leopold, a police detective in a medium-sized city in upstate New York. He introduced new characters for *EQMM*—British code expert Jeffrey Rand, thief-of-the valueless Nick Velvet—and by 1970 was represented in almost every issue.

Edward D. Hoch created 28 series characters, a dozen of which appeared in ten or more stories. While I retain a special loyalty to Simon Ark, the Leopold police stories, which included the Edgar winning "The Oblong Room" (*The Saint Mystery Magazine*, July 1967), may rank highest in terms of quality. Some of the Leopolds were adapted for the TV series *McMillan and Wife* in the 1970s, and Nick Velvet also attracted some small-screen interest. In an August 1, 1983, letter, Ed confided, "20th Century Fox has a TV option on Nick Velvet at the moment, but so far all they have is a rejection by CBS, who said, 'It's no Mike Hammer.' Well, I could have told them that!" The Velvet stories are popular for good reason: who can resist finding out how (and why) he steals a bad professional baseball team or a day-old newspaper or a firefighter's hat or tickets to a closed Broadway show? Fans of locked rooms and impossible crimes, as well as 20th-Century history and nostalgia, have a special fondness for small-town New England physician Dr. Sam Hawthorne.

When I was specializing in parodies for *EQMM*, I made Dr. Sam a target in "The Problem of the Vanishing Town" (November 1979), about Dr. Sid Shoehorn. I made casual reference to an impossible crime no one could possibly solve (certainly I couldn't): "the clown from the circus who was mauled by a lion on the fifth floor of the Northsouth Hotel when the lion was in his cage five blocks away." A quarter century later, Ed solved it, in a story called "Circus in the Sky" for the 2000 Crime Writers Association anthology *Scenes of the Crime*, edited by Martin Edwards. In acknowledgement, he named the circus after me.

Pro that he was, Hoch was able to move with the times and market demands. His early stories tended to be more hardboiled and noirish than most of his later work, and while still writing for "Doc" Lowndes in the late '50s, he was asked to turn Simon Ark into a private eye and add a bit more erotic content—the "sexy Simons" he called them, "though in truth the titles were often the sexiest thing about them." At the time, I disliked them intensely, whether out of adolescent prudery or loyalty to the more Chestertonian Simons, but of course I collected them all. When I returned to them recently, my opinion wasn't much different, though like all Ed's detective stories, they were expertly constructed and fair to the reader. His most notable 21st century series, concerning Walt Stanton and Juliet Ives, a young couple who are partners both romantically and in a courier business, reportedly raised some eyebrows among Hoch's fans. "Midsummer Night's Scheme" (*EQMM*, May 2004) includes some delightfully risqué humor.

After whatever few remain in the pipeline at *EQMM* or elsewhere, there will no more new stories by Edward D. Hoch. But we will always have those nine hundred plus, and I would venture very few are unworthy of revival. As evidence, consider two atypical early efforts: the very grim and never-reprinted account of an initially reluctant killer for hire, "Murder is Eternal" (*Saturn Web Detective Story Magazine*, August 1960), and the inventive time-travel vignette, "The Last Paradox" (*Future Science Fiction*, October 1958). To date, there have been fifteen collections of Hoch stories, including six from Crippen & Landru, two from the early days of Mysterious Press, and two from university presses. That leaves room for about another thirty volumes, figuring twenty stories to a volume. There can never be enough.

(Bibliographic note: For the full story on Edward D. Hoch's writings, fiction and nonfiction, the best source is the loose-leaf *Edward D. Hoch Bibliography*, edited by June M. Moffatt and Francis M. Nevins, annually updated and published by Moffatt House, Box 4456, Downey, CA 90241-1456.)

Postscript: I was accorded the honor of finishing the story Ed was working on when he died, "Handel and Gretel" (EQMM, November 2008). It was a humbling experience. Apparently keeping the very complicated story in his head, Ed left no notes of where he was going or what the various clues meant. I'll always wonder exactly what solution he had in mind, quite different I suspect from my own.

P. D. JAMES

(review of *The Murder Room*, Knopf, 2003)

The Weekly Standard, December 8, 2003

The setting for *The Murder Room*, P.D. James's thirteenth novel about Scotland Yard Commander Adam Dalgliesh, could hardly be more appropriate: a museum devoted to Great Britain between the world wars. With her unapologetic embrace of hallowed detective-story conventions, James is the strongest contemporary link to that era's traditional British detective fiction.

Now Baroness James of Holland Park, Phyllis Dorothy James was a hospital administrative assistant when her first novel, a country-house whodunit called *Cover Her Face*, was published in Britain in 1962. Classical British detective fiction was at low ebb. A few of the golden-age masters were still in business—Agatha Christie, Ngaio Marsh, Margery Allingham, Michael Innes, Nicholas Blake—but new talent was sparse, and the ascendant genre for popular fiction was the spy novel. So resistant were publishers to old-fashioned detection that James's first novel would not see publication in America until 1966.

James's detective Dalgliesh is a policeman and a published poet—a throwback to such literate cops as Marsh's Roderick Alleyn and Innes's John Appleby. While his cases hold fast to such classical traditions as fairly given clues and surprising murderers, James was determined to bring more reality to the pattern, emphasizing deeper characterization, recognition of the real cost of murder on the lives of the survivors, and authentic forensic detail. (Her awareness of these matters was facilitated by her administrative jobs in Britain's Home Office between 1968 and her retirement in 1979.)

And what makes James so interesting is that she sees no contradiction in taking serious explorations of character and society, and setting them against delightfully artificial plots, rich in situations like the one that begins the 1967 *Unnatural Causes*: the handless corpse of a mystery writer found floating in a boat off the East Anglian coast, a situation supposedly suggested to the victim for one of his novels. Or the bizarre opening of the 1986 *A Taste for Death*: two bodies (one a derelict and the other a minister of the crown) found bloodily murdered in a London church vestry.

After the first four Dalgliesh cases, James delighted feminists with the introduction of female private eye Cordelia Gray in *An Unsuitable Job for a Woman* (1973), with Dalgliesh in a secondary role. Gray is on her own in the theatrical mystery *The Skull Beneath the Skin* (1982), but James doubts in her diary-cum-autobiography *Time to Be in Earnest* (2000) that she will ever return to the character, having lost her to British television, which violated the author's concept of Cordelia by saddling her with an unwed pregnancy. James has confined her subsequent fiction to the Dalgliesh saga with two notable exceptions: her breakout bestseller *Innocent Blood* (1980), an unconventional detective novel about a young woman searching for her birth parents, and the science-fictional *The Children of Men* (1993), depicting a near-future world where the human race has stopped reproducing itself.

James specializes in minutely detailed institutional backgrounds: a psychiatric clinic in *A Mind to Murder* (1967), a training school for nurses in *Shroud for a Nightingale* (1971), a home for the disabled in *The Black Tower* (1975), a forensic science laboratory in *Death of an Expert Witness* (1977), a nuclear power plant in *Devices and Desires* (1989), a centuries-old London publishing house in *Original Sin* (1995), a barristers' chambers in *A Certain Justice* (1997), and a theological college in *Death in Holy Orders* (2001). Usually the institutions are threatened from without or within, and the response of the personnel drives the plot.

Her new novel, *The Murder Room*, follows this formula. The room of the title is an exhibition room in the small, family-run DuPayne Museum, which houses items from classic murder cases. For the museum to continue, all three children of the departed founder must sign the new lease. Elder brother Marcus, a recently retired government functionary, and sister Caroline, partner in a posh finishing school, have differing agendas for the museum but want to preserve it. Younger brother Neville, a psychiatrist who scorns dwelling on the past and resents his late father, is just as determined to withhold his signature and force the museum's closure. Thus, he becomes the obvious candidate for murder victim. And when his Jaguar and what may be his charred body are found burnt in the museum's garage, the circumstances echo one of the crimes the Murder Room commemorates. (The reader must ponder whether the charred body found in the car will defy detective-fiction convention by proving actually to be who it is presumed to be.)

With a solution that is satisfying if not dazzling, the latest Dalgliesh novel will not rank with the best—I would especially recommend *Shroud for a Nightingale*, *The Black Tower*, *Devices and Desires*, and *A Certain Justice*—but it's an effective job from a writer who is always worth reading. In common with most current crime novels from major publishers, however, it is longer than it needs to be. In a literary Utopia, every story would occupy its ideal length, but the market piper calls the tune. Beginning with World War II paper shortages and continuing into the 1980s, the standard detective novel ran just under two hundred pages, or about sixty thousand words. With the increasing emphasis on blockbusters in the past couple of decades, mysteries now often run to twice that length.

While some writers read as if they have been coerced to add length, the trend came naturally to James. Even her early novels move at a leisurely pace, leaving no city thoroughfare or country lane, no house or room, no character central or peripheral undescribed. In her longer novels, she sticks to the case at hand and rarely resorts to the desperate devices of lesser writers: irrelevant recurring cast members, soap-opera and situation-comedy subplots, undigested research material, characters who constantly recount to each other things the reader already knows. James adds new matter—more description, more atmosphere, more extensive back stories for her people—but runs the risk of over-balancing the plot, bringing the action to a grinding halt and encouraging the impatient reader to skip the narrative and get the story from the dialogue.

Introducing a recent reprint edition of Clyde B. Clason's 1939 novel *Murder Gone Minoan*, Tom and Enid Schantz claim that P.D. James "started out writing tightly crafted gems, but all of her books after *An Unsuitable Job for a Woman*...bog down in endless details about the contents of suitcases or in long pieces of melancholy introspection by her leading characters." This may be too harsh an assessment, but it has an element of truth. In *The Murder Room*, couldn't the life history of museum custodian Tally Clutton be summarized in a paragraph or two instead of a six-page chapter? Do we require a full chapter on the discovery of a piece of evidence in a charity shop, when a phone call to the police from offstage would have done the job?

Possibly a good detective story, even at novel length, is like a short story: a narrative in which all the elements are directed toward an overall effect and not dispersed into tangents. How often are the additional character insights brought about by extensive back stories and interior monologues profound enough to justify bringing plot movement to a halt? One could rightly argue that James is up to more than writing a detective story, that she offers real insights into society and the effect of crime on those involved, as victims, investigators, suspects, or peripheral figures. But recall how much depth of theme, character, and social observation Ross Macdonald was able to insert in his novels while providing a briskly paced story. Additional detail sometimes spells increased depth, but not always.

None of these caveats, of course, should deter James's fans from enjoying her work or new readers from discovering it. While the padding and tangents of some contemporary crime writers should be consigned to the wastebasket without looking back, James is too interesting a writer for her extraneous passages to be completely without interest. *The Murder Room* is another successful outing from a master in the genre.

Postscript 2008: Since the publication of The Murder Room, *James, among those valued writers who have continued to do first-rate work into their eighties, has added* The Lighthouse *(Knopf). In "The Jury Box" (EQMM, May 2006, I wrote the following: "This time, the threatened institution (a James specialty) is a private island off Cornwall that has become an R-and-R destination for weary VIPs. A widely hated novelist is murdered, and the isolated setting makes for a typically excellent closed-circle whodunit for Adam Dalgliesh and his team, with an enthralling cast of suspects and clues to the killer broad and fair enough to be interpreted by armchair sleuths more alert than this one."*

ELMORE LEONARD

(review of *Up in Honey's Room*, Morrow, 2007)

The Weekly Standard, June 25, July 2, 2007

When a major writer produces a sub-par book, it's no great disaster, no unforgivable affront to readers. But the biggest loser in the deal may be the new reader who picks the book up on the basis of reputation and hype, wonders what the shouting was about, and decides never to try that particular author again.

Elmore Leonard is one of the great names in contemporary crime fiction, revered and honored by his peers, rewarded with healthy book sales by a loyal readership. True, some lesser writers move more books and some arguably better writers (Donald E. Westlake, say) move fewer. It's remarkable Leonard makes the bestseller lists at all in the current thriller-dominated market given the keys to his success: plot movement, sparkling dialogue, offbeat character development, deadpan humor, economically sketched background, a wide range of pop culture references and factual nuggets, minimal use of descriptive passages (he tries to leave out the stuff readers skip), and that elusive quality known as style. There is suspense certainly, but focused on what will happen next, not on any visceral connection with the characters, whom he views at too much of a distance for the kind of emotional reader identification supposedly essential in today's popular fiction. By his own admission, he finds the bad guys more intriguing than the good guys. Readers not interested in the inner lives of small-time crooks may not fully get Leonard, but will still admire his skill.

Born in New Orleans in 1925 but resident for most of his life of Detroit, the locale of much of his fiction, Leonard worked in advertising after wartime service in the Naval Reserve. His first professional fiction sales were westerns for the 1950s magazine markets, beginning with *Argosy* and the still-flourishing pulps, finally cracking the prestigious *Saturday Evening Post* in 1956. These early stories were gathered in *The Complete Western Stories of Elmore Leonard* (Morrow, 2004), whose endpapers reproduce those colorful magazine covers. He also wrote eight western novels, notably *Hombre* (1961) and *Valdez is Coming* (1969), which became movie vehicles for Paul Newman and Burt Lancaster respectively. But after the decline of the western market, he turned to hard urban crime fiction, beginning with *The Big Bounce* (1969). By the end of the 1970s, he had become a favorite of connoisseurs, and by the time he won the Edgar Allan Poe Award for *LaBrava* (1983), he was firmly situated in the genre's pantheon.

Even in a lesser example of his work, which *Up in Honey's Room* certainly is, Leonard's strengths are at least sporadically on display. The action begins in 1939 Detroit, where Honey Deal has just left her husband Walter Schoen, a German immigrant who believes he is the twin brother (separated at birth) of Heinrich Himmler. The story jumps ahead five years to 1944. Honey is contacted by FBI agent Kevin Dean and soon she is accompanying Carl Webster of the U.S. Marshal Service on a visit to question Walter, a known Nazi sympathizer and enthusiastic reader of *Mein Kampf*, about two escaped German prisoners of war, SS major Otto Penzler and tank commander Jurgen Schrenk. The balance of the action alternates between the German group and their various plans and activities, including a venture in the black market meat industry, and Webster's investigation. A side issue is whether Honey will succeed in seducing the loyally married marshal. There are brief interludes of violent action, but most of the story is told through dialogue.

Continuing characters are rare in Leonard's work, maybe with good reason. The Oklahoman Webster was first met as the title character of the prohibition-era Feds-and-robbers saga, *The Hot Kid* (2005), a better book than its sequel, and also figured in "Comfort to the Enemy," a *New York Times Magazine* serial in the same year. The back story is filled in via a family conversation among Webster, his father Virgil, and Virgil's common-law wife Narcissa Raincrow. Three characters recounting to each other for the reader's benefit things they obviously already know makes for exceedingly clumsy exposition, particularly from a writer who has been compared with George V. Higgins as a master of dialogue-driven narrative.

The choice of names is another problem. The confusingly similar surnames Deal and Dean should have been avoided, though fortunately the FBI man is a relatively minor character. Calling one of the German fugitives Otto Penzler, in jokey homage to the well-known publisher, book dealer, and crime fiction expert, is more serious. In genre fiction, this is called Tuckerization, named after Wilson Tucker, the mystery and science fiction writer who popularized the practice. Such foolery can be cute in small doses, but to name such a prominent character after such a well-known model is dubious indeed. To some lucky readers, the name will mean nothing. Those who recognize it may find it a delightful in-joke, smugly congratulate themselves for feeling like insiders, or (most likely) be distracted from the story.

Up in Honey's Room is by no means a total disaster. There are good lines of dialogue, jokes, period details, character touches, and unexpected plot reversals to reward the patient reader. But the story doesn't move as it should, bogging down in tiresome conversations of questionable plot relevance or entertainment value. For once Leonard left in stuff readers will want to skip.

The lesson to be drawn is a simple one, though it contradicts the commercially encouraged impulse to overvalue the new. Elmore Leonard completists, those who read and/or collect everything he writes, will and should acquire this book. Those with limited experience with his work, or most crucially new readers, should first seek out his excellent past novels. For strong examples, transport to the '70s and '80s is not necessary. In *Pagan Babies* (2000), the very funny adventures of a fugitive priest and a female wannabe stand-up comic are the vehicle for exploring some serious issues, including the Rwandan genocide. *Be Cool* (1999), a sequel to the memorably filmed *Get Shorty* (1990), delivers au courant satire in hood-turned-Hollywoodian Chili Palmer's efforts to sort out the burgeoning categories of contemporary popular music. If there is any unread Leonard within reach, there's no compelling reason to visit Honey's room.

HENNING MANKELL

(review of *The Man Who Smiled*, translated from the Swedish
by Laurie Thompson, New Press, 2006)

The Weekly Standard, March 12, 2007

Swedish police detective Kurt Wallander, on medical leave for
over a year because of depression after killing a man in the line of
duty, is on the point of resigning from the Ystad force. But he is
moved to shake off his stereotypically Scandinavian gloom and
return to action when a friend, lawyer Sten Torstensson, asks him
to look into the death of his father and law partner in an apparent
road accident, then is himself murdered. As the reader knows and
the cops gradually find out, the elder Torstensson was on his way
back from Farnholm Castle, the lair of a wealthy international
businessman whose shady affairs become the focus of the investigation.

Of all the foreign writers coming on the English-language
publishing scene in the comparative bull market for translated
crime fiction, Henning Mankell may be the most commercially
and critically successful. Certainly he is the most popular Swedish
crime writer in translation since the team of Maj Sjöwall and Per
Wahlöö in the 1960s and 1970s. My own first meeting with
Mankell's work, the 2005 novel *Before the Frost*, was a major dis-
appointment, especially in light of his reputation: overlong, repetitious, and soap operatic, in common with too much contemporary
British and American crime fiction, with none of the liveliness and
humor of Sjöwall and Wahlöö. But the latest Mankell in English
translation is an earlier book, originally published in Sweden in
1994. Were Mankell's bad habits a more recent development?
Afraid not.

The fashion in crime fiction is for long books, not a bad thing
if the extra pages provide more depth of character, richness of
background, and complexity of plot. Unfortunately, what usually
comes instead is recapping of the same plot points over and over,
irrelevant details of the protagonist's daily activities, and extra
scenes and exchanges of dialogue that add nothing necessary or
useful. If the dialogue has the bite and wit of an Ed McBain, the
latter form of padding can be tolerable or even welcome. But the
exchanges between Mankell's characters are bland and flavorless,

for which I don't blame the translator: given the mundane content, they could hardly be any livelier in Swedish.

The novel is not a total waste of time. Mankell's plot is intriguing enough, though lacking in surprises, and the detective work is often interesting. The sense of a nation in the grip of unwelcome change—in crime, police work, public administration— is nicely conveyed. The interrelationships of the police characters, including the city's first woman detective, are believably sketched. As for Wallender himself, he's a well-realized character, albeit a drag to be around when off the scent and too much given to leaps of intuition and lapses of common sense. This could have been a reasonably diverting police procedural at half the length, but Mankell's inflated reputation remains a mystery.

MARGARET MILLAR

(review of *The Couple Next Door: Collected Short Stories*, Crippen & Landru, 2005)

The Weekly Standard, April 18, 2005

Under the pseudonym Ross Macdonald, Kenneth Millar became a crime fiction icon. But his Canadian wife Margaret (1915-1994) entered the field first and through most of the 1940s and 1950s was the more celebrated. Though she vocally denied the claim, some critics believe she was her husband's superior as a novelist. A new collection of her short fiction, *The Couple Next Door*, with an excellent scholarly introduction by Macdonald biographer Tom Nolan, invites a rediscovery of her work, tracing the arc of her career with two novellas by the competent but derivative neophyte of the early '40s and four short stories by the more subtle, assured, and psychologically acute author of her later mature work.

While Millar was good from the beginning, no reader of her earliest mysteries would put her in the Ross Macdonald class. *The Invisible Worm* (1941) and *The Weak-Eyed Bat* (1942) established her as a farceur in the tradition of Phoebe Atwood Taylor (a.k.a. Alice Tilton) and Craig Rice. Her amateur detective, psychiatrist Dr. Paul Prye, is represented in *The Couple Next Door* by "Mind Over Murder" (1942), which despite a promising premise, murder among an assorted group of neurotics at an island Colony for Mental Hygiene in Lake Huron, is not a particularly strong story. Though probably intended for the prestigious and well-paying slick magazine *American*, which featured a short mystery novel in every issue, it wound up instead in a pulp, *Street & Smith's Detective Story Magazine*. *American*'s editors may also have had a shot at the recently discovered "Last Day in Lisbon" (1943), a World War II spy potboiler, nicely enough written in uncharacteristic first person but minor Millar. It landed in another pulp, *Five-Novels Monthly*.

The Devil Loves Me (1942) marks a transition in Millar's work. Seeming impatient with lightweight, cozy comedies, she pairs Prye with a much more intriguing and serious professional, Inspector Sands, a Toronto policeman who specializes in middle- and upper-class murder. Prye's wedding is interrupted by the poisoning of one of the bridesmaids—she survives, but murders follow. For all their bright dialogue, the characters are not especially vivid, and many readers will anticipate the murderer, either through guesswork (based on a time-honored misdirection) or at least one very fair clue. While one element of the solution makes the Canadian background essential, otherwise the story could take place in any North American city. (In a reflection of how times have changed, one character remarks, "We hang everybody in Canada.") While amateur and pro combine to solve the case, Sands gets the final curtain call, and Prye will never appear again.

Millar would return to the wacky farcical mystery occasionally. *Fire Will Freeze* (1944), in which stranded bus passengers in Quebec ski country take refuge from a blizzard in an old house occupied by an insane elderly woman and her nurse, is reminiscent of the work of Constance and Gwenyth Little, Australian-American sisters who specialized in comic whodunits. Other forays into comedy included *Rose's Last Summer* (1952), with a clever plot based on the tax regulations of the time, and *The Murder of Miranda* (1979), the second novel about Chicano lawyer Tom Aragon. But Millar's lasting reputation would not be built on her humorous books.

Impatience with series characters may partially account for Millar's failure to establish a "brand name" commensurate with the quality of her work. Inspector Sands would appear in only two more novels, *Wall of Eyes* (1943) and *The Iron Gates* (1945), plus the fine title story of the new collection, "The Couple Next Door" (1954), which finds the Canadian cop in California retirement. Millar's novels did without a continuing sleuth for over thirty years, until the not especially memorable Aragon made three appearances between 1977 and 1982.

The Iron Gates, a sober psychological study with a well-worked-out puzzle and complex character relationships, gained Millar a Hollywood contract along with increased stature in the suspense fiction field. Lucille Morrow, second wife of Dr. Andrew Morrow, has always had a distant and uncomfortable relationship with her two stepchildren, now well into their twenties but still living in the family home. Lucille is haunted by dreams of her husband's first wife Mildred, who we gradually come to suspect may have been murdered. When a mysterious small parcel is delivered to Lucille, she vanishes from the house and eventually lands in a mental institution. According to Nolan, Jack Warner's eagerness to film the novel was dampened when both Bette Davis and Barbara Stanwyck turned the project down, not wanting to play a character who dies well before the end.

After three novels more mainstream than criminous, Millar returned to detection with *Do Evil in Return* (1950), about Dr. Charlotte Keating, a general practitioner in an unnamed California coastal city based on Santa Barbara, where the Millars now lived. Having an affair with a married lawyer while treating his neurotic wife as a patient, the doctor becomes involved in the death of a young pregnant woman and is romantically pursued by the cop on the case. The novel is another triumph, with a superb build-up of suspense, including an evocation of the Santa Ana wind to rival Raymond Chandler's and a well-prepared surprise delivered in a chilling denouement.

Beast in View, the Edgar Allan Poe Award winner for best novel of 1955, is superbly done but at a disadvantage with latter-day readers because the surprise solution, then fresh, has been re-used so often since. But the three novels that followed represent the pinnacle of Millar's achievement and retain their powerful impact more than forty years after initial publication.

In *The Listening Walls* (1959), Millar brings off a trick that is rarely attempted and even more rarely accomplished successfully: withholding the final surprise to the very last line of the novel. Two San Francisco women in their thirties, unpleasant divorcee Wilma Wyatt and her friend Amy Kellogg, are staying in a Mexico City hotel on what seems an ill-advised vacation. When Wilma falls to her death from a balcony in an apparent suicide, Amy's husband Rupert ostensibly brings her home. But Amy disappears from sight, and her brother Gill becomes convinced Rupert has done away with her. The novel is a psychological puzzle-box, somewhat like the currently popular trend in movies like *The Swimming Pool* and *Memento*, the difference being that in the end Millar reveals the truth without ambiguity. The Mexican and American backgrounds are effectively rendered, and the psychology of the characters, however deceptively it is presented, is ultimately sound.

By the author's own account in introducing a 1983 reprint, *A Stranger in My Grave* (1960) began with an idea she had jotted down in her notebook: "A woman dreams of visiting a cemetery and seeing engraved on a granite tombstone her name, the date of her birth and the date of her death four years previously. Write your way out of that one, kiddo." When Daisy Fielding Harker, troubled wife of a successful real estate broker in suburban San

Félice (another stand-in for the Millars' Santa Barbara hometown), has the dream, she goes against the wishes of her over-protective husband and mother to hire bail bondsman and private eye Steve Pinata to help her find out what happened to her on December 2, 1955, the death date on the tombstone. Eventually, they find the real-life tombstone, which bears a different name but the same date of death. Characteristically, Millar shifts the viewpoint from character to character, often in unexpected ways, as the mystery is gradually worked out with the final surprise again withheld to the very last line.

One of the standard elements of California private eye fiction is the nutty religious cult. Millar's variation on the theme in *How Like an Angel* (1962) stands as one of the best. Joe Quinn, compulsive gambler and licensed Nevada private investigator, is fleeing debts in Reno when he takes refuge for the night at the mountain compound of the Brothers and Sisters of the Tower of Heaven, a shrinking but devout fellowship who have successfully cut themselves off from the sinful influences of the outside world. The denizens have taken names like Sisters Blessing, Contrition, and Glory of the Ascension; Brothers Crown of Thorns, Tongue of Prophets, and Light of the Infinite. Initially the effect borders on the comic, but Millar takes them seriously, not in terms of believing their dogma but in convincing the reader that they believe it. Their leader, known as the Master, may be mad or deluded, but he's no charlatan. At great risk to herself, Sister Blessing uses $120, sent by her son in Chicago and squirreled away in violation of the sect's vow of poverty, to hire Quinn to go to the Central Valley town of Chicote and find a man named Patrick O'Gorman. Quinn takes the money and, somewhat to his own surprise, carries out the assignment, learning O'Gorman was a respected local citizen who died (his wife says by accident, but the police believe by murder) several years before. The investigation, beyond his initial charge, involves Quinn more and more deeply, and the rest of the complex narrative shifts between the cult's headquarters, the small town, and other California locales. Once again, the truth is gradually revealed, with one last shock withheld for the final lines of the novel. In *How Like an Angel*, the balance of elements—psychological insight, romance, suspense—achieves near perfection in the finest novel of Millar's career.

In these three novels, Millar's themes, techniques, and concerns resemble her husband's. All three involve upper middle class California suburbanites and include private eye characters. In the last two, the private eyes are the "leads" and, as in a Lew Archer case, the investigation in the present has its roots in a crime a few years in the past. Though Macdonald's books were written from Archer's first-person viewpoint, Millar uses third person, and her perfect command permits her to change course in surprising directions without any loss of narrative impetus. The reader manipulation, with a gradual and selective release of information by the author, is obvious in retrospect and sometimes as it is going on. When the case is put in terms of a private eye's investigation, as in most of *How Like an Angel*, the manipulation is less apparent. Millar's control of her characters and story elements is so surefooted that occasional lapses (too much exposition in dialogue, use of overheard conversations, unlikely confidences between characters) are easily overlooked.

Millar continued to produce distinguished work, and unlike some writers with long careers suffered no steep decline in quality. *The Fiend* (1964), about a sympathetically observed pedophile, demonstrates the effectiveness of low-key, understated, inexplicit menace, the threat of violence and horror rather than its graphic depiction. The situation of a little girl with more interest in the neighbors than her own family was foreshadowed in the paranormal short story "The People Across the Canyon" (1962), collected in *The Couple Next Door*. In *Beyond This Point Are Monsters* (1970), longtime trial watcher Millar introduced substantial courtroom action into her work for the first time, an unusual nonadversary probate action to declare dead a missing fruit-grower who may have been murdered, and delivered another of her patented surprise finishes. After the three novels featuring Tom Aragon and the non-series *Banshee* (1983), Millar returned to the courtroom for her final book-length work. By this time, her husband had died after a long battle with Alzheimer's Disease and Millar herself was legally blind as a result of glaucoma, but *Spider Webs* (1986), viewing a Santa Felicia (the now-feminized San Félice) murder trial from the points of view of various participants, is an outstanding novel and a fine windup to her novelistic career.

Millar's emphasis on the finishing surprise reflects her admiration for Agatha Christie, who in turn cited Millar as one of her favorite contemporary mystery writers. In 1979, Millar was quoted as saying, "I consider Christie an excellent plotter. When I read *Witness for the Prosecution*, I knew she really had a twisted little mind. I wished I had thought of it." In a 1957 interview, she sounded more like one of today's writers who chafe at Christie comparisons: "I happen to be able to *write* rings around her and she happens to be able to *situate* rings around me." The fact is that Millar, like Christie, plays games with the reader. She never lies but is selective in what she tells and when she tells it, including following the thoughts of characters that have more on their minds than she reveals and describing scenes in which one of the characters could be identified but isn't.

While both Millars had more on their minds than the puzzle, they recognized it as the element that made the detective novel a unique genre. They both had an allegiance, for all their interest in psychology and character development, to complex plotting and reader misdirection, providing fairly placed clues even in subgenres (the private eye novel, the farcical mystery, the psychological study) that sometimes did without them.

Margaret Millar was favorably reviewed throughout her career and was recognized by her peers with the Mystery Writers of America's Grand Master Award in 1983. Still, her novels are out of print and she is less well known to present-day readers than she should be. Whether she was actually superior to her more famous husband is open to question—if I think so at the moment, rereading a Ross Macdonald or two might change me back again. But she clearly belongs with him in the top dozen North American mystery writers and some enterprising publisher should get her novels back into print without delay.

Postscript 2008: My finishing plea was answered in 2006 when Stark House published an omnibus volume of An Air That Kills *(1957) and* Do Evil in Return, *with an introduction by Tom Nolan.*

FRANCIS M. NEVINS

Introduction, *Leap Day and Other Stories* (Five Star, 2003)

Reputations are made in the world of mystery and detective fiction in a variety of ways. Some contribute strictly as practitioners: Edgar Allan Poe, Arthur Conan Doyle, Anna Katharine Green, and Agatha Christie are prime examples. Others may never publish a word of fiction but are admired as critics, historians, bibliographers, editors, publishers, or anthologists: names like Howard Haycraft, James Sandoe, Allen J. Hubin, Joan Kahn, Douglas G. Greene, and Otto Penzler come to mind.

Then there are the all-rounders, those who have both written distinguished crime fiction and served the field in scholarly, critical, or editorial roles: a few notable examples include Dorothy L. Sayers, Ellery Queen, Anthony Boucher, Vincent Starrett, Dorothy B. Hughes, Julian Symons, and (among our contemporaries) Bill Pronzini, Edward D. Hoch, H.R.F. Keating, Marcia Muller, and Ed Gorman. One member of the latter category is Francis M. Nevins, known as Mike to his many friends.

Mike's day job has been as a St. Louis University Professor of Law. One of the qualities that must make him a great teacher has also made him an outstanding writer on and of detective fiction: boundless, infectious enthusiasm. Among his other qualities, Mike is a tireless promoter, not just of himself but of undervalued B-movie and serial directors and of mystery writers both in the canon (Queen, Cornell Woolrich, Erle Stanley Gardner) and off the wall (Harry Stephen Keeler, Michael Avallone, Milton M. Propper).

I probably first encountered the writing of Francis M. Nevins, Jr., as his byline then was, in the seventh issue (August 1967) of *The JDM Bibliophile*, a fanzine edited and published by Len and June Moffatt and devoted to the works of John D. MacDonald. His "Random Thoughts on JDM and the Frustration of the Expected" says more in three paragraphs about the conventions of popular fiction and their subversion than some scholarly essays ten times the length.

When Al Hubin's pioneering general mystery fanzine *The Armchair Detective* made its glorious debut in October 1967, many capable and knowledgeable writers, both familiar names and newer ones, emerged as contributors. It was obvious from the first paragraph of "The Worst Legal Mystery in the World" in the April

1968 issue that young lawyer Nevins would be among the most
learned and entertaining of *TAD*'s unpaid, labor-of-love contributors: "Near the end of the South Sea epic *Bird of Paradise*, when
the kahuna or witch doctor asks Debra Paget whether she is ready
to jump into the volcano as a human sacrifice, she answers, 'I have
loved (poignant pause) and been loved. I am ready.' And if around
Christmas a few years ago the kahuna had happened to ask me the
same question, I would have replied in the same tone of satiated
resignation. For I had just finished the most inane, inept, unreal,
and most purely enjoyable novel I can recall reading." The book in
question was Keeler's *The Amazing Web*.

    Though we had exchanged some correspondence, I didn't
meet Mike for the first time until 1971. By this time, his landmark
anthology of essays, *The Mystery Writer's Art*, had been published
and his fame as a detective fiction expert was growing, though his
first fiction publication was still a year away. The evening after the
MWA's Edgar Award ceremony, in the Bronx apartment of
Marvin Lachman, another pioneering fan, Mike showed my wife
Rita and me his maps of the oddball terrain in Keeler's impossi-
ble-crime novel *The Vanishing Gold Truck*, doing his best to convince us the author was not an inexplicable (and unreadable) curiosity but an unappreciated genius.

    By October 1968, Mike had begun a series for *TAD* about
Cornell Woolrich, which would culminate in the Edgar-winning
biography *Cornell Woolrich: First You Dream, Then You Die*
(1988). In the first issue of Robert E. Washer's *Queen Canon Bibliophile* (undated but mailed in September 1968), he began a serialized study of the works of Ellery Queen that would culminate
even sooner in an Edgar winner, *Royal Bloodline* (1974). Not kept
busy enough by these activities, he was also contributing regularly
to Lianne Carlin's *The Mystery Lover's* [later *Reader's*] *Newsletter*, which like *TAD* had debuted in October 1967. At the time, this
level of activity seemed amazingly copious to an observer, but in
retrospect, considering what Mike has accomplished since in his
various roles both in and out of the crime fiction field, it looks like
business as usual.

    Mike has created three series characters: first law professor
Loren Mensing, who appears in four of his six novels; then con-
man Milo Turner, who appears in the other two; and finally policewoman Gene Holt, who so far is strictly a short-story sleuth.
These three characters were emphasized in his first short story collection, *Night of Silken Snow and Other Stories* (Five Star, 2001),

and each of them makes a single appearance in the present volume. But the emphasis here is on shorter non-series crime stories with a variety of moods and backgrounds. Mike's stories represent his range of interests, from his legal specialty of intellectual property to western movies to classical music, and above all his devotion to devious but reader-fair puzzle plotting.

Mike wrote in the *St. James Guide to Crime & Mystery Writers* that his ideal mystery would combine "Erle Stanley Gardner's crackling pace and legal ingenuity, Ellery Queen's labyrinthine plot structure and deductive fair play, and Cornell Woolrich's feel for suspense and the anguish of living and compellingly visual style." The influence of these three writers is manifest in all his fiction. Of course, many writers strive to emulate Gardner's courtroom dramatics and lawyerly combat (though regrettably too few his sense of pace), and there is no shortage of writers attempting Woolrich's combination of nail-biting tension and dark pessimism. But how many of today's writers even try to plot like the Ellery Queen team? Mike Nevins does—and frequently succeeds.

Postscript 2008: I'm ashamed to admit that almost forty years later, I still haven't read The Vanishing Gold Truck, *but I've hung onto my copy and will get to it eventually. There's not much in the above introduction about Mike's novels. I think the best of them are his second,* Corrupt and Ensnare *(1978), about Mensing, and his third,* The Ninety Million Dollar Mouse *(1987), about Turner, but all are worth reading. I wrote the following about his* Into the Same River Twice *("Jury Box," September 1996): "Eighteen years after his previous book-length appearance...law professor Loren Mensing returns, seeking a lost love and a wide-ranging conspiracy in 1987 New York and St. Louis. The author's three self-identified influences are all apparent: two highly ingenious dying messages a la Ellery Queen appear, one of them in a self-contained short story in the first chapter (first published as 'Murder of a Male Chauvinist,' EQMM, May 1973); the second chapter has a lady-vanishes situation out of Cornell Woolrich; and the central plot involves citizen dissatisfaction with the adversarial justice system that was Erle Stanley Gardner's home ground. Nevins's combination of these elements is both distinctive and totally involving."*

VIN PACKER

Murder Off the Rack, edited by Jon L. Breen and Martin H. Greenberg (Scarecrow Press, 1989)

Today, any type of mystery novel from the toughest to the coziest might be published first in paperback. The paperback original of the nineteen-fifties, however, was almost entirely a hardboiled, masculine domain, directed at a male audience and created by male writers. Not until the contemporary gothic trend of the sixties and seventies did female-oriented mystery fiction become a major factor in original softcover form. There is at least one exception, however, to the overwhelming maleness of the major paperback original writers of the fifties: Vin Packer, who is unique among the most successful paperback writers of the decade in other ways as well.

Vin Packer was born Marijane Meaker in Auburn, New York, in 1927. Though she has used her birth name as a byline occasionally, notably on the novel *Shockproof Sydney Skate* (1972), the bulk of her work has appeared pseudonymously. Her best-known pen name is M. E. Kerr, which she has used for a highly successful and honored group of young adult novels, beginning with *Dinky Hocker Shoots Smack* (1972).

M. E. Kerr's autobiography, *Me Me Me Me Me* (Harper and Row, 1983), discusses her early life through her sale of a short story (under the name Laura Winston) to *Ladies' Home Journal* in 1951. The book is addressed to the readers of her young adult novels and refers frequently to characters she used in the M. E. Kerr titles, but there are occasional references to her work as Vin Packer, including her possibly unique reason for entering the suspense field: "solely because I'd heard that *The New York Times'* mystery columnist, Anthony Boucher, would review paperbacks. Encouraged by his reviews of my work, I stayed in the field about ten years before going on to hardcover under my own name, Meaker."

As the quote above suggests, Packer's original impulse as a novelist was not building either puzzles or suspense. Very few of her books can accurately be called detective or mystery stories, though they are certainly crime novels. Most are not even suspense tales in the conventional sense. Rather, they are straight novels that happen to concern a crime, and usually the action con-

sists of the events leading up to the crime, with the emphasis on
the criminal's motivation. Once the crime has taken place, the
novel is virtually over. The investigation rarely plays a major part.

A number of elements recur again and again in Packer's fiction. One of the most pervasive is the troubled adolescent character. Though many of the later novels deal entirely with adults,
equally troubled, the interest in the problems of youth that would
inspire the M. E. Kerr books is quite obvious in the early Packers.
Her ability to get inside the heads of children and teenagers, realistically reflecting their problems and attitudes, is comparable to
Stephen King's. More than once, the central character is an adolescent male being raised by a widowed or divorced mother, with a
well-meaning but ineffectual family friend attempting to serve as
father substitute.

Another recurring element is homosexuality. Under the name
Ann Aldrich, Packer wrote paperback Lesbian novels, a surprisingly viable sub-genre in the fifties, though there was no comparable market for sympathetic stories of male homosexuality, at least
from mainstream publishers. Some of the Packer novels have specifically gay subject matter, and references to homosexuality,
veiled and direct, are numerous even in those that do not.

References to college days are frequent, with much attention
to the initiation and rushing rites of fraternities and sororities.
Many characters share Packer's background at the University of
Missouri, specifically its vaunted journalism school.

Packer often employs quotations from popular song lyrics
(oddly, never with a copyright notice) and poetry, sometimes
original. The novels are always *au courant,* filled with topical references to news events, motion picture and television personalities, and concerns of the day.

Finally, and most significantly, Packer's novels are totally devoid of either heroes or villains. Virtually everyone is troubled,
mixed up, or deluded at best, psychotic at worst. No one is totally
okay, and nearly every character has at least some redeeming
qualities. Packer specializes in psychopathic killers of varying
types, and her treatment of them is never simplistic. Indeed, her
absolute refusal to provide easy answers to psychological or social
problems is one of the qualities that most endeared her to the critic
she originally sought to impress, Anthony Boucher.

Come Destroy Me (1954) was not the first Vin Packer novel.
Gold Medal, the publisher of all but one of Packer's paperback
originals, lists three earlier books opposite the title page. *Spring*

Fire, a Lesbian-themed book published in 1952, was her first major success and perhaps her most famous single title of the period. Also listed are *Dark Intruder* (1952) and *Look Back on Love* (1953), both of which are identified as crime fiction in Allen J. Hubin's bibliography, *Crime Fiction, 1749-1980.* But *Come Destroy Me* was the first of her books to be reviewed by Boucher and the earliest I have examined for this article. It sets a pattern for many of the Packer suspense novels to come. Only from the publisher's cover blurb and the chapter epigraphs would the reader know until very late in the story that the book was a crime novel. Packer is interested in exploring the roots of violent crime, and most of the novel is concerned with setting up the circumstances that eventually lead to murder.

The setting of *Come Destroy Me* is Azrael, Vermont, in the Green Mountains. Sixteen-year-old Charlie Wright is a quiet library habitué, a brilliant, Harvard-bound student who is constantly teased by his college-age sister Evie. Most prominent older male figure in the fatherless household is irritating lawyer-widower Russel Lofton, who is mildly courting Charlie's mother, Emily. Epigraphs from trial testimony and psychiatric reports let us know that Charlie will kill, but the suspense lies in whom, how, and why. Although the reader knows Charlie will do murder, he initially doesn't seem all that much more troubled and confused than most adolescents, and therein lies much of the case history's fascination.

Object of Charlie's sexual fantasy is book dealer Jill Latham. Their first meeting foreshadows the classic coming-of-age movie *Summer of '42,* though this meeting is considerably less innocent on both sides. Jill is an odd-mannered heavy drinker with affected speech patterns, very much like a Tennessee Williams character.

Boucher was immediately impressed. As he would later, he praised Packer's reluctance to offer easy answers—"she never quite answers her own questions with any pat psychiatric diagram." The novel is "well and subtly written, with acutely overhead *[sic]* dialogue, full-length characterizations in brief compass, and excerpts from hearings that capture the exact flavor of authentic transcripts" *(New York Times Book Review,* March, 7, 1954).

Whisper His Sin (1954), though very different in cast and milieu, follows a similar pattern. New Yorker Ferris Sullivan—a poetry reader, personally fastidious, a "hopeless eccentric"—arrives at Jackson University in Virginia. He is clearly homosexual, though the term is waltzed around in the first part of the novel. His mother has tried throughout his life to erase those "tendencies," also seen in his Uncle Arnold. At Jackson, senior Paul Lasher becomes Ferris's protector and the wealthy Carter Fryman IV his chief tormentor. Again, the chapter epigraphs foreshadow the crime to come, though the questions of who will be killer and who victim are more ambiguous. (As is often the case, Gold Medal's blurb tells far too much.)

The treatment of homosexuality in the novel is fascinating, since the author is apparently trying to satisfy the moral qualms of the public and depict gays sympathetically at the same time. Lasher, a closet homosexual who wants to be "double gaited," takes Sullivan to a gay party at a New York apartment, then is angry when Sullivan, for the first time in his life not an outsider, fits in with this world all too well. The host is a Capote-ish outward queen known as Rug (because people walk all over him). At the party, the discussion of the homosexual and his options in a straight society becomes franker. Of the guests, only a Merchant Marine, a very minor character, seems well-adjusted to his sexual identity, so this is not what the present-day gay community would be likely to hail as a "positive" depiction. Still, in a mass market 1954 paperback, the scene seems far ahead of its time.

Packer appealed to Anthony Boucher's keen interest in true crime cases. His review identified the murder with a "startling recent New York parricide" and described the book as "a forceful and tragic novel of college life, homosexuality (handled with a surprising combination of good taste and explicitness), and the bitter after-the-fact relationship between collaborators in murder" *(NYTBR,* October 31, 1954).

Following two more novels of troubled youth, *The Thrill Kids* (1955) and *The Young and the Violent* (1956), both centered in New York, Packer published the first of two novels concerned with race relations in the deep South.

In the opening pages of *Dark Don't Catch Me* (1956), Harlem youth Millard Post is sent unwillingly to Paradise, Georgia. His grandmother is reported to be dying, and his father can't get off work to make the trip. As Millard travels south, and is gradually introduced to the horrors and inconsistencies of Jim Crow, we are filled in on the explosive situation that awaits him, all revolving around the household of wealthy landholder Thad Hooper: his long-dead twin sister, his sexy wife, his children, his black servants, and his white friends and neighbors, who are all busy debating the implications of Brown versus the Board of Education of

Topeka, the Supreme Court decision mandating school integration. More than anything else, however, the large cast of black and white characters is obsessed with and motivated by one thing: sex.

This time, all the specific foreshadowing of crime is in the cover copy rather than the text. Even more than its predecessors, this is a straight novel for most of the distance. Like all Packer's work, the novel is ambiguous and lacking in easy answers, but it is less successful than *Come Destroy Me* or *Whisper His Sin*. The reader has the feeling that the eventual crime and its aftermath could have been treated in greater detail—indeed, the story could support a book twice the length. It could have been an interesting example of the Big Trial novel, but legal proceedings were usually employed by Packer only in her chapter headings.

The overemphasis on sex brought the first mildly negative notice from Anthony Boucher, who found the book "dominated and distorted by an obsession with sex so powerful as to make John O'Hara's view of life seem somewhat bowdlerized." Packer made the root of "the entire Problem of the South . . . purely sexual in origin" *(NYTBR,* December 21, 1956). The anonymous reviewer in *The Saint Detective Magazine,* which reviewed paperback original novels in a monthly feature called "The Saint's Ratings," awarded the novel two halos (the next to highest rating) but groused that the novel "tries to take the 'color problem' into a barely modernized Uncle Tom's Cabin. Outstanding craftsmanship is wasted on what any Southerner will recognize as strictly Yankee plumbing" (June 1957). Both reviews referred to the story's origin in a recent real-life case, pegged by Boucher the "wolf-whistle" case.

3 Day Terror (1957) has several similarities to its predecessor, being set in a small southern town (Bastrop, Alabama), also faced with the imminent integration of its schools and also visited by someone from New York. Dee Benjamin, who once had a celebrated local romance with editor Jack Chadwick, now returns from the North a divorcee. Stranger Richard Buddy is in town to campaign against school integration. His racist tracts consist of a chilling burlesque of songs from *My Fair Lady.* The novel continues the previous book's theme: that virtually all the racial troubles in the South are based on lust and sexual fear. Again, the body of the book is a build-up to a violent finish, but a less criminous one than in the earlier novels. Boucher did not review the book, and the *Saint's* rater awarded only one halo, while introducing similar caveats: "We fail to recognize too clearly Vin Packer's South and her Southern dialect seems to have a faint ring of the north in it.

The story itself seems at times to get as confused as the lives of the people who tread not too ably through it" (December 1957).

The novel is clearly not one of Packer's best, but it contains the kind of social observation that makes the least of her work worthy of attention, as when politico Troy Porter discourses on the requirements for a southern politician: "Even God himself had to produce a son to get some respect down here, and a good politician's got to do a hell of a lot more. He's got to go to church, and he'd better have gone to war. He's got to have a wife, kids, a dog and a low-priced car. He can't get caught sinning, but he better seem capable of it."

Packer's next novel, *5:45 to Suburbia* (1958), seems to be guiding the reader to a shock ending that never happens. Though listed with Packer's crime novels in Hubin's bibliography, it really isn't a crime novel at all but rather a combination of two fifties bestseller genres: the executive-suite novel and the adultery novel. Despite the title, there is very little about life in the suburbs. Main character is 50-year-old publishing executive Charlie Gibson, who objects to his company's new *Confidential*-type scandal magazine, yet unnamed but called *Vile* around the office. We meet Charlie on his fiftieth birthday, then flash back to earlier birthdays, beginning with his eighteenth when he was a student at the University of Missouri. A former classmate, now a TV commentator, is scheduled for exposé in *Vile* concerning an old pederasty charge.

Another 1958 book, *The Evil Friendship*, is definitely criminous, fictionalizing New Zealand's Parker-Hulme case of four years before. In his review, Boucher characterized the case as a Lesbian Loeb-Leopold and pronounced Packer "as relentlessly tough-minded as any of the best 'hard-boiled' writers" *(NYTBR,* September 7, 1958).

The Twisted Ones (1959) may be the finest of Packer's novels. The narrative alternates the lives of three troubled youths: Brock Brown, 15, handsome, puritanical New Yorker, a compulsive thief subject to blinding headaches; Charles Berrey, 8, a precocious New Jersey boy who is a big-money quiz show contestant; and Reginald Whittier, 19, a shy stutterer, mother-dominated with a friend-of-the-family father substitute. Parents in Packer novels are full of well-meant but excruciatingly harmful advice. Whittier's mother exhorts him, "Be a bush if you can't be a tree!"

All three boys have serious problems, though Brock is the most obviously disturbed, and in the closing chapters all three commit murder. Though the trio of well-drawn central characters never meet, they are linked by Packer in inventive ways, and a simplistic *Time*-style epilogue about Memorial day murders by members of the "shook-up" generation ironically brings them together at the end.

Though the novel was written before the quiz scandals hit, the quiz-show sequences in *The Twisted Ones* provide a good example of Packer's ability to use the events that define the times in a way that is successful both artistically and commercially. Her next novel, *The Girl on the Best Seller List* (1960), was inspired by another phenomenon of the day: Grace Metalious and her bestselling novel of small-town scandal, *Peyton Place*. In this novel, Packer flirts with the whodunit form for the first time, as several residents of Cayuta, New York, have good reason to contemplate the murder of novelist Gloria Whealdon, author of the best-selling *roman à clef, Population 12,360*. What makes the subject matter especially interesting is that Packer, though obviously a more serious and admirable writer than the fictional Whealdon (and probably the real-life Metalious), admits to drawing freely on real people and experiences for her own fiction. Typically, the expected crime occurs very late in the book. Though Packer answers the question of who committed the crime, there is a fine irony in the solution.

Both *Twisted Ones* and *Girl on the Best Seller List* have a character named Dr. Mannerheim. His first name changes from Clyde to Jay, but in each case he is a Ph.D. who practices or wants to practice psychology. Clyde has an art history doctorate but teaches psychology at Brock Brown's school. Jay actually practices psychology, but much is made of the fact that he is not a "real" doctor, and there is some question whether his bills can be taken as income-tax deductions. In a later Packer novel, *Something in the Shadows,* there is a reference to still another Dr. Mannerheim, though he never appears in the story. Prolific writers for the pulps and paperback originals often repeated character names out of haste and carelessness, but Packer never strikes the reader as a careless writer. She seems to know exactly what she is doing in using Dr. Mannerheims in three books, though what significance the name has for her is grist for a deeper study than this one.

The author's choice of character names is often intriguing. She would return to the title character's name in *The Damnation of Adam Blessing* (1960) for the main character in one of her M. E. Kerr novels, *The Son of Someone Famous* (1974). *Adam Blessing* drew another admiring review from Boucher, who wrote that

Packer, "consistently the most sensitive and illuminating writer of paperback originals, is at her perceptive best" in "a full-scale and disquieting portrait of a psychopath" (*NYTBR,* February 26, 1961).

In what may seem an extreme example of drawing on real life, Packer uses her own real surname for the main character in *Something in the Shadows* (1961). Folklorist Joseph Meaker (yet another former University of Missouri student) has moved to a Pennsylvania farm with wife Maggie, who is employed in advertising in New York. Joseph is a confirmed, indeed extreme animal-lover, and when his cat Ishmael is run over by a doctor's Mercedes, Joseph begins to plot revenge. His plans take an odd course when he insists that he and Maggie befriend Dr. and Mrs. Hart, inviting them to dinner. The story is more like a standard suspense novel than most of Packer's, the reader suspecting that Meaker will murder but not knowing whom or how. The crime comes earlier in the book than usual, though still in the second half. Maggie's occupation provides the vehicle for some advertising parodies, notably a soft-sell cigarette commercial. ("Ladies and gentlemen, Pick cigarettes bring you three minutes of uninterrupted silence....The public is tired of noisy commercials. They're irritating"). Early in the novel, Joseph receives a letter from a Hungarian woman and former left-wing activist he knew at Missouri. The real-life origin of this character can be seen in the author's relationship with a Hungarian man, described in *Me Me Me Me Me.*

The writer Packer is most often compared to by reviewers is John O'Hara. That the influence is a real one is suggested by the O'Hara parody contained in *Something in the Shadows,* where one character imagines some O'Hara dialogue.

Indeed, Anthony Boucher, in reviewing Packer's next novel, *Intimate Victims* (1962), credits her "eye and ear for nice distinctions of culture and usage as acute as those of . . . O'Hara and Nancy Mitford" (*NYTBR,* November 11, 1962). Reviewing the novel in tandem with Ross Macdonald's *The Zebra-Striped Hearse,* he finds in Packer "an almost comparable amount of meat," high praise indeed considering Boucher's view of Macdonald. A closer comparison in the crime/suspense field might be Patricia Highsmith, as the relationship between main characters Robert Bowser and Harvey Plangman has something of a *Strangers on a Train* flavor. For once, a crime appears at the very beginning of the book. The treasurer of an investment firm, Bowser has embezzled over $100,000, and he is planning his imminent escape to Brazil when, through an unfortunate stroke of fate, he inadvertently trades jackets and wallets with Plangman in a service-station restroom. Obsessive social climber Plangman, a pitiful collector of brand names and foreign phrases who is one of Packer's most memorable characters, finds the evidence of Bowser's plans and takes the opportunity for an odd and elaborate blackmail plan: Bowser must take Plangman's place as superintendent of a boardinghouse near the University of Missouri, while providing him evidence by mail on which clothes to wear, brands to buy, and dishes to cook while futilely courting a rich man's daughter. Of course, the scheme will culminate in murder, but again who will murder whom is left to the end of the book.

Alone at Night (1963) is Vin Packer's last novel for Gold Medal. In fact, only two more novels under the pseudonym would appear, one a hardcover. Once again, the setting is Cayuta, New York, in the Finger Lakes. This novel may represent Packer's closest approach to a detective story, albeit an inverted one. Buzzy Cloward went to prison for causing the death of Carrie Burr, running her down while drunk and driving her husband's car. Now he returns to Cayuta, where Carrie's husband Slater Burr has remarried. The reader soon comes to suspect that Cloward may not be guilty, but any whodunit element is short-lived: Slater is the person really responsible. Awkward questions begin to arise—how, for example, could the drunken Cloward immediately figure out how to drive Burr's difficult and unfamiliar Jaguar?—and the novel's suspense lies in how (or whether) Burr will ultimately be found out.

The novel, though competent enough, lacks Packer's usual zest. Boucher again reviewed a Packer book in tandem with others, and again the company he chose for her shows how highly she was regarded. *Alone at Night* is bracketed with John D. MacDonald's *On the Run* and Donald E. Westlake's *Killy* as examples of sub-par performances by good writers. Boucher said the "polish seems machine-made, without the exciting creativity we have associated with these writers" (*NYTBR*, June 2, 1963).

The last Packer paperback original is better, though still not in a class with the best books of the fifties and early sixties. *The Hare in March* (Signet, 1966), like several of the novels from Gold Medal, is given a cover blurb that emphasizes its trendiness: "A shattering novel about the college boys and girls who fly high on violence, sex, and L.S.D." As usual, it is far less conventional and predictable than the blurb might suggest. The first chapter suggests a traditional mystery, as two Far Point, New York cops on patrol discover a dead girl next to a spaced-out college boy in a car at the local lover's lane. But the novel then flashes back to the events leading up to the crime, in a pattern like that in Packer's earliest books, albeit somewhat more complex in plot. The scene is Far Point College, where L.S.D. is used in a fraternity hazing. Undersized Arnold Hagerman is a chilling figure in the grand tradition of Packer psychopaths. That Packer kept her finger on the pulse of the times is indicated by her topical references—Vietnam protest (still fairly early in 1966), Timothy Leary, camp, and a couple of names that remain quite current today: Ronald Reagan and Cher.

Following one more novel, the hardcover astrology comedy *Don't Rely on Gemini* (Delacorte, 1969), the Packer byline was retired. In 1972, with the first M. E. Kerr book, the author almost immediately attained a firm place among the most celebrated authors of young adult "problem" novels. Few if any of the Kerrs could be classified as mystery and suspense, until the most recent one, *Fell* (1987), which is not only a mystery but introduces an element that could not be more foreign to the world of Vin Packer: a series detective!

M. E. Kerr's continued fame seems secure. But her alter ego Vin Packer is one of many authors of suspense fiction who are unjustly forgotten and deserve revival. She was a big seller in the fifties—the back cover of *Dark Don't Catch Me* is already claiming 4 1/2 million copies sold—and Boucher considered her one of the best crime novelists of her day, regardless of format. A rereading of her novels today bears out his opinion. Though all her novels are of interest, the following seem to this reader the most deserving of rediscovery: *Come Destroy Me, Whisper His Sin, The Twisted Ones*, and *Something in the Shadows*.

Still, with all the recent reprinting activity in the mystery/suspense field, the Packer novels remain unavailable. Most of the major reference works—*Encyclopedia of Mystery and Detection, Twentieth-Century Crime and Mystery Writers, 1001 Midnights, A Catalogue of Crime*—omit her from coverage. It seems safe to predict, however, that this neglect won't continue. With the current surge of feminisim in the crime-fiction world, no woman writer as outstanding as Vin Packer can be ignored for long.

Postscript 2008: It took a while, but my prediction came true when Stark House reissued six Packer novels, two to a volume, between 2004 and 2006, and Cleis Press reissued her pioneering Lesbian novel Spring Fire *in 2004. Also of criminous interest are her 2003 memoir (as by Marijane Meaker)*, Highsmith: A Romance of the 1950s *and the 2007 return of the Packer byline with* Scott Free, *a mystery introducing a transgender detective.*

REBECCA C. PAWEL

(review of *Law of Return*, Soho, 2004)

The Weekly Standard, June 21, 2004

With the growing popularity of mystery fiction set in the past, every historical period may eventually have its own sleuthing series. Post-Civil War Spain has been staked out by one of the most capable new crime writers to emerge in recent years: a young New York City high-school teacher. On April 29, Rebecca Pawel's *Death of a Nationalist* won an Edgar Award from the Mystery Writers of America for best first novel of 2003, and her second, *Law of Return*, has already confirmed that debut's high promise.

As Pawel's work opens, the Civil War that ravaged Spain in 1936 is effectively over, and Generalísimo Francisco Franco has assumed a control he won't relinquish until his death in 1975. But times continue to be hard. Food shortages leave much of the populace hungry, parts of the cities are in ruins, and raw political wounds continue to fester. Carlos Tejada Alonso y Léon is an officer of the Guardia Civil, charged with validating Franco's dubious claim that Spain is now at peace. Though such matters are always more complicated than they look, it's clear Tejada and his colleagues are on the winning side for the moment—but on the wrong side of history. Tejada is a Falangist, a Fascist, and thus seemingly an obvious villain. But he is not a Gestapo officer or death-camp custodian. He functions credibly as an essentially decent man who thinks he is doing the right thing, however it may look from a different time or place.

Like many fictional policemen, Tejada has educational and class advantages over most of his fellow officers. He came to the Guardia relatively late and from the university rather than the military academy, but achieved accelerated promotion to sergeant before his thirtieth birthday. Attracted to the military as a youth, Tejada followed his wealthy landowner father's wish that he study law, with the understanding he could join the army after graduation if he still wanted to. His interest in criminal law made the Guardia "an obvious compromise," though not one that pleased his family.

To his hero-worshipping young partner Jiménez, Tejada has the aura of both war hero and supersleuth. The police relationships follow a familiar pattern in procedural fiction: the tough, complex, sometimes ruthless but basically decent cop protagonist; his semi-competent partner; his demanding, difficult superior. But setting them against a historical background little explored in crime fiction makes all the difference. Pawel's treatment of Tejada's ambiguous position as a likeable, even heroic figure representing a questionable regime is one of the keys to her two novels' appeal, along with the solid realization of time and place and the creation of vivid secondary characters.

One of the measures of a new practitioner is how mystery fiction's many conventions will be followed, tweaked, or (sometimes) subverted. Observe how Pawel plays with the reader's expectations in introducing Tejada's first case. It is early April 1939. Seven-year-old Maria Alejandra, walking home from school through the Madrid streets, hears gunshots and finds the body of a Guardia corporal who has been shot to death. In her panicked run home, she leaves behind her half-filled school notebook, an unthinkable thing to lose in a time of strict paper rationing. The child's aunt Viviana, a Nationalist sympathizer in her early twenties, sets out to retrieve the notebook. Meanwhile, Tejada and Jiménez have been dispatched to the scene by their superior, Lieutenant Ramos, with clear instructions to "arrest anyone in the neighborhood who seems suspicious" and "if they're Reds, put them up against a wall" and summarily execute them. Finding Tía Viviana crouching by the body, Tejada reasonably assumes she has committed the crime and that the notebook in her hand has some sinister significance.

Pawel has set up a classic dramatic situation: The wrongly accused murder suspect is a Communist; the good-guy cop investigating the case is a Fascist. How will justice be done? Will a star-crossed romance ensue? The possibilities for suspense and conflict are more than sufficient, but what happens next shockingly undercuts the reader's expectations. Tejada feels certain Tía Viviana is guilty of murder, and he knows gang rape awaits a female prisoner. So he decides the most humane course, as well as the most expedient, is to follow the letter of his instructions from his superior. He shoots her in cold blood. Later, of course, Tejada will realize he has executed an innocent person, and he will be sorry. But given how cheaply human life can be valued in wartime, he is far from being as devastated by the knowledge as the reader might wish.

The murdered member of the Guardia proves to be Francisco López Pérez, with whom Tejada served during the Civil War. Tejada investigates his friend's murder, certain at first of who did it but unsure as to why. Meanwhile, Viviana's lover Gonzalo, a loyalist soldier severely injured in battle, is released from the hospital to the news of her death and vows to find the man who killed her, though emerging from hiding will risk his own life. The rest of the narrative alternates between Tejada's search for the truth and Gonzalo's search for Tejada.

When he visits the little girl's school, Tejada reminds the director he should have a Spanish flag in his office, along with a picture of Franco and posted words to the national anthem, but he offers the educator an out, suggesting the flag must have been burned by the Reds. Tejada is attracted to Maria Alejandra's teacher, Elena Fernández, a Nationalist sympathizer who is subsequently dismissed from her job because merely being questioned by the Guardia has made her politically suspicious. From their meeting gradually develops the romance of political opposites the reader might have anticipated earlier. Tejada and Elena find they both have connections to the university town of Salamanca, where he studied and her father was a professor.

The novel ends with the mystery solved but Tejada and Elena separated, their relationship calculatedly unresolved. Purely as a whodunit, the book is nothing exceptional, but as an exploration of its time and place, it is remarkable. One might carp about the occasional narrative clichés ("burst into tears," "exchanged glances") or the politically correct anachronism "chalkboard" for "blackboard," but generally the telling is fluid and graceful.

Tejada's first case has surprisingly little specific comment on the merits of the political situation in Spain but is more about the atmosphere of fear, mutual distrust, and distorted personal relationships that develop in such an environment. Pawel makes it clear there are decent people and knaves, true believers and pragmatists, on both sides of the divide. In her second novel, however, the stakes become clearer as the true face of Fascism is displayed in sharper relief.

Law of Return opens in the summer of 1940, over a year after the action of the first book. Tejada, now promoted to lieutenant, and Corporal Jiménez have commandeered a first-class carriage on the train to their new posting in Salamanca. Part of Tejada's new job is performing weekly interviews with a group of "parolees," suspicious characters kept under government surveillance, one of whom proves to be Elena Fernández's classics-professor father.

When she accompanies her father to his weekly meeting, the pair unexpectedly meet again.

Another parolee, Manuel Arroyo Díaz, a law professor from whom Tejada took a class in his university days, has gone missing. Arroyo, along with Elena's father, was one of four Salamanca professors who lost their university posts over a petition they signed in support of a colleague. Though the four professors are fictional, their protest was in reaction to a real event: the removal of Miguel de Unamuno from his post as rector of the University of Salamanca in 1936 after insulting Falangist General Millán de Astray. When a murder victim, found bludgeoned to death at a warehouse under renovation, is identified as Arroyo, Tejada doubts the body is really his.

In search of Arroyo, who he believes has faked his own death and fled the country, Tejada travels to Biarritz in Nazi-occupied France. There he again unexpectedly encounters Elena, who has gone to aid the escape of Joseph Meyer, a German Jew who is a family friend. When Tejada meets Meyer, he seems never to have encountered a Jew and to view him as an alien creature. Still, he helps Meyer to escape into Spain and offers him a strategy to save himself in the event he is found without identity papers. Under the 1924 Law of Return, he can claim descent from Sephardic Jews expelled from Spain centuries before and thus gain Spanish citizenship.

The mystery is brought to a satisfactorily dramatic and surprising conclusion. The personal story of Tejada and Elena proceeds along happy lines, though briefly derailed by the kind of boy-meets-girl-boy-loses-girl misunderstanding that is exasperating in fiction. The direction of their relationship at the end of the book opens the way for unlimited sequels.

Rebecca Pawel is a writer to watch. Her instincts will delight those readers who value intelligence over fireworks. Both novels have a continuous sense of menace but little in the way of contrived action scenes or choreographed suspense set-pieces. Instead, Pawel depicts the personal friction between fully-fleshed and credibly-motivated characters that produces much more satisfactory fictional conflict.

Postscript 2008: Pawel has continued the saga in two additional novels. The Watcher in the Pine *(Soho, 2005)is up to the standard of its predecessors. My "Jury Box" review (EQMM, June 2005): "In spring 1941, Carlos and Elena, married and ex-*

pecting a child, arrive at his new posting in the war-ravaged town of Potes, where his predecessor was murdered and bandits menace the Guardias. While you may more easily identify with Elena, very mildly feminist by current standards, Tejada and a local priest are made sympathetic despite attitudes today's readers will find antiquated at best, repellent at worst. Traditionalists note: Pawel honors the detective form with fair-play clues."

ELLERY QUEEN

The Weekly Standard, October 10, 2005

Literary reputation is as fragile in crime fiction as anywhere else, but the precipitous decline of Ellery Queen may be unique, one of the most total, and in some ways inexplicable, cases of devalued stock in the annals of American letters. From the 1930s into the 1970s, Frederic Dannay (1905-1982) and Manfred B. Lee (1905-1971), the two cousins behind the joint pseudonym, justified the mid-century pronouncement of New York *Times* critic Anthony Boucher that "Ellery Queen *is* the American detective story." Today, in their centenary year, most of their books are out of print, and the contribution of the team is frequently understated or even ignored in historical accounts. Some reasons, if not good ones, can be identified for their fall, but first, the happier story of their rise.

Lee and Dannay, drawing on experience in publicity and advertising, made an ingenious marketing decision when they used the same unforgettable name for their byline and their gifted amateur sleuth. First appearing in *The Roman Hat Mystery* (1929), Ellery the character was an erudite and somewhat annoying bibliophile along the lines of Philo Vance, the creation of S.S. Van Dine (Willard Huntington Wright), whose novels were bestsellers in the 1920s. Detective novelist Ellery aided his New York police inspector father in much the same way Vance advised District Attorney Markham. In their first novel, the cousins included some of that puzzle-minded time's familiar accoutrements—a mock non-fictional preface, a floor plan of the crime scene (New York's Roman Theatre), a list of characters—and added a refinement of their own: fifty pages from the end, they interrupt the action to present a challenge to the reader, who now has been provided the necessary clues to name the murderer "by a series of logical deductions and psychological observations...."

Through the early '30s, the team took the intellectual game that was the formal detective novel to greater heights than any American writer, arguably raising it from a craft to an art. They mined the mystery potential of specialized backgrounds—a department store in *The French Powder Mystery* (1930), a hospital in *The Dutch Shoe Mystery* (1931), a Madison Square Garden rodeo in *The American Gun Mystery* (1933)—and concealed among their characters a succession of master killers with god complexes who carried out seemingly inexplicable or even impossible murders of victims who left helpful if initially misleading or impenetrable dying messages. In the single year of 1932, Dannay and Lee published four novels that are considered classics by proponents of formal detection: *The Greek Coffin Mystery* and *The Egyptian Cross Mystery* as Queen, and *The Tragedy of X* and *The Tragedy of Y* as Barnaby Ross, the second byline they adopted for a four-book series about deaf actor sleuth Drury Lane. At some point in those early years, they hit on the division of labor that would continue throughout their collaboration: detailed plot outlines by Dannay would be expanded into novels, short stories, and later radio plays by Lee.

The partners, unlike their model Van Dine, were able to adapt to changing fashions. In the late thirties, they dropped the nationality/object title pattern and the overt challenge to the reader (though it would always be there implicitly) and took pains to humanize Ellery, while introducing more romantic interest in an effort to crack the slick magazine serialization market.

Through their peak period of the 1940s and 1950s, they deepened their exploration of psychology and serious social themes in landmark novels like *Calamity Town* (1942), first of four books set in the small New England town of Wrightsville. *Cat of Many Tails* (1949) vividly depicts the trauma to the collective psyche of Manhattan's citizens from fear of a serial killer. *The Glass Village* (1954), a rare Queen novel without Ellery as a character, confronts xenophobic hysteria and lynch-mob justice in response to the murder of an elderly small town artist resembling Grandma Moses. *Inspector Queen's Own Case* (1956) is a study in gerontology, in which the elder Queen detects on his own while exemplifying the adjustment problems of a new retiree. Experiments with style and theme continued through *The Finishing Stroke*, a 1958 novel looking back nostalgically on 1929, originally intended to be Ellery's final case.

Through it all, they never renounced the allegiance to the pure fair-play puzzle that was their early hallmark. While they were quite capable of creating effective sequences of action, menace, and pursuit, they knew their readers relished the intellectual pleasure of those extended scenes in which Ellery explained his reasoning in careful, painstaking detail.

As the Queen novels grew in quality and prestige, the name was advancing on other fronts, including ten fairly unremarkable

B movies between 1935 and 1942, a long-running radio series between 1939 and 1948, and several TV series in the 1950s that were
neither very good nor very Queenian, but helped to keep the brand
name before the public. A final series in 1975-76, with Jim Hutton
as Ellery, sought to approximate a genuine Queen style, including
the challenge to the viewer. Of these media adaptations, only the
radio show had direct involvement of Dannay and Lee.

In a more literarily significant event, the cousins edited the
high-class pulp magazine *Mystery League*, which lasted a mere
four issues in 1933 and 1934 but foreshadowed the 1941 launch of
Ellery Queen's Mystery Magazine, still the leading crime fiction
periodical 64 years later and the most prominent surviving institution to carry on the Queen name. Editorial work on the magazine
and a long series of influential anthologies was done almost entirely by Dannay, whose separate identity as the premiere editor in
the field put an added strain on his relationship with Lee, which
always had an element of Gilbert-and-Sullivan combativeness.

In 2005, the Queen centenary has been marked by a single
book, *The Adventure of the Murdered Moths*, a collection of radio
plays published by Crippen & Landru; a one-day symposium at
Columbia University, which houses Dannay's papers; and a series
of commemorative issues of *Ellery Queen's Mystery Magazine*.
For all the biographies and book-length studies accorded writers
like Agatha Christie, Dorothy L. Sayers, Dashiell Hammett, Raymond Chandler, and even the writer the Queens emulated (in the
true meaning of that abused word) earlier in their career, Van
Dine, there still is no full-scale biography of the Queen team and
only one book-length critical study, Francis M. Nevins's *Royal
Bloodline* (1974), now out of print. Indeed, the only in-print
Queen study is *The Sound of Detection* (2002), a reference on the
radio show by Nevins and Martin Grams, Jr.

How did Ellery Queen fall so far? I'll advance five possible
explanations.

First, the standard version of the genre's history has hardened
into an over-simplified conventional wisdom: classical detective
fiction, the artificial kind based on clues and deductions and puzzles for the reader to solve, is British and feminine and concerned
with the upper classes, thus the continued obeisance paid Christie
and Sayers. Tough fiction noir, allegedly but not necessarily more
realistic, is American and masculine, thus the admission into the
literary canon of Hammett and Chandler. In the British classical
model, the detective's activities restore order to a basically stable

society, while the American hardboiled model assumes that in a corrupt and chaotic world, there is no order to restore. The result of this pigeonholing is that American male classicists, the greatest of whom was Ellery Queen, tend to be marginalized, not fitting the handy historical grid. Opposing points—that the Queen team wrote in a proudly American idiom, that they explored many corners of life beyond the activities of the rich and privileged, that they did more experimenting with theme, approach, and subject matter than any of their contemporaries, and that they did not always claim everything in the garden of rationality is lovely—are lost in the discussion.

Second, the distinctive Queen prose style, which some find ornately over-decorated, may be a taste today's readers find it harder to acquire, as Jacques Barzun and Wendell Hertig Taylor suggest in *A Catalogue of Crime* (second edition, 1989), when they refer to "the chat and comment that enliven the Queen cases for some and make them a trifle too rich for others." Both cousins loved the English language, strove for the perfect word to convey their meaning, and wanted to reflect their times vividly and accurately. One of their hallmarks from the beginning was the accretion of details that would capture a time and a place and a mood, as in this example from an extended account of a New York heat wave in the early pages of *Cat of Many Tails*: "Some would seek the subways. The coupled cars kept their connecting doors open and when the trains rushed along between stations there was a violent displacement of the tunnel air, hellish but a wind." In Dannay's one solo novel, *The Golden Summer* (1953), published under his birth name Daniel Nathan, he recounts what two, four, six, eight, and ten cents would buy in the small-town 1915 world of ten-year-old Danny, with a prose poem whose rhythm foreshadows the rap song that leads off Meredith Willson's *The Music Man*: "When eight cents would buy a man's tie, or a whisk broom, or a white cotton-duck clothespin apron (big enough to hold 10 dozen clothespins) or a flaring open-top tin milk pail, or a fiber shoe brush with a dauber, or a leather money or tobacco pouch with a button clasp and Indian-head design...." For some readers, the Queen style remains a marvel; for others, it's a barrier.

Third, there is a general critical prejudice against literary collaboration. Two-handed fiction may be good commerce, but how can distinct creative visions combine to achieve the status of art? Both Dannay and Lee had serious literary aspirations, but their artistic visions were frequently at war. Dannay, a very good amateur poet as well as a puzzle-making genius, sought to break down artificial barriers and get the detective story taken seriously as literature. Lee, who would have pursued an academic career had he not been convinced his Jewish identity would prevent it, frankly did not think the detective form could ever achieve the heights of great literature.

That the unlikely result of this collision of competing sensibilities was a cohesive whole is illustrated by their disagreements over the 1948 novel *Ten Days' Wonder*, written while they were living on opposite coasts and communicating by long, often acrimonious letters. It's clear from surviving correspondence that both were unhappy with the finished product: Dannay thought his original concept had been distorted and violated by Lee's efforts, while Lee thought the elaborate puzzle was too far-fetched and psychologically implausible to render believably. Their mutual friend Anthony Boucher hated the book, whether because he shared Lee's concerns about the psychology or because (according to Dannay's theory) "it offended his deep sense of religiousness and theological purity, though he won't admit it." Still, many commentators consider this troubled project one of the team's greatest works. Though only a genius could piece together the clues of the incredibly complex early Queen cases, an attentive and thoughtful reader might actually figure out *Ten Days' Wonder*, both Ellery's initial mistaken solution (a Queen specialty) and the final true solution. Certainly, the Biblical references that begin in the very first line are a major clue.

Fourth, and possibly the biggest blot on the Queen image, is an early-sixties decision of the partners, no doubt fiscally and commercially wise at the time but disastrous in its effect on their claim to a serious literary reputation. Apart from juvenile books and radio scripts, Dannay and Lee did not use ghostwriters or third collaborators through the end of the 1950s. But in the 1960s, the Queen byline appeared on a series of paperback original novels, edited by Lee but written by a variety of popular fiction pros. Ellery the character did not appear in them, and most did not even try to approximate a Queenian writing or plotting style. At least the difference in format helped American fans to separate the real from the ersatz, but in Britain the wholly ghosted works appeared in hard covers from the same publisher, Victor Gollancz, as the genuine Queen novels.

Further confusing matters, several of the "real" Queen novels that appeared in hard covers in the 1960s and actually featured

Queen the sleuth involved uncredited third collaborators. Lee, suffering from various health problems and a severe case of writer's block, was unable to perform his usual function of fleshing out Dannay's detailed outlines, and the job fell to Theodore Sturgeon on one book and Avram Davidson on three.

Just how damaging was the whole ghostwriting business? Once their employment of ghosts became known, its extent became blurred in the minds of readers. One of the best Queen novels and one of the few currently in print (in the omnibus volume *The Hollywood Murders*) is *The Origin of Evil*, published in 1951 and unequivocally the sole work of Dannay and Lee. A few years ago, a friend remarked to me how impressed he was with the book and then asked who had actually written it. His suspect was Ross Macdonald.

Are all of these explanations for the Queens' decline just an advocate's straw men? Or do the Ellery Queen team really deserve higher stature in the history of detective fiction and American fiction generally? I believe they do, but the lack of contemporary appreciation may have more to do with their detective-puzzle style than their thematic explorations, literary aspirations, or elegant prose. Ellery Queen practiced a lost art. When I read a contemporary mystery novel that has one or two fairly placed clues to guide the alert reader to the solution, I tend to celebrate it as a classical throwback. But nobody today is even attempting the kind of ornate puzzles the EQ team put together—and did better than anybody, even Christie and Sayers and John Dickson Carr.

Reportedly one of the lessons producers William Link and Richard Levinson drew from the short-lived Queen TV series of the '70s was that you mustn't make the puzzles too hard. They dumbed down the clues in their subsequent project, *Murder, She Wrote*, and it was a triumphant success. Thus, my fifth possible explanation: that Ellery Queen has fallen from public attention because our respect for intelligence, our cultural literacy, and our attention span are all in steep decline.

SECTION TWO

SHORT TAKES ON 100 WRITERS

Catherine Aird. In a long career, she has given great pleasure with her low-key, humorous, traditional British mysteries. Her 1970 book *The Stately Home Murder* (*EQMM*, December 1, 1980) was "one of the funniest, deftest, and generally most delightful classical specimens of recent years." On *The Body Politic* (*EQMM*, March 1992): "The complex plot, involving local Members of Parliament from opposing parties, a medieval battle reenactment, and commercial relations with a Middle Eastern sheikhdom, is entertainingly worked out with a key clue that could be described as a dazzler or a groaner—I can't decide which." On *Stiff News* (*EQMM*, July 1999): "Detective-Inspector C.D. Sloan and his feckless (or is it gormless?) partner Constable Crosby look into a suspicious death at Almstone Manor, a retirement home for survivors and wives of a World War II regiment. There are serious issues at the root of the plot, but as always Aird's touch is as lightly comic as her plot is deftly cunning."

Boris Akunin. The Russian author of 19th-Century historicals is one of the best foreign-language writers to crack the 21st-Century British and American markets. In the Agatha Christie homage *Murder on the Leviathan* (*EQMM*, November 2004), about diplomat Erast Fandorin, "a murderer lurks among the passengers and crew of the luxury steamship...on its 1878 maiden voyage from Southampton to Calcutta....The multiple revelations and reversals of the latter chapters display Golden Age gamesmanship at its most playful." *The Turkish Gambit* (*EQMM*, December 2005), set during "Russia's war with the Ottoman Empire" is "a classically plotted whodunit as much as a war or spy story, with 1877 period details, bright style, and well-drawn characters to appeal...especially to those with an interest in military history and tactics." In *Sister Pelagia and the White Bulldog* (*EQMM*, November 2007), introducing a nun detective, "The period-style narrative includes such old-fashioned touches as overheard conversations, direct addresses to the reader, and announced tangents not directly related to the story that the impatient may safely skip. The forms of name make it challenging to keep the characters straight, and this author is clearly a specialized taste, but those who share his interests will be delighted."

Richard Aleas. Behind the anagram lurks Charles Ardai, founder editor of the retro noir imprint Hard Case Crime. In *Little Girl*

Lost (*EQMM*, March 2005), "a formidable first novel, young New York private eye John Blake tries to find out why his high school girl friend...wound up in the *Daily News* as a murdered stripper. The relationship of Blake and his aging boss reminded me of Fredric Brown's excellent Ed and Am Hunter series." On *Songs of Innocence* (*EQMM*, January 2008): "Three years after quitting detective work for the Columbia University writing program, John Blake tries to prove the apparent suicide of a girlfriend and fellow student, who had a secret life in the Manhattan sex industry, was really murder. Aleas...tops his Edgar-nominated debut...in this man-on-the-run thriller, expertly crafted in every way and ending with one of the most shocking and chilling conclusions in recent memory."

James Anderson. Editor Ellery Queen (Frederic Dannay) thought I overrated the first novel about Inspector Wilkins, *The Affair of the Blood-Stained Egg Cosy* (*EQMM*, June 1977): "The scene is an English country estate (floor plan provided) called Amberley, where the eccentric Earl of Burford plays host to a widely assorted house party. Among the elements are state secrets, a society jewel thief known as the Wraith, a rare gun collection, a secret passage, and a threat of thirteen at dinner, all climaxed by a lengthy gathering-of-the-suspects scene....Despite the tongue-in-cheek title, Anderson has not set out to burlesque or parody the classical mystery in *Murder by Death* style. What he has done is much more difficult: to write a '30s mystery in the style of the time, straight-faced throughout, patiently constructing the kind of plot few writers today would even attempt, rich in misdirection and complication, clues plentiful and audaciously showcased, all loose ends accounted for. It's a beautiful performance." Was I overly generous? Nearly three decades later, I was unrepentant when considering Wilkins's third case, *The Affair of the 39 Cufflinks* (*EQMM*, June 2004), which "even manages to avoid the mid-novel sag that is one of the biggest pitfalls of this sort of book."

John Ball. Has the reputation of *In the Heat of the Night*'s author declined unfairly since his death in 1988? Two reviews highlight his strengths and weaknesses. On *The Murder Children* (*EQMM*, January 14, 1980): "This intensively researched novel of Chicano gangs in Southern California offers its author's usual sure-footed technique and authentic procedural details, and the final shock is very effectively done. On the debit side, the book sometimes reads a little too much like a public-relations handout for the L.A. County Sheriff's Department, and the attitude to the Mexican-American community seems somewhat patronizing." On *Then Came Violence*, (*EQMM*, August 18, 1980): "Early in his latest case, Pasadena cop Virgil Tibbs makes a string of Sherlock Holmes-style deductions from examining the body of an unidentified murder victim....[I]t's a refreshing touch. This time, though, the mystery plot carries less interest than the dignified, decorous, painfully noble romance Ball allows his sleuth with a woman he's assigned to protect."

Robert Barnard. This British author of the best book-length critical study of Agatha Christie, *A Talent to Deceive* (1980), was an outstanding mystery novelist from the beginning. On *Death of an Old Goat* (*EQMM*, October 1977): "A second-string Australian university is the setting for a delightful first mystery, reminiscent in style of Emma Lathen, Joyce Porter, and Colin Watson. It's fairly clued with a nice extra shock at the end. Inspector Royle rivals [Porter's] Dover for undiluted obnoxiousness, and the victim is a delightful character." On *Death of a Literary Widow* (*EQMM*, January 1, 1981): "The most memorable character (or caricature) in this satirical mystery is one of the most venomously drawn comic Americans to appear even in British detective fiction, a professor of English named Dwight Kronweiser, who is determined to resuscitate the reputation of British working-class novelist Walter Machin. Kronweiser may be a trifle overdone, but the quotation from his critical prose is a priceless parody of the worst academic literary analysis." Though he never lost his sense of humor, later Barnard novels are less comedic. On *Dying Flames* (*EQMM*, January 2007): "In a typically literate and enthralling entry..., novelist Graham Broadbent is visited at his hotel by a teenage girl claiming to be his daughter and becomes involved in the complicated mendacities of a former girlfriend. Like most of Barnard's work, the novel refuses to develop along predictable lines. Much is written about plot-driven versus character-driven novels, but in the best mysteries (like this one), the elements are blended too well for the reader to tell who's driving." Barnard wrote some fine historical mysteries under the name Bernard Bastable. On *To Die Like a Gentleman* (*EQMM*, January 1994): "...[T]yrannical gout sufferer Sir Richard Hudson...has surrounded himself with potential murderers among his family, employees, and other acquaintances. Partly written in letters and diaries, the novel reveals a mastery of period style plus the irony and deft plotting for which his contemporary mysteries are so notable."

Lawrence Block. Four series suggest the versatility and overall mastery demonstrated in a half-century career. On *The Burglar Who Traded Ted Williams* (*EQMM*, August 1994): "His book business threatened with an impossible rent increase, [Bernie] Rhodenbarr yields to temptation and returns to his larcenous vocation in a funny and complex puzzle involving collectible baseball trading cards and a body in a bathroom. This novel has as good an example of Golden Age-style puzzle-making as you are likely to find in the current market, including even a short-lived locked room problem and one of the most extended gathering-of-the-suspects scenes since they stopped making *Thin Man* movies." On *A Long Line of Dead Men* (*EQMM*, May 1995): "Unlicensed New York private eye Matt Scudder is consulted by a member of a 'last man' club whose members are dying off at an alarmingly accelerated pace. The investigation is fascinating, and the sidebar discourses on death and alcoholism are less tangential to the story than they may at first seem." On *Tanner on Ice* (*EQMM*, August 1998): "Evan Tanner, an unsleeping, multi-lingual, profligately political, sexually adventurous spy [is revived] after 28 years by the Buck Rogers method: Tanner has been in cryonic storage and thus has not aged....His rapid assimilation to a world of computers and political correctness, along with his mission to destablize the government of Burma, makes for a funny, compulsively readable, surprisingly philosophical travelogue thriller." In *Hit Man* (*EQMM*, January 1999) "ten linked stories tracing the professional career and evolving outlook of murderer-for-hire Keller...add up to an episodic novel...[O]ne of the great books of '90s crime fiction..., it will leave the thoughtful reader pondering: why are we so easily able to like and identify with an amoral killer?"

Michael Bowen. Of the many contemporary lawyers writing crime fiction, Bowen is one of the least likely to get into the courtroom and one of the most likely to produce oscarwildean one-liners. *Worst Case Scenario* (*EQMM*, January 1997) "combines contemporary concerns like the health care crisis and Washington political intrigue; computer technology, and the kind of puzzle-spinning practiced in the Golden Age thirties by writers like John Dickson Carr (yes, Bowen provides a locked room mystery) and Ellery Queen (he also deals in elaborate wordplay clues). Bowen's wit and literate prose invite further comparison with the masters of an earlier day." *Screenscam* (*EQMM*, February 2002) adds to his stature as "one of crime fiction's wickedest satirists, with showbiz mores, law firm politics, and online kinkiness among his targets. (This lampoon of the movie world would make a good movie.)"

Simon Brett. I summarized his finest work as follows (*L.A. Federal Savings Quarterly*, Winter 1983): "Next to [Ngaio] Marsh, Brett is probably the most effective delineator of a theatrical background in detective fiction. Since his debut in *Cast in Order of Disappearance* (1976), actor-detective Charles Paris has entered a different sphere of British show business in each of his appearances—the Edinburgh festival in *So Much Blood* (1977); musical theatre in *Star Trap* (1978); non-professional theatre in *An Amateur Corpse* (1978); comedy in *A Comedian Dies* (1979); radio drama in *The Dead Side of the Mike* (1980); and series television in *Situation Tragedy* (1981). Be warned that Brett is to be read more for wit, style and satire than for plot, strictly a secondary feature in the Charles Paris novels."

Ken Bruen. Cops and crooks alike are extraordinarily literate in this Irish writer's tough minimalist noir. On *Her Last Call to Louis MacNeice* (*EQMM*, November 1998): "Cooper, London bankrobber and repo man, comes under the spell of Cassie, an American *femme fatale* who turns him onto the works of MacNeice but can only be bad news. Low-life crooks with pervasive literary obsessions seem to me even more unlikely than the poetry-quoting Scotland Yard detectives of more traditional British fiction—so much for realism—but the punchy, slangy, jokey narrative, rich in allusion to British and American popular culture, achieves an almost hypnotic quality." On *A White Arrest* (*EQMM*, December 1999): "Brit Noir, in which the violence and stylized slang of American hardboiled fiction is applied to British characters and settings, is not my favorite current school of crime writing, but paradoxically Bruen *is* one of my favorite newer writers. His police team of Roberts and Brant may be the least likeable in fiction, and their search for a serial killer of English cricketers turns the reader's expectations on their heads in the *anti*-detective story manner loathed by traditionalists. But Bruen is essentially a brilliant satirist….I loved it; you may hate it."

James Lee Burke. I've gone back and forth on one of the most honored writers in contemporary crime fiction. On *In the Electric Mist with Confederate Dead* (*EQMM*, November 1993): "Dave Robicheaux, the stand-up police sleuth of New Iberia, Louisiana, confronts a number of possibly related problems: the discovery of the remains of a black man lynched in 1957, a present-day rapist-killer, and the return to the area of gangster Julie 'Baby Feet' Balboni, who is bankrolling a movie being filmed locally. While delivering a well-wrought conventional detective story, Burke takes the artistic risk of also introducing a possibly supernatural element: Robicheaux's encounters with the ghost of a Civil War general. Burke is one of the half dozen or so finest stylists in the mystery genre, and this is as good a novel as I've read this year...." But the best-novel Edgar winner for 1997, *Cimarron Rose* (*EQMM*, November 1998), showed his "reputation has been inflated beyond reason by evidence of this succession of confrontations and macho posturings." On *Purple Cane Road* (*EQMM*, February 2001): "There is nothing especially original in Burke's plots, his stagecraft, or the macho/sensitive paces he puts his lead character through. But as a wordsmith, he has few peers....[T]he sounds and smells and warm damp of the Bayou setting palpable." On *Jolie Blon's Bounce* (*EQMM*, December 2002): "Burke's descriptive powers are extraordinary; some of the incidentals (scenes in a jail holding tank and at two contrasting AA meetings, a reflection on the ironies of capital punishment) have immense power. But the tough-guy confrontations, physical and verbal, become tiresome, and the climactic rescue seems too contrived in a novel with such serious literary pretensions."

Lee Child. Why is the creator of former military cop Jack Reacher one of the hottest crime writers of the new century? Reviewing *One Shot* (*EQMM*, November 2005), I advanced a theory: "Mixing detection and thriller elements, Child is a writer to treasure, a master of all the keys to first-rate crime fiction: style, plot, pace, and character. What other writer gives you Sherlockian deduction, a Bondish storming of the bad guys' lair, and even a Poirotian gathering of the suspects?" On *The Enemy* (*EQMM*, January 2005): "...Reacher is not quite celebrating the new year of 1990, having been abruptly transferred from the action in Panama to a backwater posting in North Carolina. Aided by a young female lieutenant, he covers ground from Paris to California in a career-threatening effort to connect a series of murders that certain fellow officers want left alone. Child has a narrative knack comparable to Donald Hamilton or Adam Hall, and his complex hero offers much to ponder about the limits of duty and honor."

Mary Higgins Clark. Mastery of story structure explains the bestseller status of a writer who will never win high honors for her prose. On *All Around the Town* (*EQMM*, September 1992): "Laurie Kenyon, who was abducted at age four and rescued at age six, has blocked out all memory of her captivity. At age 21, she is menaced again by her captors, now fronting a national TV ministry and fearful of exposure, and accused of the murder of a college professor..." Style, characterization, and dialogue that are all bestseller (or miniseries) simple have kept me from fully appreciating the novels of Mary Higgins Clark, but it's hard not to admire the intricate construction and cunning design of this one. The author knows how to keep the pages turning, wisely combining the pure suspense situation of an antagonist who is known (to the reader, that is) with a whodunit element. (Sharing the present book's stalker-out-of-the-past situation is the author's famous *Where are the Children?*..., the effective 1975 novel that...presaged a whole sub-genre of children-in-jeopardy novels.)" On *Remember Me* (*EQMM*, September 1994): "The cross-cutting style works like clockwork; surprises are plentiful; and one minor character, an Alzheimer's-afflicted local historian, is memorably drawn."

Harlan Coben. He's a bestseller for good reasons, but his inconsistency of tone is bothersome. On *One False Move* (*EQMM*, December 1998): "Sports agent Myron Bolitar, asked to protect a young woman basketball star who has received threatening letters, does more real detective work than some current amateur sleuths. The tone ranges from the stand-up comic school at its most smartass to overwrought tearjerking. Bolitar's friend Win, though in deliberate contrast to Spenser's trusty Hawk in many respects, still represents a tiresome contemporary cliché: the hero's dangerously violent, morally ambiguous sidekick. Reservations aside, Edgar-winner Coben lives up to his reputation with a strong narrative drive, a satisfactorily complex and surprising plot, and a solid sense of pace and structure." On *Promise Me* (*EQMM*, January 2007): "Coben keeps the pages flying with a complex plot and a masterful final surprise, while addressing serious societal issues, but some of the comic-book supporting characters belong in another book."

Max Allan Collins. My statement in reviewing *The Slasher*, one of a paperback series about killer-for-hire Quarry, that the young author was "a good bet for future glory" (*EQMM*, January 1978) has proven a good prophecy. While Collins has written almost every type of crime story, his specialty is the 20th-Century historical in which real-life celebrities emerge as fictional characters. On *Blood and Thunder* (*EQMM*, November 1995): "Chicago private eye Nate Heller was apparently on the scene for every major 20th-Century crime....[The investigation of] the 1935 assassination of Louisiana Senator Huey P. Long...shows some parallels to the JFK case: an alleged 'lone nut' assassin who is too dead to speak for himself and questions involving entry and exit wounds. This is one of the best Hellers, sticking close to the historical record while providing a fresh theory of who was really behind the Long killing." *Flying Blind* (*EQMM*, July 1998) concerns "the disappearance of Amelia Earhart during her 1937 round-the-world flight. The surprisingly credible solution is a variant on one of the more sensational theories. Earhart comes across as a complex, likeable, believably flawed heroine; her husband G.P. Putnam as one of the most despicable villains of recent memory." On *The Titanic Murders* (*EQMM*, June 1999): "Jack and May Futrelle play pre-WWI Nick and Nora Charles in investigating the smothering murder of a sleazy blackmailer plying his trade among the first class passengers....While the whodunit is nicely handled, with some elements chosen to reflect mystery fashions of the period, the historical fidelity and the impression of what the great ship was like for its passengers in the days before the iceberg are the novel's strongest attributes. For once, a *Titanic* story does not focus on the sinking, which is dealt with only in an epilogue, but the reader's knowledge of what is to come gives the account an extra melancholy resonance. No more adventures for this happy detecting couple."

Michael Collins. The very prolific Dennis Lynds (a.k.a. William Arden, John Crowe, and Mark Sadler) used the Collins name for his best series, about one-armed New York private eye Dan Fortune, whose shorter cases were collected in *Crime, Punishment and Resurrection* (*EQMM*, mid-December 1992): "This stunning collection...demonstrates why Collins is one of the giants of private-eye fiction. The kind of puzzle-spinning mind that can create a locked-room mystery like 'Who?' coexists quite nicely with an uncompromising and unapologetic social conscience that relishes swimming against the prevailing tide. The longest piece, 'Resurrection,' is unusual among the many p.i. mysteries about crazy cults in its very serious exploration of religion." On *Circle of Fire* (*Wilson Library Bulletin*, October 1973), as by Sadler: "Private-eye writers are divided into...those who can plot both logically and comprehensibly (e.g., Ross Macdonald) and those who can't (e.g., Raymond Chandler). Sadler is among the can's. [Paul] Shaw has the Archer sensitivity but expresses private-eye values that date back to Hammett. ('It's good to work for your partner, necessary, but money is better.')"

K.C. Constantine. Most crime fiction isn't realistic, nor would we want it to be. But an exception is this pseudonymous author's series about Rocksburg, Pennsylvania police chief Mario Balzic, which is of such transcendent quality, I stretched to find comparisons. On *Upon Some Midnights Clear* (*Los Angeles Federal Savings Quarterly*, Winter 1986): "He is one of the best writers of realistic crime fiction ever to enter the field....better than George V. Higgins, better than Elmore Leonard, and so far superior to Robert B. Parker as to be on a different planet....Balzic [is] a man of contradictions: profane in his language, determined not to be used or taken advantage of, even more determined to do the right thing in every circumstance and inclined to agonize over what the right thing is." On *Grievance* (*EQMM*, January 2001): "...[D]etective Rugs Carlucci, who has succeeded retired police chief Mario Balzic at center stage of Constantine's novels, investigates the murder of a wealthy and hated local industrialist while confronting a crisis in his psychologically and physically painful relationship with his demented mother. Rugs is a brilliant cop and as complex and sympathetic a character as his mentor....You have to evoke the names of major American playwrights like David Mamet, August Wilson, Amy Freed, Sam Shepard, and Richard Greenberg to find parallels for Constantine's extraordinary gift for dialogue that captures the poetry and eloquence of everyday speech. He also writes a genuine detective story, albeit a highly unconventional one with some mysteries left unsolved."

Thomas H. Cook. Reviewing the Edgar-winning *The Chatham School Affair* (*EQMM*, November 1996), I declared that "Cook may be the best American writer of crime fiction currently practicing. Stress the word American, for his range of locales is unusually varied, from New York in his first novel *Blood Innocents*

(1980) and others to Salt Lake City in *Tabernacle* (1983), Atlanta in *Sacrificial Ground* (1988), Birmingham in *Streets of Fire* (1989), and, in his two most recent novels, small towns on Cape Cod and in Alabama. Though not inclined to repeat himself, Cook employs similar structures in 1995's...*Breakheart Hill*...and [*Chatham School Affair*]. In each case, the narrator is an adult recalling a traumatic incident from his schooldays; the circumstances are hinted at and gradually revealed; the narrator has a guilty secret, mysterious until near the end of the book; there are flashbacks to trial transcripts; an interesting father-son relationship is explored; and the not-always-linear narrative style keeps the reader clear on the frequent time shifts. Each book can be called a detective story, but the detective is the reader, who may not foretell the surprises but can trace the fairly-laid clues when the truth is finally revealed. *Breakheart Hill*, in which a small-town Alabama doctor looks back to events of the early sixties, is an outstanding novel, but its successor is even better....Narrator Henry Griswald recalls the twenties when he was a pupil in his father's Cape Cod school and new art teacher Elizabeth Channing, a world traveler and thus an exotic figure, took up her duties. Any more information would endanger the reader's pleasure. Suffice it to say the elegiac prose is beautiful and the gradual unraveling of the truth masterfully accomplished. Though Cook is one of a kind, the closest comparison might be the brilliant British author Peter Dickinson." On *Places in the Dark* (*EQMM*, January 2001): "Two keys to Cook's success are his evocative, lyrical writing style and his mastery of story structure, including an ability to shift in time and dole out information selectively without losing clarity or antagonizing the reader. His finishing revelations meet the three-way test: they are surprising, believable, and fairly clued." On *Red Leaves* (*EQMM*, May 2006): "Photo-shop proprietor Eric Moore's seemingly perfect life all starts to unravel when an eight-year-old girl disappears from her home on a night his teenage son had babysat her. This grim study in suspicion, loss, and multigenerational family relationships explodes artificial distinctions between literary and category, character-driven and plot-driven fiction."

Mat Coward. He may be best as a writer of short stories. *Do the World a Favour and Other Stories* (*EQMM*, July 2003) offers "droll narrative and dialogue, in a range of quirky and sometimes iconoclastic British voices, and a continuing theme of 'specious moral logic'...." But his novels feature a memorable addition to the ranks of odd-couple police partnerships. On *In and Out* (*EQMM*, July 2002): "The London team of Detective Inspector Don Packham, the manic-depressive veteran, and Police Constable Frank Mitchell, his straight-arrow family-man subordinate, may occasionally remind you of earlier combos like Joyce Porter's Dover and MacGregor or Colin Dexter's Morse and Lewis, but they are as fresh and original as their creator's droll narrative voice. In their second case, following *Up and Down*, they investigate murder among the members of a pub darts team. The suspects are vividly characterized, and the observations of the customs and rituals of the sport are vastly entertaining." In *Over and Under* (*EQMM*, February 2005), "Coward, one of the funniest writers in the history of crime fiction, provides observations on comedy fandom, European-vs.-American sport, and health delivery systems, along with a nicely twisted whodunit."

Robert Crais. Always insistently readable, he grew in stature as his career progressed. On *Lullaby Town* (*EQMM*, June 1992): "Los Angeles private eye Elvis Cole spends most of his time in Connecticut and New York in his third case, seeking the long-lost wife and son of Peter Alan Nelsen, a quintessential jerk who is third only to Spielberg and Lucas in power and influence among Hollywood action directors. The first third of the book is fine, but it tails off some once the main mystery is solved. My interest wavered with every appearance of some standard-issue gangsters ....[T]he book will appeal to fans of Robert B. Parker's Spenser and other wisecracking-but-oh-so-sensitive tough guys." In *L.A. Requiem* (*EQMM*, January 2000), "Cole is asked by silent partner Joe Pike, a tough and taciturn ex-LAPD officer with a shadowed past, to help search for the missing daughter of tortilla king Frank Garcia. Alternating first and third person narration, the novel probes the characters and their problems, illuminates the Los Angeles scene, and keeps the reader guessing in masterful fashion. If you had Crais pegged as a west-coast...Parker (i.e., magical style but invisible plot), this complex and enormously entertaining novel should change your mind."

Michael Crichton. Since starting his career as a paperback original writer (under the name John Lange) and winning an Edgar with the outstanding 1968 medical thriller *A Case of Need* (as by Jeffery Hudson), Crichton has combined mystery, adventure, and science fiction elements in his often controversial bestsellers. According to *Rising Sun* (*EQMM*, October 1992), "set in an indeterminate near future in which the Japanese own most of Los Angeles…, U.S. business policies must be changed to be competitive with Japan, which plays by different rules. Only occasionally does the lecturing about international trade slow down the story, usually in the second half when the reader has already been hooked by Crichton's sure and practiced storytelling skills." *Disclosure* (*EQMM*, July 1994) "has all of the characteristics you associate with Crichton: compulsive readability; an efficient, inconspicuous prose style; vividly if not deeply realized characters; and a strong strain of technology (in this case, some fascinating stuff about virtual reality).…Despite finding a bit of stop-picking-on-the-guys whining along the way, I believe Crichton's critics are once again off base: by showing a sexual harassment case from the point of view of a male victim, he doesn't minimize the plight of a woman in that situation but rather illustrates it in a way that permits more readers to identify with it."

Bill Crider. One of the best and most prolific novelists to emerge from mystery fandom has proven remarkably versatile. In *Blood Marks* (*EQMM*, December 1992), the "Houston serial killer has the distinction of never following the same *modus operandi* and almost never leaving a clue at the remarkably tidy crime scenes.…Crider, in a more explicitly violent novel than the gentle small-town stories he is best known for, both keeps the pages flying and gets maximum mileage out of only three suspects." On *The Texas Capitol Murders* (*EQMM*, October 1992): "The usual humor is present in abundance; a large cast of varied characters is efficiently managed; the background is exploited to full advantage; and the murderer is an especially interesting and memorable one." In *…A Dangerous Thing* (*EQMM*, August 1994), "[m]urder once again comes to Hartley Gorman College, the St. Mary Mead of academia, after a newly-appointed feminist dean introduces the campus to political correctness. Crider's satirical approach will comfort neither PC proponents nor their loudest detractors." In *A Romantic Way to Die* (*EQMM*, February 2002), about his best-known character, Texas sheriff Dan Rhodes, "the background of a romance writers' conference is well imagined and the sly, deadpan wit is on target."

Deborah Crombie. Every time I review this author, I make the same point: of the three prominent American women turning out British police procedurals, she is much the best. On *Kissed a Sad Goodbye* (*EQMM*, July 1999): "Duncan Kincaid and Gemma James, Scotland Yard detectives and discreet lovers, return for their sixth case. Their present-day investigation of the mutilation murder of a beautiful woman alternates with flashbacks to the experiences of a child evacuated from London's East End in the early days of World War II. The two story lines eventually dovetail in an admirable denouement. This is a smashing effort right down to the evocative epigraphs about London's docklands. Crombie manages to avoid the main pitfalls of her two better-known colleagues: [Martha] Grimes's tendency to cultural solecisms (so I understand from British critics of her work) and [Elizabeth] George's excessive length and plodding prose."

Amanda Cross. The mystery-writing persona of Columbia University scholar Carolyn Heilbrun started strongly but slipped badly later in her career. On *Death in a Tenured Position* (*EQMM*, July 15, 1981): "The first woman English professor at Harvard is the object of dirty tricks and worse in the latest from Dorothy L. Sayers's most prominent descendent in the field of the academic feminist mystery. Professor Kate Fansler investigates....The writing is witty, the clueing fair (if you are a graduate student in English literature), and the solution, of a hard type to bring off successfully, ultimately satisfying. Cross chooses some of the best epigraphs in detective fiction." On *The Puzzled Heart* (*EQMM*, February 1998): "Though beginning with a dramatic kidnapping and including the usual intelligent talk, this is a weak entry in the Kate Fansler series. The lack of Cross's trademark great-author theme may disappoint some fans, and the whole enterprise lacks credibility. (Even liberals like your reviewer may be bothered by the author's facile assumptions about the right wing.)"

Barbara D'Amato. Starting with a delightfully unfashionable throwback to the '30s, the Chicago author found success in the newer style without losing her classical touch. *The Hands of Healing Murder* (*EQMM*, April 22, 1981) is "pure detection with scarcely a concession to the action, menace, and personal involvement expected by contemporary readers. Dr. Gerritt De-Graaf, neither as colorful nor as irritating as Philo Vance, is the sleuth. The solution to the impossible crime...is both enormously ingenious and of doubtful workability. The reader has every chance to solve it. I liked this book, but not everyone will." On *Hard Tack* (*EQMM*, January 1992): "The second novel about Chicago journalist Cat Marsala is a terrific example of both the locked-room mystery and the closed-circle whodunit. A dozen are aboard the luxurious yacht *Easy Girl* on Lake Michigan when storm, murder, and other disasters strike. The cast members are almost universally likable, so that virtually every one qualifies as a least-suspected-person candidate. The puzzle plotting, brisk telling, sailing action, and character drawing are all first-rate. The first Marsala novel, *Hardball* (1990) was impressive, but this one is miles better."

Lindsey Davis. Marcus Didius Falco ranks second only to Steven Saylor's Gordianus the Finder among Ancient Roman private eyes. On *Venus in Copper* (*EQMM*, mid-December 1992): "...Falco is asked by the female members of a non-blood-related family of freed slaves to investigate the fiancée of the one single male: her last three marriages have been shortened by sudden death of the husbands. Though some of the slang and other modern terminology may occasionally jar, the novel is well-plotted, well-peopled, and exceedingly well-told. The background is captured brilliantly, with more view of the underside of Roman society than provided in most other Roman detective novels: we first meet Falco viewing the rats in jail." *Time to Depart* (*EQMM*, August 1997) was "rich in humor, domestic details, action, and devious plotspinning...." *Three Hands in the Fountain* (*EQMM*, June 1999), "involving a serial killer who leaves body parts in the city's water system, is one of the best in the series, illustrating my belief that the Roman sleuths perform most impressively when they stay home. True Falco and his highborn wife Helena Justina seem suspiciously like a twentieth-century couple who time travelled to the ancient world, and only Falco's past visit to Britain can explain all the Yorkshire slang he uses."

William L. DeAndrea. The first novel about TV network troubleshooter Matt Cobb won an Edgar, while the author's even better second, a paperback original introducing Prof. Niccolo Benedetti, won another. On *Killed in the Ratings* (*EQMM*, August 1978): "The author has much fun with similes and metaphors, quotes from old TV shows as epigraphs to the chapters, and a satisfying old-fashioned gathering-of-the-suspects finale." In *The HOG*

Murders (*EQMM*, February 11, 1980), Benedetti finds "a worthy opponent in HOG, perhaps the most terrifying versatile serial killer in mystery annals. Fair play is manifest, and the solution is so logical and inevitable that many readers will probably anticipate it." On *Killed in Paradise* (*EQMM*, mid-December 1988): "...Cobb escorts the winner of a radio prize contest featuring a murder game....DeAndrea does a nice job with the comic possibilities of confusing a real-life mystery with a manufactured one and resists overdoing the 'in' references." On *Fatal Elixir* (*EQMM*, September 1997): "The author, who died last year at the tragically young age of 44, is at his best in what may prove to be his last novel: the second western mystery about paralyzed lawman-turned-newspaperman Lobo Blacke and his dime-novel biographer Quinn Booker. The mystery is both surprisingly resolved and clued with scrupulous fairness, the telling bright and humorous."

Jane Dentinger. Actor detectives were numerous in the 1980s, but there was no American in a class with Simon Brett's Charles Paris until Dentinger introduced Jocelyn O'Roarke. *Murder on Cue* (*Los Angeles Federal Savings Quarterly*, Summer 1983) has "the same combination of wit, incisive characterization, and knowledgable theatrical background found in Brett's series. If [Dentinger] is not yet quite as scintillating as Brett, she may be a somewhat more skilled plotter. Herself an actress with off-Broadway and regional theater experience [she] knows her setting well and can convey effectively the joys and tensions of preparing a play for production." On *The Queen is Dead* (*EQMM*, December 1994): "...Jocelyn O'Roarke returns to her upstate New York alma mater to star in a production of Shakespeare's *A Winter's Tale*—replacing former mentor Tessa Grant who has died suddenly and (apparently) unmysteriously....Aside from vivid characters and background, Dentinger also provides a well-developed puzzle. Right at home in a pure whodunit is the local police chief, a cop dumb enough to inhabit a B-movie mystery of the thirties or forties."

Colin Dexter. Oxford's Chief Inspector Morse, whose immortality was secured by a long-running series of excellent television adaptations, is one of the towering figures of recent detective fiction. On *The Way Through the Woods* (*EQMM*, February 1994): "When a young Swedish woman disappears north of Oxford, clues to her fate are offered in a poem published in the *Times*, whose readers fill its letters column with ingenious speculation. While many fictional detectives, like characters in comic strips, become less grotesque and more conventional as they go along, Morse— lover of music, women, puzzles, and *The Archers*; squeamish in the presence of blood and gore; always quick to let Sergeant Lewis pay for the drinks—seems to grow quirkier." *The Daughters of Cain* (*EQMM*, August 1995) "is in many ways typical of the author/sleuth team: the aging Morse has a quasi-romantic involvement with a much younger character; each of the seventy chapters plus prologue and epilogue is headed with an apposite quotation, most from familiar authors and sources but others so obscure the reader may wonder if they are invented; Morse's cheapness and quirkiness, Lewis's patience and solidity seem more notable than ever; and a crossword puzzle clue ('Kick in the pants,' eight letters) introduced in the opening pages is dazzlingly solved near the end." On *Death is Now My Neighbor* (*EQMM*, June 1997): "...[A] pair of local murders on a single quiet street may be connected to the contest for Master of Lonsdale College, from which Sir Clixby Bream is stepping down and for which two professors (and their wives) have ambitions. (The parallel to C.P. Snow's wonderful novel *The Masters* is duly noted.) This is among the best books in the series, with puzzle-building in the Golden Age tradition...as well as a study in friendship....[W]e learn what Morse's first initial (E) stands for, and even that revelation is prepared for by a group of clues that might lead some especially keen readers to the answer before Dexter chooses to give it on the final page. (My wife got it; I didn't.)"

Michael Dibdin. A writer of great versatility and literary ambition began with an inflamatory addition to the pastiche shelf. On *The Last Sherlock Holmes Story* (*Wilson Library Bulletin*, June 1978): "Although the novel is well written and constructed, the Sherlockian purists who are most likely to peruse such an effort are also the most likely to shout foul: Dibdin's distortion of the canon puts the earlier offenses of Nicholas Meyer...and Robert Lee Hall...in the shade." *The Dying of the Light* (*EQMM*, June 1994) "combine[d] the broad parody of the classical detective story found in Tom Stoppard's play *The Real Inspector Hound*...with a harrowing account of the treatment of residents in an English retirement home whose operators have a motive to thin the ranks of guests. Rosemary Travis and Dorothy Davenport make their existence at Eventide Lodge bearable by casting their fellow residents in an imaginary murder mystery, but a real mystery develops, investigated by Stanley Jarvis, a memorable cop who carries in his head all the scores of the obscure and defunct English football club Accrington Stanley for the years 1956 to 1962. With its unity of place and variety of interesting characters, this short novel would make a fine play." On *And Then You Die* (*EQMM*, December 2002): "Someone is trying to kill Italian cop Aurelio Zen before he can testify against members of the Mafia. If you have to assign to a subgenre this intelligent, sophisticated, funny, romantic, and genuinely suspenseful novel, pure thriller comes the closest. A quoted review from Britain's *New Statesman* evokes Agatha Christie, Elmore Leonard, and Ian Fleming—justified comparisons but all off the mark in pigeonholing one of crime fiction's most original writers. Watch how Dibdin teases the reader in the closing pages: is he or isn't he going to resort to a time-honored surprise twist?"

Peter Dickinson. If I were choosing the greatest crime novelist of the past thirty years, Dickinson would be on the short list. On *One Foot in the Grave* (*EQMM*, June 30, 1980): "Jimmy Pibble, police sleuth of the author's early novels, is now retired and, seemingly senile before his time, a patient in a high-class nursing home called Flycatchers. During an abortive suicide attempt, he finds a body in the building's tower, beginning his gradual return to detection and a meaningful life. The novel is rich in insights into the old and sick and contains some exceptionally fine prose." On *The Yellow Room Conspiracy* (*EQMM*, January 1995): "Aging lovers Paul Ackerley and Lady Seddon, she one of the five famous Vereker sisters (not really, we are told, so much like the Mitfords), recall in alternate chapters events beginning in the thirties and leading up to locked-room murder and government scandal in 1956. This is an astonishing novel, written with its author's usual elegant style and unerring sense of place, period, and character. It also has a formal puzzle with several alternate solutions, and readers will not all agree on which of them Dickinson believes is the correct one." On *Some Deaths Before Dying* (*EQMM*, November 1999): "Nonagenarian Rachel Matson, a lifelong photographer who is physically helpless but mentally acute, tries before her imminent, inevitable death from a wasting illness to solve the mystery surrounding a split pair of antique duelling pistols owned by her late husband Jocelyn, survivor of a Japanese prison camp during

World War II. The mystery is not so much who done it as what happened, which is gradually revealed through Rachel's memories and the legwork of her full-time nurse Dilys, one of several marvelously drawn characters. The best of Dickinson's elegantly written novels deserve the label classic, arguably representing the ultimate detective story: a real mystery, logically, fairly, and surprisingly resolved, and solidly rooted in character."

Susan Dunlap. The cases of Berkeley policewoman Jill Smith comprise an exceptionally pleasurable and reliable series. *Time Expired* (*EQMM*, October 1993) "delivers an especially fine combination of quirky characters, complex plot, and strong sense of place....Who is behind the series of generally applauded pranks directed at the city's meter maids, who come in both genders? And why is a terminally ill local attorney, whose support of radical clients has made her the object of a police dart-board, murdered in a nursing home? Dunlap is one of the best active proponents of the classical-style police procedural." In *Sudden Exposure* (*EQMM*, April 1996), "Smith doesn't let a transfer from detective back to uniformed patrol officer cramp her style in a case involving a galloping nudist, a feminist Olympic diver who runs a health club called the Girls' Team, and various shadows from the university town's radical political tradition. Why do I admire Dunlap's work so much? For her classical plots maybe, or her characters or style. But mostly because she nails Berkeley, California, as well as any mystery writer has nailed any city from Poe to Chandler to Grafton and beyond."

James Ellroy. Here are two conflicting views of a formidable and controversial writer. I stand by them both. On *White Jazz* (*EQMM*, March 1993): "...Ellroy is the rare writer who tries to do something new and different in the crime fiction genre, and as a result, he will never appeal to everyone. Tip for readers: read this book in extended sittings rather than in fits and starts, for you'll have to acclimate yourself anew to the eloquent but quirky telegraphic writing style every time you pick it up. Ellroy writes a highly individual stream-of-consciousness prose, like a shorthand description of a dream, which like Raymond Chandler's quite different narrative can compel you along even when you lose track of the story. *Unlike* most of Chandler's, Ellroy's complicated plot is masterfully constructed and comes together brilliantly at the end. In 1958 Los Angeles, mob-connected cop Dave Klein narrates a case involving characters both fictional and real (Mickey Cohen, Howard Hughes)....This one may turn out to be a classic." On the mixed collection *Destination: Morgue! L.A. Tales* (*EQMM*, May 2005): "Ellroy is one of the most talented writers around, uniquely powerful but uniquely exasperating. The four fictional entries...take his pretentiously prurient sex-crazed stylistic self-indulgence, with its annoying alliteration and numbing nastiness in destructively deadening and dumbed-down density wending its way over the tiresome top. The nonfiction is better: a boxing article is a weak curtain raiser, but the punchy, violent, profane, semi-poetic style (an unconventional vehicle for conservative political views and Christian witness) works much better in the confessional autobiography and true crime pieces."

Aaron Elkins. The fourth book in the series about physical anthropologist Gideon Oliver, known as the Skeleton Detective, won the Edgar for best novel of 1987. *Old Bones* (*EQMM*, March 1989) "is a hugely enjoyable classical puzzle, the kind of book I most value in the mystery field simply because it offers what is not available outside the genre (save possibly in some hard science fiction)." That intellectual appeal continues to be delivered painlessly in later books like *Cold Blood* (*EQMM*, August 2004): "With real detection from physical evidence and the author's customary bright dialogue, this is a welcome walk down detective fiction's Main Street. (Gideon must be the Dagwood Bumstead of mystery fiction: you never get the impression he's fat, but he certainly spends a lot of pages eating.)" On *Little Tiny Teeth* (*EQMM*, September 2007): "...Oliver joins an Amazon River cruise arranged by a secrets-bearing botany professor surrounded by those who hate him most. Elkins has done stronger puzzle plots in the past, but background and humor carry the day. The introduction to the travelers of the spaced-out expedition guide is one of the funniest scenes in recent memory."

Howard Engel. The careers of one of the key figures in Canada's crime-fiction renaissance and his most memorable character took the same unexpected turn. On *Getting Away with Murder* (*EQMM*, December 1998): "...Grantham, Ontario, private eye Benny Cooperman reluctantly accepts employment from menacing gangster Abram Wise, who wants to know who is trying to kill him. The plot also involves an old domestic murder case revived in a true-crime book by a writer friend of Benny's. As usual, the narrative is humorous, detailed, and leisurely, and the puzzle (elucidated in a *Thin Man*-ish gathering-of-the-suspects) will delight traditionalists. The story starts with a possibly unique fictional murder method, and another of the book's crimes involves a most unusual accessory to homicide." In *Memory Book* (*EQMM*, February 2007), "Cooperman wakes up in a Toronto hospital, victim of a brain injury that has robbed him of the ability to read, though not to write. Author Engel, whose stroke in 2000 produced the same rare condition, gives a good-humored and intensely involving insider's account of his affliction, while producing one of the most abundantly clued puzzle plots in recent memory, solved by a detective who has trouble remembering the names of the suspects."

Janet Evanovich. For good or ill, the creator of this number-coded series must be one of the most influential mystery writers on the current scene. On *High Five* (*EQMM*, December 1999): "Many current novels can be described as lightly plotted detective stories straddling the tough and cozy extremes with a wryly funny female narrator, often but not always a private eye. In her fifth case, New Jersey bounty hunter Stephanie Plum looks into the disappearance of her Uncle Fred and encounters a gallery of characters almost as weird and wacky as her family. There are a few laughs here, but the plot is thin and uninteresting and the old stalked-by-escaped-or-released-enemy bit is a very tired sub-plot. A mystery novel should focus on the mystery, not go off on six different tangents to avoid it, and it should resemble a sitcom or a slapstick two-reeler only if it's funny enough. Few are." Either *To the Nines* (*EQMM*, December 2003) was better or the reviewer mellowed: "Stephanie Plum,...whose gross, gritty, and romantic adventures in slapstick have gained her creator bestsellerdom, looks for a vanished Indian alien and becomes the target of the Carnation Killer. Highlights include a side trip to Las Vegas and colleague Lula's search for the perfect diet. Even if you miss a very broad clue, you may guess who did it, but no one reads Evanovich, who can be very, very funny, for her plots."

E.X. Ferrars. One of the longest careers in classical detective fiction began in 1940 and continued through the year of her death in 1995. My statement that of active writers she was "closest to Christie in style, plotting, and general milieu" was often quoted on dustjackets, and she continued in fine form well into her eighties. On *Danger from the Dead* (*EQMM*, June 1992): "Schoolmaster

Gavin Cleaver comes to vacation in the guest cottage of his brother Nigel and wife Annabel, a famous romance novelist recovering from a stroke. Also in attendance is Annabel's actress sister Caroline, the principal attraction for shy bachelor Gavin. Murders follow and are resolved with Ferrars' customary knack for plot and people. In addition to wondering who the murderer is, the reader can ponder who will be the detective." On *Beware of the Dog* (*EQMM*, June 1993): "Virginia Freer and her estranged husband Felix, a charming crook and inveterate liar who likes to play Great Detective, form one of the more unusual Holmes-Watson teams in current detective fiction....Ferrars uses some of the most time-honored mystery ingredients (a will, a dog who does not bark, a claimant from Australia) in fresh combinations to produce a typically well-constructed and agreeably-told puzzle. Part of the surprise solution may suggest itself early, but only a sharp reader will work out all of it." *A Hobby of Murder* (*EQMM*, November 1995) describes "retired professor Andrew Basnett's investigation of the poisoning at a village dinner party of a well-known crime novelist. In fact, octogenarian Ferrars was superior to octogenarian Christie, bamboozling the reader with a tricky variation on the Least-Suspected-Person solution that is undeniably clever whether you believe it or not."

DeLoris Stanton Forbes. Known as DeForbes in 1950s mystery digests and as Tobias Wells in a series of Boston-based police procedurals, she has continued to search for fresh angles and approaches into the new century. *One Man Died on Base* (*EQMM*, August 2001) "follows the inning-by-inning action of a baseball game with flashbacks from the troubled thoughts of aging slugger Zack Amidon. The reader may anticipate the tragic climax, but both the psychology and the baseball ring true in a novel of gathering tension by an undervalued writer." On *The Perils of Marie Louise* (*EQMM*, June 2004): "Marie Louise DelOrio narrates the saga of the wealthy and tradition-bound Snodgrass family, of whom she is her generation's only female offspring. The story, never too specific on dates, ranges over many decades and makes for compelling reading, though you may wonder how the account of her eventful, privileged, but sometimes seemingly cursed life can be resolved satisfactorily. Forbes, one of the most consistently inventive and unconventional of crime writers, manages the trick."

Katherine V. Forrest. The series about Lesbian LAPD detective Kate Delafield deserved and achieved a wider audience than the gay community. On *Murder by Tradition* (*EQMM*, October 1991): "…[I]t is known early on who was responsible for the stabbing death of gay restaurateur Teddie Crawford. The question is whether defendant Kyle Jensen will be let off the hook by a homophobic justice system—and whether Jensen's defense attorney will try to discredit Kate's testimony by exposing her lifestyle on the witness stand. An unusual novel and a totally enthralling one." On *Liberty Square* (*EQMM*, May 1997): "Kate Delafield's youthful lover almost has to trick her into attending the Washington, D.C. reunion of old colleagues (male and female, gay and straight) from her days as a Marine lieutenant in Vietnam. Forrest spins a nifty puzzle, but as always she has more on her mind, including the contribution of women and gays to America's war effort and the nation's general attitude to those who fought that most unpopular of wars."

Dick Francis. The former steeplechase jockey's virtuoso thrillers attracted a wider audience than horse racing enthusiasts. On *Smokescreen* (*Wilson Library Bulletin*, April 1973): "His great virtues are a pure narrative facility comparable to Alistair MacLean's, expert characterization, and scrupulous authenticity in the portrayal of specialized backgrounds. The facts on film-making and South African gold-mining in this novel are as thoroughly researched and entertainingly conveyed as the racing and flying lore of earlier novels." On *Comeback* (*EQMM*, January 1992): "The former jockey's thirtieth novel finds him near top form, as usual dispensing fascinating specialized information—this time on the British diplomatic corps and equine veterinary surgery—along with a masterfully controlled plot and a remarkably large cast of vivid characters. Concerning an inexplicable series of deaths among a top surgeon's racehorse patients, the novel continues a trend in Francis' work to less physical action and more cerebral detection." *Wild Horses* (*EQMM*, May 1995) found him "operating at as high a level of craft as ever—and possibly an even higher level of character insight….As always, the specialized detail is fascinating, and the dovetailing of plot and theme in the final pages demonstrates how complete is Francis's mastery of crime writing technique."

Tess Gerritsen. She is one of the best writers to come to prominence at the turn of the 21st Century. On *Gravity* (*EQMM*, February 2000): "In a medical thriller as much science fiction as suspense, a mysterious malady afflicts astronauts working on an international space station....A believable picture of the politics and
procedures of NASA combines with the internist author's medical
expertise and gift for pace, character, and construction to make
this an absolutely riveting novel, one that will send new readers
scurrying to find her previous three." On *Body Double* (*EQMM*,
November 2004): "The Boston team of pathologist Maura Isles,
whose previously unknown identical twin sister becomes a murder
victim outside her home, and police detective Jane Rizzoli, now
very pregnant, return in a deviously plotted and expertly executed
thriller that takes full advantage of the current fascination with
forensic detection. Gerritsen gets extra points for avoiding a trite
climactic situation she seems to be leading up to." On *The Bone
Garden* (*EQMM*, February 2008): "In 1830 Boston, the continuing
need for fresh cadavers and the crimes of a slasher known as the
West End Reaper complicate the lives of several medical students,
including the young Oliver Wendell Holmes....Before going
slightly off the rails in a tidy sentimental conclusion, the novel
delivers superbly its harrowing account of early 19th-century
medical practice."

Joe Gores. An Edgar winner for his first novel and the creator of
the Daniel Kearney Associates private-eye procedurals did his best
work on a couple of non-series books. On *Interface* (*Wilson Library Bulletin*, February 1975): "To put things in perspective,
though graceful style, sensitive characterization, and concern for
the eternal verities all have their place in the mystery field, there's
no substitute for technical trickery....[Gores's] best novel yet...is
grim, hard, and often depressing, but is written with great skill and
understanding of people and a mastery of detective story construction rare among current writers." On *Hammett* (*Wilson Library
Bulletin*, January 1976): "Gores gives a vivid impression of the
time and place without the overdose of period detail that often
marks fiction on recent history. He offers a credible and admirable
portrait of a great writer...."

Ed Gorman. Apart from founding *Mystery Scene*, editing numerous anthologies, and tirelessly encouraging the careers of fellow
writers, Gorman is one of the best and most versatile living writers

of novels and short stories in a variety of popular genres. On *Prisoners & Other Stories* (*EQMM*, November 1992): "As Dean R. Koontz points out in his afterword, Gorman loves and draws upon any number of fictional genres—westerns, horror, mainstream short stories a la Irwin Shaw. Nearly all the stories deal with some form of crime, though many are not amenable to conventional punishment. His favored backgrounds run to the darkside—bars, buses, truck stops, hospitals, prisons—and his characters to disillusioned middle-agers, threatened children, discordant families, though the bleak world view is seldom unleavened by some gleam of hope for the human species." On *Shadow Games* (*EQMM*, February 1995): "Charting the career of child actor Cobey Daniels, from TV stardom to shopping-mall sex scandal to psychiatric institutionalization to murder-plagued young adulthood, Gorman makes some pointed observations about the way Hollywood exploits its young performers." On *Black River Falls* (*EQMM*, September 1997): "A sharply observed middle-American background, a painfully recognizable view of adolescent rites of passage, a dark but not completely pessimistic slant on family relationships, a Woolrichian incursion of crime and terror into recognizable everyday life, a rapidly paced narrative full of unexpected but fully believable twists and turns—these are some of the features of Gorman country, to which this novel's visit is one of the best." On *Save the Last Dance for Me* (*EQMM*, April 2002): "The fourth Sam McCain novel involves a rattlesnake-handling church and a pending visit to Black River Falls, Iowa, by Presidential candidate Richard Nixon, one of many powerful friends of lawyer McCain's colorful boss, Judge Esme Ann Whitney. Continuing the nostalgic but clear-eyed picture of period middle America, the series' best to date is even funnier than usual, as well as offering a stronger mystery plot than some of its predecessors."

Ron Goulart. The science fiction humorist and pop culture historian made a detective of one of his prime comedic influences with *Groucho Marx, Master Detective* (*EQMM*, December 1998), "who, assisted by a radio-writer Watson, looks into the death of a young actress in 1937 Hollywood. The plot is negligible, but Goulart's sure feel for the period and perfect duplication of the verbal rhythms and offbeat humor of the public Groucho mark him a Marx Brothers scripter born too late." On *Groucho Marx and the Broadway Murders* (*EQMM*, November 2001): "The fourth in the very funny series includes rides on the Super Chief and Twentieth

Century Limited, a visit to the 1939 World's Fair, a passable who-dunit featuring one genuine fair-play clue, and Marxian dialogue that would not have disgraced George S. Kaufmann, Morey Riskind, S.J. Perelman, or the great man himself." *Adam and Eve on a Raft: Mystery Stories* (*EQMM*, April 2002) includes "sixteen stories, five about frustrated stand-up comic and dying message explicator Scrib Merlin, the rest about an unnamed California Adman who numbers many murderers and victims among his show biz acquaintances....The plots vary in quality, but not the window dressing: comically named restaurants, unlikely product campaigns, parodic descriptions of movies and TV series."

Sue Grafton. Californian Kinsey Millhone, whose alphabetical cases began with *"A" is for Alibi*, and Sara Paretsky's Chicagoan V.I. Warshawski, the two most famous female private eyes, de-buted in the same year, 1982. In the September 1994 *EQMM*, I compared and contrasted them: "Both characters are independent professionals in their thirties who jog for exercise, live alone, are divorced, have elderly protective landlords, and confront ethical dilemmas as well as criminal problems. While Warshawski oper-ates in big-city Chicago, imbibes Scotch, and dresses snappily, Millhone works in a small California city based on Santa Barbara, sticks to white wine, and has one all-purpose dress for situations where jeans won't do. Both are certainly feminists, but War-shawski is much more intensely political, her worldview un-ashamedly if unfashionably liberal. Millhone's politics are both more subtle and more 'mainstream.' In a sense, the Millhone nov-els are about the case at hand, while the Warshawski novels are about Warshawski, an angry, somewhat wired person who is both the more complex and intriguing character and potentially the harder to take if encountered in real life. Certainly she continually exasperates her circle of friends, whom she is always exposing to danger, sometimes irresponsibly. Paretsky writes at greater length than Grafton—Warshawski's latest case, at over 400 pages is al-most exactly double what used to be the standard length for a mys-tery novel—and generally places less emphasis on the formal puz-zle. While Warshawski has appeared on the big screen in a roundly-panned feature starring Kathleen Turner, Grafton swears she will never sell movie or TV rights to Millhone and will come back to haunt her children if they do so." On *"I" is for Innocent* (*EQMM*, August 1992): "Grafton always writes lively and amus-ing prose, full of quotable lines and comic set-pieces, but her plots have been highly variable. This one is first-rate, as cunningly constructed and surprising a pure whodunit as I've read in quite a while. The denouement provides a fresh take on a standard mystery-novel situation." On *"Q" is for Quarry* (*EQMM*, April 2003): "...Millhone helps two aging and ailing cops (great characters both) reopen the twenty-year-old investigation of a Jane Doe found murdered in a quarry in 1969. Plotting and writing are reliably strong. It's overlong, to be sure, but Grafton pioneered the no-move-unreported method and practices it better than nearly anyone else."

Carolyn G. Hart. Though she has been celebrated for a series of cozies about a mystery book dealer, her best is probably a non-series novel. On *The Christie Caper* (*EQMM*, October 1991): "...Hart's continuing homage to Agatha Christie...is especially overt in this account of a week-long celebration of the Christie centenary masterminded by mystery bookdealer Annie Laurence Darling. The book won't serve to lower hostilities in the continuing (and increasingly ludicrous) toughs-vs.-cozies war. Obnoxious editor-critic Neil Bledsoe, a sneering proponent of the hardboiled crime novel, seems determined to spoil the week for the tea-imbibing Miss Marple fans, while an unknown hand seems just as determined to end Bledsoe's life. There are at least two Christie-like Least-Suspected-Person possibilities veteran buffs may anticipate, but Hart keeps the reader guessing over which of them she will choose. The fun-and-games will be a bit much for some readers, but hard-core traditionalists should ultimately embrace this book for its classical misdirection." On *Letter From Home* (*EQMM*, May 2004): "In 1944, 14-year-old Gretchen Gilman gets a summer job on her small-town Oklahoma paper and winds up reporting on the murder of a friend's mother. Was Faye Tatum a goodtime girl who cheated on her recently furloughed G.I. husband, or did she hang out at a locally notorious nightspot because she loved to dance? Evoking the town, its people, and the problems and attitudes of the World War II home front beautifully while constructing a deceptive but fairly clued mystery, this is by far the best novel I've read by Hart."

John Harvey. Nottingham cop Charlie Resnick, a much admired character, put his creator on the police procedural map in the 1980s and '90s. On *Living Proof* (*EQMM*, mid-December 1995): "When American private-eye writer Cathy Jordan receives ugly threats prior to her appearance at Nottingham's Shots in the Dark mystery festival (a real event), ...Resnick takes on her protection. Harvey does one of the best jobs I've seen of incorporating mystery world material into his story without seeming too self-indulgent, and his pastiche of first-person-female private eye writing is on the money." In *Still Waters* (*EQMM*, June 1998), "Resnick wonders if a young teacher, the subject of abuse by her dentist husband, is the victim of a random serial killer or someone closer to home. Though Harvey deliberately gives his police procedurals some of the untidiness of real life, the central case is resolved quite satis-factorily, and the pace, prose, and characterization are superb." On *Gone to Ground* (*EQMM*, June 2008): "Occasional excerpts from the script of a 1950s British film noir hint that the murder of a gay academic arose from his research into the female star, who died mysteriously and whose family resists cooperation. Most interest-ing feature of the first book-length case for police detectives Will Grayson and Helen Walker is Harvey's depiction of the triangle, benign and friendly but potentially dangerous, of male detective, wife, and female partner."

Reginald Hill. Though it took him a while after his early '70s de-but to gain a foothold in the American market, the creator of Yorkshire cops Andy Dalziel and Peter Pascoe is one of the most respected and formidable novelists on both sides of the Atlantic. On *Arms and the Women* (*EQMM*, January 2000): "The real pro-tagonist here is aspiring novelist Ellie Pascoe, whose current pro-ject, an Ancient Greek historical of which we read several seg-ments, helps take her mind off the hoped-for sale of her first novel and threats from a mysterious source. Ellie is as complex and in-teresting a character as Dorothy L. Sayers's Harriet Vane, and the other women of the title are both varied and well-realized. Hill's ear for Yorkshire speech, especially that of Andy Dalziel, is sharp as ever." On *Dialogues of the Dead* (*EQMM*, July 2002): "The detective story in its finest between-the-World-Wars flower was an author-vs.-reader game as much as a literary genre. And how literary it was, could be, or should be was a matter of controversy. In the crime fiction field today, one of the writers with the greatest literary ambition is also one of its most ardent games players. Though some readers might call...Hill, as one of his Yorkshire characters might say, too clever by half, he has produced the most elaborate, deceptive, dazzling, and (to the right language-obsessed reader) fair puzzle I've seen in years....A series of otherwise unconnected deaths are linked by anonymous entries in a short-story contest, sponsored by a local newspaper and public library. As the carnage rises, the pressure mounts on plain-spoken Fat Man...Dalziel and university-educated...Pascoe, one of the great odd-couple police teams in the literature. The attentive reader who shares Hill's love of wordplay may foresee at least some of the novel's unfolding secrets, but it will take a genius to get them all. The manner of Hill's final revelation must be unique in detective fiction annals."

Tony Hillerman. The many detective series focused on Native American culture owe a debt to the creator of Navajo cops Joe Leaphorn and Jim Chee. In an introductory essay to *The Tony Hillerman Companion* (1994), too long to reprint here, I wrote that *A Thief of Time* (1988), the author's own favorite of his novels, "may well be the high point of the series....Besides including one of Hillerman's best-woven plots, with all elements coming to-gether like a perfect mosaic, [it] has some of his deepest explora-tion of religious values and the varieties of religious belief and expression." Other highlights were *People of Darkness* (1980), including "one of the most elaborate and unusual murder weapons in fiction"; *The Dark Wind* (1982), "with a stronger whodunit element that usual and possibly Hillerman's best fair-play puzzle spinning"; and *Skinwalkers* (1986), in which Chee and Leaphorn appear together for the first time.

Robert Irvine. After some early novels drawing on his back-ground in the Southern California TV news business, this author struck his richest vein in the state of Utah with Salt Lake City pri-vate eye Moroni Traveler. *The Spoken Word* (*EQMM*, December 1992) "has a terrific opening situation: the grandniece of Latter-Day Saints Prophet Elton Wooley has been kidnapped. The condition of her release is one only the Prophet is in a position to deliver: a reve-lation from God giving equal rights to women in the Mormon church." Reviewing *Pillar of Fire* (*EQMM*, April 1996), one of the best in the series, in the Los Angeles *Times*, "Dick Adler in a sin-gle sentence compared the author to Tony Hillerman, Umberto Eco, and Ross Macdonald. An exaggeration? Read it and see." With wife Angie Irvine, he has written several novels as Val Davis, including *Flight of the Serpent* (*EQMM*, April 1999): "In her second case, archaeologist Nicolette (Nick) Scott witnesses a desert plane crash and helps the pilot's grandfather, World War II flyer John Gaunt, determine what happened and why. Gaunt summons his old crew to fly their B-24 bomber one last time. The story, involving contemporary computer technology as well as vintage aircraft, builds to a thrilling conclusion. It's well-designed for the big screen, offering great parts for older actors, including a leading man of advanced years (Paul Newman or Clint Eastwood maybe?) opposite a younger actress." I found *Wake of the Hornet* (*EQMM*, June 2000): "the best adventure yet for aircraft archaeologist...Scott. The background of a Pacific Island, whose natives follow the teachings of the Cargo Cults and have constructed a phony airfield to attract planes, is both fresh and fascinating, and the payoff is as good as the buildup."

Stuart M. Kaminsky. The very prolific film professor and historian has created three memorable long-running detectives: forties Hollywood private eye Toby Peters, Russian cop Porfiry Petrovich Rostnikov, and the finest of them all, Chicago police detective Abe Lieberman. On *The Big Silence* (*EQMM*, February 2001): "In their sixth appearance, Lieberman and his Irish-American partner Bill Hanrahan, who address each other as Rabbi and Father, work on several cases: a con game targeting senior citizens with a driveway repaving offer, the crime spree of a black/white team of convenience store robbers, the murder of a homeless former football star, and the kidnapping of a protected witness's teenage son." On *The Last Dark Place* (*EQMM*, February 2005): "The first chapter..., set in 1969, is a self-contained short story of extraordinary impact and resonance, and the rest of the book lives up to the opening. This is a superb example of the modular police procedural....The personal lives of Lieberman (whose grandson is about to have his Bar Mitzvah) and...Hanrahan (whose Chinese-American wife faces family objections to her marriage) are not the wearisome interruptions that mark too many contemporary mysteries but indispensable plot and thematic elements."

H.R.F. Keating. The British novelist and critic has written crime fiction of many types and backgrounds, but he is inevitably bracketed with his most famous character, Bombay's Inspector Ganesh Ghote. On *Doing Wrong* (*EQMM*, May 1995): "Though the style, the central character, and the semi-comic dialogue, strewn with *only*s and *itself*s, remain constant, the moods, themes, and structures change from book to book. This time it's an inverted detective novel, as Ghote jousts Columbo-style with H.K. Verma, a killer known to the reader from the beginning." *On Bribery, Corruption Also* (*EQMM*, February 2000): "Inspector Ghote, whose heart belongs to Bombay, travels to Calcutta when wife Protima, a native of that quite different city, inherits a large house she remembers fondly from her childhood. The couple encounter one setback after another and gain new insights into the shady practices of the title. Like some other latter-day Ghotes, this is more a seriocomic mainstream novel than a mystery. Keating's eye for detail and ear for dialect are typically sharp in a novel notable for Protima's largest role ever, insights into Indian city rivalry, and probing of the complexities of ethics and morality."

Faye Kellerman. She is best known for her series about Rina Lazarus, married to LAPD detective Peter Decker, e.g. *Jupiter's Bones* (*EQMM*, January 2000): "When cult leader Father Jupiter, formerly known as a major academic physicist, is reported dead at the Order of the Rings of God compound,...Decker heads the investigation. Along with the expected tidbits on Orthodox Jewish life, Kellerman provides fascinating background on cult psychology, deprogramming, and theoretical physics along with superb character interplay. I was sorry to see a promising detective story turn into an unconvincing action thriller in the latter stages, but Kellerman's people kept me involved." On the historical novel *The Quality of Mercy* (*EQMM*, mid-December 1989): "The family of Roderigo Lopez, a Portuguese *converso* (i.e., a Jew who has at least ostensibly converted to Christianity) and physician to Queen Elizabeth, continue to follow the old religion in secret while working to help Jews escape the Spanish Inquisition. Daughter Rebecca...becomes romantically involved with a Christian writer-player named William Shakespeare, who is trying to solve the murder of his theatrical mentor. An extraordinary novel, equally laudable for the fascination of its history, the non-stop readability of its story, the explicit (and appropriate) bawdiness of its dialogue and action, and the flesh-and-blood realization of its characters."

Jonathan Kellerman. In a piece for an unpublished reference book, I wrote that "the first three books about child psychotherapist Alex Delaware quickly established [Kellerman] as one of the contemporary mystery's best practitioners. A painstaking builder of complex, well-clued plots and a prose stylist reminiscent of Ross Macdonald, Kellerman is at his best in the development of characters. At the center of each story is a troubled child or adolescent, an over-medicated seven-year-old girl who may be a witness to murder in the Edgar-winning *When the Bough Breaks* (1985), a five-year-old cancer patient whose parents want to remove him from treatment in *Blood Test* (1986), and a mentally ill teenage genius in *Over the Edge* (1987)." *Gone* (*EQMM*, August 2006) "begins with a publicity stunt—the faked abduction of two acting students—that turns more serious with the murder of the female half of the team. Kellerman recalls the late Ed McBain in his one-word titles, prolific output..., mesmerizing perfect-pitch dialogue, and in this case a distinctly 87th Precinct-like touch: a reproduced Homicide Investigation Progress Report listing four pages of physical evidence gathered."

Harry Kemelman. In a beloved series of novels, mystery plots were used as a vehicle for illuminating Judaism to both Jews and non-Jews. On *Monday the Rabbi Took Off* (*Wilson Library Bulletin*, June 1972): "Oddly enough, the best novel to date about Rabbi David Small is the one in which he functions least as a detective. The whodunit aspect is only one of several subplots connected to the Rabbi's visit to Israel. Kemelman's great strength is his ability to make his background and his characters real and moving. Strictly as a puzzle-maker, he is more impressive in the Nicky Welt short stories." On *The Day the Rabbi Resigned* (*EQMM*, August 1992): "Some of the highlights are only tenuously related to the plot: an amusing description of the very casual Barnard's Crossing Symphonic Orchestra..., and the inventive theological arguments of the Rabbi's atheist/agnostic cousin known as Simcha the Apicorus. (Rabbi Small is the rare fictional sleuth who has aged with the calendar: he was in his twenties when he came to Barnard's Crossing in *Friday the Rabbi Slept Late* [1964], and he's now in his fifties and contemplating a mid-life career change.)"

Stephen King: I had no idea who was behind the pseudonym Richard Bachman when I wrote the following about *Rage* (*EQMM*, February 1978): "A mentally ill high school student holds a full classroom captive in a genuine horror novel without a hint of the occult. The book's chilling exploration of a sick mind may remind some of Jim Thompson's *The Killer Inside Me*. Bachman's beautifully written first novel is easily the best paperback original I've read in the past year." While King has more or less disowned that book, presumably for its subject matter rather than its quality, crime and mystery have figured in most of his novels since, supernatural or not. One reason that his well-deserved Grand Master Award from MWA was controversial may be inferred from this note on another paperback original, *The Colorado Kid* (*EQMM*, May 2006): "Told mostly in dialogue, between two veterans of a small Maine weekly and the young woman they are training in the journalist's art, this…novel makes for compelling reading: the author has a matchless narrative gift, and the characters are beautifully drawn. It sets a tantalizing mystery puzzle and examines it from all angles with near Queenian thoroughness, and it makes valid points about news media and human nature. But it will help to know…going in [that] this is not a detective story but an *anti*-detective story."

Dean Koontz. Before he became a perennial genre-bending bestseller, he wrote popular fiction under such pseudonyms as Brian Coffey, Leigh Nichols, and David Axton, author of *Prison of Ice* (*EQMM*, February 1977): "How will the Arctic scientific team escape from an adrift hunk of ice scheduled to blow to bits at midnight, and who is the homicidal maniac in their midst? A real nail-biter, perfect for the movies." On *Intensity* (*EQMM*, June 1996): "With its known villain, claustrophobic atmosphere, and tension-packed 24-hour timeframe, this is as pure a novel of suspense as you are likely to find. Twenty-six-year-old college student Chyna, haunted by demons from a miserable childhood, is the lone survivor of mass murder on a Napa Valley wine estate. She goes from trying to escape the nutty murderer to courageously going after him in the hope of saving another of his many victims." On *Velocity* (*EQMM*, May 2006): "In a fresh variation on a familiar situation, the nutty games-playing serial killer's antagonist is not a cop but a Napa Valley bartender. The wild and tricky plotting, hyped-up suspense, moral ponderings, and unconventional romance demonstrate that over the top can be a good thing." On *The Darkest Evening of the Year* (*EQMM*, May 2008): "…Koontz's two most recent books have several elements in common apart from expert writing, construction, pacing, and suspense: a strong demarcation between good and evil, darkness and light; strong male and female leads with secrets in their past and murderous sociopaths as their adversaries; valid if curmudgeonly cultural criticism, a plea for old-fashioned morality, and a belief in the psychic sensitivities of dogs."

Joe R. Lansdale. The debut novel of this much-acclaimed writer of mystery and horror fiction suggested what was to come. In *Act of Love* (*EQMM*, October 7, 1981), "A black/white team of cops hunt the Houston Hacker in this first novel, characterized by relentless blood and gore and a wrought-up, mannered writing style reminiscent of McBain or [John] Wainwright. The explicit horrors (shades of EC comics!) may turn some readers off, but Lansdale is a fine natural storyteller who knows how to keep the pages flying. [Other books reviewed in the column] have more polish but less gut-level reader interest." On *Mucho Mojo* (*EQMM*, November 1994): "The two main characters from the author's 1990 novel *Savage Season*, Texas field workers Hap Collins, white and straight, and Leonard Pine, black and gay, return in a beautifully-written whodunit, in some ways closer to Agatha Christie (who is referred to several times) than to the fifties paperbacks evoked by their previous adventure. The pair find the skeleton of a small child wrapped in porno magazines under the floorboards of Leonard's late uncle's house and work to clear Uncle Chester of complicity in a series of child murders. Lansdale offers a fresh answer to the question that Ellery Queen and other spinners of elaborate puzzles always had to address: why did the deceased resort to tantalizing and esoteric clues instead of delivering his message straight out? If you've been put off by Lansdale's wildman reputation, this may be the book with which to discover his extraordinary gifts. Its gross-out factor is no greater than that of the average contemporary crime novel, and the humor and decency of Hap and Leonard may surprise you."

Dick Lochte. The well-known critic is fond of structural experiments. His much-admired debut novel *Sleeping Dogs* (1985), alternates the very different first-person viewpoints of private eye Leo Bloodworth and precocious teen Serendipity Dahlquist. *The Neon Smile* (*EQMM*, October 1995), about New Orleans private eye Terry Manion, "features the kind of complex structure its author specializes in. Hired by a tabloid TV show to look into the thirty-year-old murder of a black militant Tyrone Pano, Manion finds connections to another mid-sixties case, the brutal crimes of a serial killer known as the Meddler. The book flashes back to the 1965 investigations of Manion's mentor, outsider homicide detective J.J. Legendre. Lochte sets the scene and deploys the characters and plot elements with a pro's practiced touch." On *Croaked!* (*EQMM*, June 2007): "In 1965 Los Angeles, young Harry Trouble works on his potential best-selling novel *Child of the Gap* while writing advertising and promotion copy for *Ogle*, a high-class girly magazine second only to that one in Chicago with the rabbit. In a workplace whodunit somewhat in the mode of Dorothy L. Sayers's *Murder Must Advertise*, the circulation director dies when a sculpture of the magazine's trademark frog falls on his head. Lochte's satirical eye captures the period flawlessly, and there's even a broad clue to the surprising murderer."

Peter Lovesey. A pioneer of the historical detective novel with his series about Victorian cops Cribb and Thackeray, followed by a later comic series narrated by Bertie, the Prince of Wales, later Edward VII, finally turned to the contemporary mystery in *The Last Detective* (*EQMM*, May 1992), which "introduces Detective Superintendent Peter Diamond, a sleuth unenamored of modern aids to police work like computers and DNA typing who longs for the real detective work of figures like Fabian of the Yard. When a woman's body is found in a reservoir south of Bristol, Diamond heads the investigation of a complicated case involving some newly-discovered letters of Jane Austen. Lovesey is one of the best writers of pure detection now active, and this ranks with his best." *Bloodhounds* (*EQMM*, July 1997), "in which the members of the titular mystery fiction discussion group become murder victims and suspects, is a natural for lovers of classical detection, including a clever locked boat mystery (amid John Dickson Carr references) and a theft of the same rare stamp that formed the title of the first Ellery Queen short story: the One-Penny Black....If I summarized the killer's motivation, you'd be sure I was putting you on, but Lovesey is such a solid pro, he may convince you."

Richard A. Lupoff. Best-known for science fiction, he entered the mystery field in a big way in the late 1980s with his series about insurance investigator Hobart Lindsey and Berkeley cop Marvia Plum. *The Bessie Blue Killer* (*EQMM*, February 1995) "continues the preoccupation with collectibles [begun in *The Comic Book Killer* and *The Classic Car Killer*], in this case vintage World-War-II aircraft, and with odd corners of Twentieth-Century American history and culture, including sidelights on jazz musicians and the Negro baseball leagues....[A]n exciting blend of enthusiastically conveyed information and a cleverly-wrought crime puzzle. An author's note carefully separates fact from fiction and provides a bibliography of further reading." I recommended *The Sepia Siren*

Killer (*EQMM*, February 1995) "to anyone, like me, who is fasci-
nated both with the history of the motion picture industry and with
African-American contributions to American culture....Pioneering
black film-maker Edward J. 'Speedy' MacReedy is an especially
interesting and well-realized character whose memories have the
ring of truth." On *The Radio Red Killer* (*EQMM*, December 1997):
"Lupoff knows just how far to go with the historic radio lore—I
could have taken a great deal more of it, but that might have lost
those less enchanted with the subject." On *Marblehead: A Novel
of H.P. Lovecraft* (*EQMM*, August 2007): "In 1927, the plot confronting New England's horror master includes the Ku Klux Klan,
German agents, Houdini's surviving brother, Lindbergh's flight,
the Sacco-Vanzetti case, Hitler's *Mein Kampf*, and various U.S.
and European political issues. Lupoff manages to make a man as
odd and as full of repellent opinions as Lovecraft a sympathetic
protagonist."

John Lutz. Though he may be even better as a short-story writer,
his many novels are expertly crafted, with a wide variety of backgrounds and moods. *Shadow Man* (*EQMM*, November 4, 1981)
"poses an irresistible problem: how can a multiple-personality political assassin, known to be locked up in a maximum-security
mental institution, be seen on the streets by people who knew him
in his various identities?...The complicated puzzle culminates in a
rousing action finish and a succession of neat twists." On *Spark*
(*EQMM*, April 1993): "Florida private eye Fred Carver is asked by
Hattie Evans, a resident of the Solartown retirement community,
to look into the recent heart-attack death of her husband....With a
clever scam at the center of the plot and Lutz's typically eloquent
prose giving freshness to scenes of action, sex, and torture, this is
one of the best in an outstanding series." On *Thicker Than Blood*
(*EQMM*, April 1994): "St. Louis's sad-sack private eye Nudger,
still popping antacids and avoiding Danny's Dunker Delites (while
loading up on the sly on a competitor's MunchaBunches), is asked
to look into a supposed securities fraud and winds up entwined in
the affairs of a dysfunctional family a la Ross Macdonald while
taking a stock-market flyer on dubious inside information picked
up during his investigation. The plot is more complex than usual,
and many of the events are very dark and very serious, but as usual
the main attractions are the likable central character, the Lutzean
humor, and one of the most admirable prose styles in the mystery
field."

Ed McBain. As Evan Hunter, he wrote the classic novel about teaching and juvenile delinquency *The Blackboard Jungle* (1954), followed by several more bestsellers. But he became even more famous as McBain, not the first but arguably the best and certainly the most influential author of police procedural novels. On *Nocturne* (*EQMM*, November 1997): "87th Precinct cops Steve Carella and Cotton Hawes investigate the murder of Svetlana Dyalovich, an octogenarian former concert pianist—one of the suspects is her cabaret-singer granddaughter. Over forty years after launching the series with the paperback original *Cop Hater* (1956), McBain['s]...mix of neat plotting, sharp dialogue, and prose cityscapes [is] as fresh as ever." On *Fat Ollie's Book* (*EQMM*, March 2003): "The 88th Precinct's obese bigot and aspiring novelist Ollie Weeks tries to recover his manuscript, stolen by a transvestite male prostitute who mistakes it for nonfiction, while investigating with the 87th's Carella and Kling the murder of a politician. Fat Ollie's observations on writing are classic satire, and the text of his story, told from the unconvincing perspective of a policewoman and including an absurd finishing surprise, is hilarious." On *Fiddlers* (*EQMM*, February 2006): "The final 87th Precinct novel meets the standard of freshness, currency, vitality, and quality the late author maintained over fifty years..., combining inverted detection and whydunit with a teasing hint of a subgenre McBain embraced late in his career: the woman in jeopardy."

Sharyn McCrumb. This honored and gifted author's contributions to mystery fiction range from the lightly humorous to the very serious. On *Zombies of the Gene Pool* (*EQMM*, July 1992): "In a delightful sequel to the Edgar-winning *Bimbos of the Death Sun* (1987), professors Marion Farley and James Owen Mega (a.k.a. science fiction novelist Jay Omega) travel to Wall Hollow, Tennessee, to attend the thirty-year reunion of a group of s.f. fans called the Lanthanides, some of whom have gone on to greater fame in the field, others of whom may or may not be dead. The cast is well-drawn, the whodunit puzzle deftly accomplished, and the writing has McCrumb's customary charm and humor." On *She Walks These Hills* (*EQMM*, mid-December 1994): "The third in McCrumb's Appalachian series is a masterpiece of complex construction, intercutting among several major characters...and addressing three murder problems: one in the present, one from the late 1960s, and one from 1789, involving a girl who was kidnapped by the Shawnees and escaped to make her way home. An elegy to a vanishing culture with a wealth of character insights and a touch of the supernatural, this novel ranks with the best books by one of the mystery genre's stellar performers." On *The Ballad of Frankie Silver* (*EQMM*, September 1998): "While recuperating from wounds suffered at the end of *The Rosewood Casket* (1996), Sheriff Spencer Arrowood passes the time researching a historic North Carolina case: the 1832 trial of young backwoods wife Frankie Silver for the murder of her husband. In contrast to its de-tective-fiction precedents (Alan Grant's investigation of the Rich-ard III case in Josephine Tey's classic *The Daughter of Time* [1951] and Chief Inspector Morse's reexamination of a fictional nineteenth century Oxford crime in Colin Dexter's *The Wench is Dead* [1989]), this novel spends a good deal of time in the histori-cal period, as the local court clerk describes the course of the Sil-ver case with a fine combination of humor, character observation, and telling detail."

John D. MacDonald. In *The Mystery Scene Reader* (1987), I wrote, "If there were a 'future book' on which 20th Century writers will still be read a hundred years from now, John D. MacDonald would be at shorter odds than all but a handful of his contemporar-ies, whether classed as 'category' or literary. MacDonald was the ultimate professional storyteller, skilled in every aspect of popular fiction writing—his characters live; his prose sings; his plots co-here; and his pages seem to turn themselves. But the detailed pic-ture he gives of his times in America will give his works their staying power….To many readers, John D. MacDonald and Travis McGee are inseparably associated. But it should be remembered that at the time the first McGee novels appeared, MacDonald al-ready had a gargantuan reputation among serious crime fiction fans and scholars. It seemed unthinkable that creation of a series, though clearly a wise commercial move, could eclipse in general acclaim his early non-series novels, but that is what has hap-pened….Along with reading and rereading the McGees and Mac-Donald's latter day non-series bestsellers, readers should redis-cover those novels of the fifties."

Ross Macdonald. Comments on a reprint of 1963's *The Chill* (*EQMM*, December 1996) sum up this iconic writer: "…[W]ith his emphasis on past events haunting the present and the bittersweet observations of the sad and wise and brave and deluded characters

Lew Archer meets, [Macdonald] has probably influenced the current crop of private eye writers even more than Hammett and Chandler. How does...*The Chill*...stack up against the books being published today? Few contemporaries could match the extremely complicated but ultimately comprehensible (as well as satisfactorily fair and surprising) solution of this whodunit, and the bits of description and character touches are as deft as you remember—with all that, Macdonald manages to keep his story zipping along nearly as briskly as a Perry Mason, a trait more of his present-day disciples should try to emulate." Reviewing an audio recording of 1962's *The Zebra-Striped Hearse* (*EQMM*, December 2002), I called it "one of the finest detective novels ever written....The elements that make Macdonald so extraordinary are his characters, his prose, his themes of search and loss, and his surprising yet credible plot edifices. For all the artifice of the mystery puzzle, Archer is a more realistic private eye than most: when he has evidence related to a murder, he immediately makes a full report to the police; he is concerned about getting paid by someone when his initial client appears ready to fire him; and he asks for money back from an informant to assure he can testify later that no one paid him for his evidence. Although there are a few very brief interludes of violence, the emphasis is more on the mental and emotional than the physical aspects of detection."

Margaret Maron. Early New York police novels about Sigrid Harald included some fine work, but this author hit her full stride when she returned to her Southern roots. On *Southern Discomfort* (*EQMM*, November 1993): "If [James Lee] Burke represents the masculine South of writers like William Faulkner and John D. MacDonald, Maron's is the feminine South of films like *Passion Fish* and *Steel Magnolias* and the plays of Beth Henley. In this sequel to [the Edgar-winning] *Bootlegger's Daughter* [1992], Deborah Knott, as if not busy enough as newly appointed judge in her small North Carolina town, devotes her weekends to WomenAid's all-female house-building project and becomes embroiled in a murder case close to her own large family." In *Winter's Child* (*EQMM*, February 2007), "Knott...confronts two mysteries: the shooting of a local ne'er-do-well while driving his pickup truck and the disappearance of new husband Dwight Bryant's ex-wife and eight-year-old son. Maron's expertly plotted and written books are less often sidetracked from the main narrative than some series with large continuing casts. Unusual weather-related chapter epigraphs are a plus."

Walter Mosley. Easy Rawlins, the African-American private eye operating in Los Angeles, is one of the most significant creations in contemporary crime fiction. Reviewing *White Butterfly* (*EQMM*, January 1993), I called him "multi-faceted and painfully real," adding, "With Mosley's narrative gift and way with people, he could probably get away with eschewing plot altogether in the current market, but the puzzle, concerning a serial killer of black bar girls who gets more police and press attention when a white college girl is added to the list, is both complex and surprising." In *Little Scarlet* (*EQMM*, January 2005), Rawlins takes on an unconventional role "in the aftermath of the 1965 Watts riots: working with the police to solve a young woman's murder and avert further violence in the Black community. The subsequent search for a serial killer is minor as detection but major as a view of the African-American experience." On *Cinnamon Kiss* (*EQMM*, January 2006): "L.A. in the sixties is beautifully captured, the plot will keep you guessing, and Easy (who may make the private eye record book for most dreams described) continues to be a likeably conflicted character."

Marcia Muller. San Francisco's Sharon McCone beat both Grafton's Kinsey Millhone and Paretsky's V.I. Warshawski to the post in the female-private-eye stakes with her debut in *Edwin of the Iron Shoes* (1977). I found *The Cheshire Cat's Eye* (*EQMM*, mid-July 1983) "a smoothly written, fairly clued pure whodunit with an interesting background of Victorian house restoration." But *The Legend of the Slain Soldiers* (*Los Angeles Federal Savings Quarterly*, Fall 1985) featured a shorter-lived character whom I found "an even more intriguing and fully-developed protagonist": Elena Olivarez, Director and Curator of the Museum of Mexican Arts in Santa Barbara. I might not say that now, McCone having grown as a character and her cases increased in complexity. Muller uses the large cast of continuing characters, a drag on many series, masterfully. On *The Broken Promise Land* (*EQMM*, December 1996), I noted that her cases "always manage to combine a suitably complex mystery plot with the continuing soap opera of her extended family of relatives and co-workers....Muller's solid professionalism never falters." On *Cape Perdido* (*EQMM*, August 2005): "In the third entry of the locale-driven series about Soledad County,

California, a North Carolina company plans to load water from the depressed former lumbering town of the title into huge blue bags and float it down to Southern California without compensating the residents. A variety of local and outside environmental groups want to derail the plan, whether through legal means or dirty tricks....This is a typically expert Muller product, with a good sense of place, a well-managed large cast, and clues so fair, you'll kick yourself if you don't spot the main criminal. (Yes, I'm kicking myself.)" On *Vanishing Point* (*EQMM*, February 2007): "Family is important to...Sharon McCone—consider how many continuing characters in her immediate, extended, and professional families appear in every book....An unusual whydunit in the rare literal use of the term, this novel takes an unsentimental and ultimately unsettling look at family dynamics."

Joyce Carol Oates. Sometimes using pseudonyms, but more often under her own name, one of the most celebrated contemporary American authors has increasingly identified herself with crime fiction. On *The Collector of Hearts: New Tales of the Grotesque* (*EQMM*, January 1999): "The very prolific Oates is able to assume a wide variety of styles and voices: though there are a fair number of middle-aged academics among her central characters, the title story (from *Seventeen*) is believably narrated by an African-American teenage girl." On *The Barrens*, writing as Rosamond Smith (*EQMM*, August 2001): "Matt McBride, New Jersey husband, father, real estate agent, and (under the cognomen Nighthawk) photographer, becomes a suspect in the disappearance and possible murder of a young artist in circumstances remarkably similar to an earlier case of rape-murder in his high school days. Obsessed with the similarity of the two cases, McBride has plenty to hide from the police and (especially) his wife, but the reader is also invited into the twisted mind of the real killer, who, significantly, is also an artist. The novel, voyeuristically compelling as a road accident, is full of psychologically troubled characters, including the protagonist. An Internet serial-killer expert who appears briefly late in the book is especially vivid and repellent. Oates' work exemplifies dark suspense in that you have no idea where the story is going—but there's not much reason for optimism." On *Blood Mask*, writing as Lauren Kelly (*EQMM*, August 2006): "Even without the cover disclosure 'Joyce Carol Oates writing as...,' the unmistakably edgy and energized style would tip off the true authorship of this modern gothic, in which teenage

Annemarie Straube comes to live with her beautiful, mercurial, and very weird aunt Drewe Hildebrand, operator of a Hudson River artists' colony. The mystery may keep you guessing even after you turn the last page, but most memorable are the descriptions of avant-garde art gimmicks, including the frozen-blood death masks of the title. The aunt's summary of her old friend Andy Warhol ('an utterly empty man, a vacant space....There can be greatness in such emptiness, I think') is especially remarkable."

Leonardo Padura. One of the best of the many international writers who have been introduced to the 21st-Century English-language market comes from Cuba. In *Havana Red* (*EQMM*, December 2005), "a novel first published in Spain in 1997, Havana cop Mario Conde investigates the strangulation murder of the transvestite whose father is a powerful diplomat. Among the suspects is an elderly gay playwright and theatre director whose career was cut short in a less bloody Cuban equivalent of China's Cultural Revolution. This novel has extraordinary originality and power, combining serious literary ambition and achievement with a sound mystery plot, including a distinctively Cuban main clue. Though the characters' strivings, failures, and regrets are universal, their story illuminates their country's culture and conditions, with the political elements neither ignored nor allowed to overwhelm the human story. With an excellence of prose not lost in translation, this novel may be regarded as a crime fiction classic and its author a major figure in the genre." Published under a different form of his name (Leonardo Padura Fuentes), *Adiós Hemingway* (*EQMM*, December 2005) "is much shorter but just as ambitious. Conde, retired to a life as book scout and aspiring writer, takes on the mystery of a decades-old corpse found on the grounds of Papa's Havana estate, now a museum. The narrative shifts between the present-day investigation and an imaginary recreation of the novelist's last days in Cuba."

Katherine Hall Page. Readers with a knee-jerk aversion to so-called cozies risk missing some excellent writers. On *The Body in the Bookcase* (*EQMM*, June 1999): "Given the small town's murder rate in recent years, I'm amazed it takes a string of burglaries to finally get the residents of Aleford, Massachusetts, to start locking their doors. Caterer and clergyman's wife Faith Fairchild again does the detecting in a highly enjoyable novel, based on author Page's own harrowing experience as a burglary victim. Though the subject matter is essentially serious, the cast of humorously observed characters keep the reader smiling most of the way....[T]his is not an especially bookish mystery, but there's plenty of interesting background on the antiques trade." On *The Body in the Snowdrift* (EQMM, August 2005): "...Faith Fairchild agrees to spend a week at a Vermont ski resort with her minister husband's family in celebration of her father-in-law's seventieth birthday and promptly finds a dead body in the snow. The background is expertly rendered; the characters and their sometimes-tense relationships are believable; the writing has humorous flair; and every loose end is elucidated with commendable tidiness. Page does the malice-domestic-with-recipes number as well as anybody and better than most."

Sara Paretsky. Chicago private eye V.I. Warshawski was one of the first and most important of the female private eyes to debut in the 1980s. In *Indemnity Only* (*EQMM*, July 1982), "V.I. (for Victoria, but call her Vic)...emerges as a likeable and fully realized figure to the novel's advantage. Paretsky has chosen a great name for her corrupt and mob-connected labor union: the International Brotherhood of Knifegrinders. A...strong debut." Reviewing *Blood Shot* (*EQMM*, March 1989), I called Warshawski "surely the toughest and possibly the best of the current crop of female private eyes....Paretsky has the ability to build plots that are both complex and believable and to create characters that have all the inconsistency and unpredictability found in real people." *Total Recall* (*EQMM*, March 2002) "is...a masterful example of the recent mystery-fiction trend of blending past and present. The wonderfully complicated plot involves insurance fraud, recovered memory therapy, and (most strikingly) the experiences of V.I.'s friend and surrogate mother Dr. Lotty Herschel as a beneficiary of the World War II kindertransport." (For a comparison to Sue Grafton's Kinsey Millhone, see the Grafton entry.)

Robert B. Parker. While there's no argument that the earliest novels about Boston private eye Spenser, especially *God Save the Child* (1974), are excellent, or that his creator often composes the kind of beautiful sentences other writers would like to frame and hang above their computers, my ambivalence about his long career is summed up by my comments on *The Widening Gyre* (*EQMM*, mid-July 1983): "...Spenser, attainer of one of the highest wise-crack-per-utterance ratios in all shamusdom, becomes chief of security for a right-wing Senate candidate. Strengths (as usual): dialogue (except for the pop-psych speechifying...), descriptive passages, general readability. Weaknesses (also as usual): thin plot, pretentiousness, superficiality (especially when compared to writers like Chandler and Ross Macdonald)." By *Hugger Mugger* (*EQMM*, November 2000), the approach had changed somewhat: "Parker now plays the wisecracking macho p.i. genre almost entirely for laughs. This one, more of a real detective story than most in the series, is his *Thin Man* homage—Spenser's climactic speech to the gathered suspects cries out for interpretation by William Powell." I found the non-series *Wilderness* (*EQMM*, February 11, 1980) "a genuinely suspenseful tale of outdoor revenge, centered on a middle-aged writer and his college professor-wife" but couldn't resist a backhanded compliment: "Parker...involves his readers in the lives of his characters so completely they will even put up with some laughably pretentious dialogue."

George P. Pelecanos. An early book that foretold future fame was *Shoedog* (*EQMM*, January 1995): "[This] medium-sized caper novel concerns an interestingly assorted group of criminals, most participating because the boss has something on them, and their meticulously-planned effort to knock over two Washington D.C. liquor stores the same day for a take of about $300,000. Reminiscent of the works of writers like Jim Thompson and Lionel White, the book would be right at home with the sexy cover and yellow spine of a 1950s Gold Medal original. Even the length is right, an economical 200 pages of classy, suspenseful prose. Few books in the current market are as genuinely hardboiled as this one. The story is a natural choice for adaptation to a contemporary *film noir*, which will be better if the film-makers resist the temptation to step up the action and violence and concentrate on the gallery of well-drawn characters."

Anne Perry. Her combination of detective story and family saga set in the society world of Victorian London, especially claustrophobic for women, made the creator of Charlotte and Thomas Pitt one of my favorite writers of the '80s and '90s. On *Highgate Rise* (*EQMM*, September 1991): "The socially active wife of a prominent London doctor dies in a fire. Was he the real target, or did the woman's efforts on behalf of the poor make her a threat to powerful exploiters? It's disconcerting that a novel about the social injustices of Victorian England can seem so relevant in the United

States one hundred years later." On *A Breach of Promise* (*EQMM*, February 1999), from her secondary series about amnesiac private detective William Monk and Nurse Hester Latterly: "Perry is a great storyteller whose sure hand with plot, background, character, Victorian social commentary, and (in this series) even a touch of humor makes even her most minor work worth the reader's attention, and this is one of her best. The mid-book shocker is both genuinely surprising and fairly clued, and the feminist message is powerfully delivered." But my longtime favorite has become increasingly problematic in recent novels, not I think because of any decline in her powers but in unfortunate decisions on the direction to take. On *Funeral in Blue* (*EQMM*, February 2002): "When Dr. Kristian Beck is accused of the strangling murder of his wife and an artist's model, his father-in-law defends him in the Old Bailey while William Monk investigates in Vienna the possible roots of the crime in the 1848 revolution. Readable and involving as the novel is, two unhappy trends of the series continue: tiresome padding and courtroom scenes that grow more absurd with each book. As for Monk's exchanges on feelings with other male characters, men don't talk like that now and I suspect did even less in Victorian times."

Elizabeth Peters/Barbara Michaels. While the author has had a long and successful career under both names, her greatest fame has come from the series that began with the classic *Crocodile on the Sandbank* (1975). On its sequel *The Curse of the Pharaohs* (*EQMM*, December 2, 1981): "Amelia Peabody (Victorian in narrative style if not completely so in attitude) has married archaeologist Radcliffe Emerson, settled in England, and given birth to an alarmingly precocious son known as Ramses. The couple return to Egypt to complete the work of a dead colleague (Sir Henry Baskerville, one of several Sherlockian names in the book) and confront the titular curse. There's plenty of fun and action, even some detection, but the tongue-in-cheek style is the key." Among the novels by Michaels, the most unusual is *Other Worlds* (*EQMM*, August 1999), in which "a detecting club…, Houdini and Conan Doyle the most famous members,…meet out of their own time in a shadowy, fog-enshrouded netherworld to listen to accounts of psychic mysteries and offer solutions both rational and occult. The problems, concerning haunted houses, poltergeists, and troubled children, are so distinctively odd I'm sure they must be drawn from actual records rather than invented. The author has a sure hand with atmosphere and period writing styles, along with an enthusiasm for real detection that was somewhat submerged in her early romantic suspense novels under the Michaels name (less so in the novels written as Elizabeth Peters). Though you're free to accept the mundane solutions, the very nature of the club gives the supernatural ones an automatic advantage."

Ellis Peters. The author, well-known as a historical novelist under her real name Edith Parteger, began to attract notice with contemporary mysteries about the Felse family but gained her greatest fame with the medieval monk-detective Brother Cadfael. *Monk's-Hood* (*EQMM*, November 4, 1981), "concerning the murder by poison of a potential benefactor of Shrewsbury Abbey, is a gem of a historical whodunit, written, plotted, and peopled with consummate skill. It has the added virtue of insight into a time and background rarely explored in mystery fiction. The material on medieval Welsh and English property law is fascinating." That next-to-last sentence was true at the time but, thanks to Peters's trailblazing, far from it today.

Gary Phillips. The creator of African-American L.A. private eye Ivan Monk is one of many contemporary writers to counter the claim that Florida has overtaken California as a prime locale for hardboiled fiction. In *Bad Night is Falling* (*EQMM*, January 1999), "Monk investigates murder and racial tensions in an inner-city housing project. Greater attractions than the serviceable plot are the author's unapologetically liberal social, political, and historical observations....When the history of L.A. detective fiction is written, Phillips will be a subject alongside Chandler, Ellroy, Mosley, and the rest." On *Only the Wicked* (*EQMM*, April 2001): "A complex case involving blues history, civil rights activism, and the murder of a disgraced cousin who once played in baseball's Negro Leagues takes...Monk from his familiar Los Angeles surroundings to Mississippi, where race relations prove complicated as ever. Phillips combines politics and storytelling as well as any writer of crime fiction."

Nancy Pickard. The books about foundation director Jenny Cain began light and comic but became more serious as the series continued. In *But I Wouldn't Want to Die There* (EQMM, December 1993), "Jenny...is offered an interim position previously occupied by a friend—along with a chance to solve the friend's murder.

Though the job, troubleshooting problems with potential donors and recipients, is similar, the locale is quite different. The mystery plot is typically well-worked-out, but small-town Jenny's interaction with the New York City milieu is the most memorable feature of the book. Pickard's New York is alternately funny and frightening, attractive and nightmarish, peopled by a vividly realized cast of quirky characters." On *Storm Warnings* (*EQMM*, July 1999): "Pickard...produces relatively conventional (though outstanding) mysteries at novel length and experiments with a wide range of themes and backgrounds in her few short stories. The nine in this first collection ring some unusual variations on standard suspense situations and characters: domestic betrayal, murder for hire; private eyes, crooks and con men....The collection can only enhance Pickard's reputation as one of the best and most inventive current practitioners of crime fiction." On *The Virgin of Small Plains* (*EQMM*, February 2007): "In 1987, the body of an unidentified young woman is found in a snowdrift, bringing consequences for three families in a small Kansas town. By the time the truth comes to light in 2004, local legend has brought people seeking healing to the dead woman's grave. The deceptive but logical plot, supernatural overtones, well-realized plains background (including a twister), and familiar romantic-suspense elements will satisfy a wide range of readers."

Bill Pronzini. This recent MWA Grand Master has been reviewed in "The Jury Box" by the present juror more frequently than any writer but Max Allan Collins. On *Blue Lonesome* (*EQMM*, April 1996): "An author who has demonstrated an ability to write any kind of crime, mystery, or suspense novel here delivers a tale of loneliness and obsession to a jazz beat that insistently recalls the work of Cornell Woolrich. CPA Jim Messenger saw the terribly unhappy and lonely woman numerous times at San Francisco's Harmony Cafe and even spoke to her once, unsatisfactorily. When she commits suicide and is designated a Jane Doe by the police, Messenger is determined to find out who she was and where she came from, an ex-library book his only clue....This may not be Pronzini's very best—novels like *The Running of Beasts* (1976, with Barry N. Malzberg) and *Shackles* (1988) come to mind—but it probably belongs in his top half dozen." On *Bleeders* (*EQMM*, March 2002): "San Francisco's 'Nameless Detective,' working on a complex blackmail case, survives death through pure luck when a killer's gun misfires. Questions of mortality and personal priorities, including his duty to his wife and adopted ten-year-old daughter, occupy the realistically traumatized sleuth as he tracks the shooter down. The route to a unique and satisfying denouement is marked by sharp prose, crisp pace, and the ability to involve the reader emotionally." On *The Crimes of Jordan Wise* (*EQMM*, March 2007): "To win the heart of a beautiful woman who wants to live on the edge with the finer things, San Francisco accountant Wise engineers a complex embezzlement scheme that allows the couple to escape to a new and carefree life in the Virgin Islands, until complications ensue. This is an extraordinary piece of pure storytelling, with the noirish mood, pounding narrative impetus, and unsparing character insights of the best 1950s Gold Medal paperbacks."

Robert J. Randisi. The astoundingly prolific author of mysteries and westerns has advanced steadily as a writer since his earliest efforts. In *Hard Look* (*EQMM*, December 1993), "New York private eye Miles Jacoby goes to Florida to search for a client's missing wife, with only a sexy postcard of her posterior as a clue. In his best form, Randisi offers a user friendly whodunit, with an agreeably intriguing but easy to follow plot and a likeable, unpretentious sleuth, who embraces Florida like a wide-eyed tourist....The effect is relaxing, even soothing, a hardboiled cozy." On *Stand-Up* (*EQMM*, February 1995): "The low-key approach and self-effacing humor that characterize the author are here, along with a briskness of pace, complexity of plot, and taut buildup of dramatic scenes that puts the novel ahead of its predecessors." On *The Offer* (*EQMM*, December 2003): "Museum employee Robin Lobianco, stalked by a murderous threesome-loving married couple, is helped by a St. Louis police detective married to a stripper. Erotic suspense novels often run to 400 or 500 bloated over-heated pages—I for one prefer this stripped-down version." Randisi's very best may be *The Turner Journals*, published under the pseudonym Robert Leigh (*EQMM*, April 1997): "The jacket blurbs emphasize the finishing twist of this fresh, suspenseful, fast-moving New-York-cop-vs.-serial-killer police procedural, and the surprise of the last two sentences lives up to the hype."

Ian Rankin. It's not hard to see why the Scottish exemplar of Tartan Noir is reportedly the bestselling crime writer in Great Britain. On *The Falls* (*EQMM*, May 2002): "...[M]averick cop John Rebus and colleagues are looking for a young woman...[possibly] the

victim of a killer who leaves dolls and miniature caskets to com-
memorate his victims. Also involved are an anonymous online
games player known as Quizmaster and Edinburgh history going
back to those over-zealous resurrection men, Burke and Hare. Like
all the best procedural writers, Rankin manages to involve many
continuing characters while sticking to the case at hand." Even
better is *The Naming of the Dead* (*EQMM*, June 2007): "Increased
length, a broad canvas, a multitude of apparently unconnected
cases, and an emphasis on the personal lives of the cops are not
always happy trends in the hands of lesser writers, but Rankin is a
master....In 2005 Edinburgh, the G8 economic summit and associated demonstrations complicate life for Rebus, now approaching
retirement age and mourning the death of a brother, and his colleague Siobhan Clarke, whose aging hippie parents have traveled
north to join the protests. A Scottish Member of Parliament has
died by fall, jump, or push from Edinburgh Castle, and a serial
killer has apparently used a weird shrine to witchcraft and
superstition called a Clootie Well to link three seemingly unrelated
crimes. One of the best mystery plots in recent memory accompanies a detailed and harrowing account of the historic events attending the summit, peopled by a wide range of vividly drawn characters."

Ruth Rendell. One of the most respected literary talents in the
crime fiction field pays close attention to its structural requirements, and not only in her long-running series about Chief Inspector Wexford. On *Master of the Moor* (*EQMM*, February 1983):
"Stephen Whalby, a young part-time journalist and unenthusiastic
partner in his father's furniture business, lives for his opportunities
to walk on his beloved moor. This exceptional novel of psychological suspense begins with his discovery there of a young
woman's body. Rendell's virtuosity allows her to do a whodunit
and a study of criminal mentality at the same time....[T]his is even
somewhat of a fair-play detective story, with ample clues for the
reader-detective to anticipate (or not) the surprise ending." On
Anna's Book, written as Barbara Vine (*EQMM*, 1994): "The tale is
told partly through the diaries of Anna Westerby, a Danish woman
who recorded an account of her family life in England from 1905
to 1967, and partly through the present-day narrative of her granddaughter Ann Eastbrook, who has inherited literary rights to the
diaries, now international bestsellers. Ann becomes intrigued with
dual mysteries: the real identity of the aunt, Anna's daughter

Swanny, who willed her the diaries, and the possible connection of the Westerby family to a notorious murder case of the day. The carefully laid clues in the diaries allow for as many alternate solutions as a vintage Ellery Queen novel, and Rendell's gradual unpeeling of the truth is dazzling."

Peter Robinson. The British-born Canadian belongs in the front rank of contemporary crime novelists. On *Wednesday's Child* (*EQMM*, January 1995): "Chief Inspector Alan Banks and his fellow Yorkshire cops search for a seven-year-old girl abducted from her home by a couple who claim to be social workers investigating an abuse accusation. This is police procedural writing at its best, achieving the illusion the reader is following a real investigation rather than a contrived one." On *Innocent Graves* (*EQMM*, February 1997): "The smooth style and the complexity of plot and character make quoted evocations of P.D. James and Ruth Rendell credible.." *In a Dry Season* (*EQMM*, November 1999) "provides a textbook example of parallel narratives, either of which would provide an enthralling and comprehensible story on its own, drawing strength from each other to form a whole greater than the sum of its parts. The investigation...of the origin of some World War II era bones, found in a deserted village that had been flooded for a reservoir, alternates with a first-person narrative of village life in the early forties." On *Aftermath* (*EQMM*, June 2002): "We've read about plenty (too many) serial killers in recent fiction, but how about a novel that begins with the serial killer's identification and capture and spends the balance of the book exploring some questions left unanswered?...All the questions are answered, satisfactorily if not happily, in a serious examination of our attitudes toward and definitions of crime and criminals, plus the effects, great and small, a series of horrible crimes have on everyone even remotely connected to them. This is virtuoso work...."

Kate Ross. The gifted attorney-novelist's tragic death in her early forties was a significant loss to historical and classical mystery fiction. On *Whom the Gods Love* (*EQMM*, November 1995): "In his third recorded case, Julian Kestrel, detecting dandy of Regency London, is asked by barrister Sir Malcolm Falkland to discover the murderer of his son. Warning the bereaved father of the possibility of unwelcome revelations, Julian takes the case and along the way gives himself (via a wager with a rival dandy) a deadline for solving it. With a sleuth closer than most to the Great Detective model and the provision of plentiful fair-play clues, the author is a throwback to the Golden Age of the twenties and thirties. Style and characterization are not stinted, nor is a well-researched evocation of the time, but puzzle-spinning is the name of the game and few contemporary writers do it as well as Kate Ross." In *The Devil in Music* (*EQMM*, November 1997), "Kestrel travels to…Italy to look into the murder of a Milanese nobleman and opera patron whose last singing protégée, an English tenor known as Orfeo, seems the most likely suspect. But no one knows what the vanished Orfeo looked like, his singing teacher being blind. Ross demonstrates mastery of period, locale, character, and fair-play detection, producing one of the most daring stunt solutions in recent memory."

Jennifer Rowe. Though such comparisons are usually empty hype, Rowe really deserves to be called the Australian Agatha Christie. On *Stranglehold* (*EQMM*, August 1995): "When radio personality Max Tully uses his seventieth birthday party to announce both his retirement from the airwaves and his engagement to his young Vietnamese housekeeper, his friends and family are thrown into a tailspin and murder results. Series sleuth Verity Birdwood, the daughter of his radio employer, naturally winds up on the case….Rowe shares with Christie a devotion to the Least Suspected Person that really fools the reader, as well as an ability to make her suspects, if not deeply characterized, vivid and individual. Finally, it is easy to imagine Rowe's novel as a successful stage play." *Suspect* (*EQMM*, May 1999), about Senior Detective Tessa Vance, is "in the gritty, realistic police-procedural tradition, but the serial-murder plot of this ingenious novel and its reader-teasing alternate solutions will recall the work of Christie, Queen, Van Dine, and Philip MacDonald more than any contemporary."

James Sallis. The distinguished biographer of Chester Himes has written excellent crime novels of his own. On *Cypress Grove* (*EQMM*, November 2003): "Turner, ex-cop, ex-shrink, and ex-con, has come to a small southern town to hide from his past, until the out-of-his-depth local sheriff asks his help in a murder investigation. Sallis juggles past and present story lines with ease while spinning a plot with special appeal to movie buffs. The lyrical prose is reminiscent of James Lee Burke, but most of Burke's male characters are full of hostile testosterone, while even Sallis's prisoners display the manly reasonableness of characters in a

Howard Hawks western." On *Drive* (*EQMM*, November 2005): "The protagonist, appropriately known as Driver, is an automotive movie stunt man with a sideline criminal specialty that threatens to bring him to grief. Don't tell him the details, he insists, for all he does is drive. Some novels are said to be plot-driven, others character-driven. While it provides both of the above, this short novel is primarily style-driven, with superb fiction noir prose and a fine sense of locale, be it Phoenix, Los Angeles, or Brooklyn."

Steven Saylor. Of the many writers of Roman detective fiction, Saylor was not quite the first but is undoubtedly the best. On *Roman Blood* (*EQMM*, May 1992): "Gordianus the Finder is...something like Sherlock Holmes (he amazes his client's slave/messenger with off-the-wall deductions in the first chapter) and something like the hardboiled American p.i. (he tells his own story, has an active sex life, engages in much physical action, and repeatedly describes his dreams). Employed by the young advocate Cicero, preparing to defend Sextus Roscius in the Forum on a charge of parricide, Gordianus visits all strata of Roman life and gives a vivid (and obviously exhaustively researched) picture of ancient society to go with the complex puzzle, patterned on a real case. This [first novel] is a remarkable achievement." *The Venus Throw* (*EQMM*, November 1995) is "another astonishing performance, with a strong sense of time and place and a terrific final surprise. In the opening sequence, philosopher and Egyptian ambassador Dio, fearing for his life, comes to visit his old pupil Gordianus dressed in drag and accompanied by a eunuch priest of Cybele. Though Gordianus turns down the case, he eventually solves Dio's subsequent murder. A Roman trial, with Cicero in fine form defending Marcus Caelius, is one of the novel's highlights."

Julie Smith. Her debut was the first of several novels featuring Rebecca Schwartz, a San Francisco lawyer. In *Death Turns a Trick* (*EQMM*, June 1983): the "very likeable new feminist sleuth enters the scene in colorful fashion playing whorehouse piano. She represents an organization called HYENA (Head Your Ethics toward a New Age), dedicated to the legalization of prostitution." But Smith reached her best stride when she returned to her Louisiana roots. On *The Axeman's Jazz* (*EQMM*, February 1992): "...[P]olicewoman Skip Langdon searches for a serial strangler who (in his love for jazz and his Jack-the-Ripper-like letter-writing proclivities) invites comparison with the city's Axeman of seventy-plus years ago—and who seems to have some connection with the various twelve-step recovery programs active in the community. Smith's first Langdon novel, *New Orleans Mourning* (1990), was a deserving Edgar winner, and this one, proving again a pure whodunit need not fake character to surprise, is at least as good."

Martin Cruz Smith. Though his most famous book, *Gorky Park* (1981), about Moscow cop Arkady Renko, has had several sequels, this perennial bestseller loves to vary his subject matter. In *December 6* (*EQMM*, May 2003), "Smith's cultural concerns, his mastery of well-integrated research, and his irresistible narrative drive are all on display....The son of American missionaries, Harry Niles has spent most of his life in Japan, most recently as a representative of Hollywood film companies in Tokyo. Now, with war imminent in the last month of 1941, his dilemma is how, when, and whether he should get out of the country. The characters are vividly realized, the twists and turns of the plot unpredictable, the prose and dialogue expert, but the best feature is the detailed and often surprising picture of Japan on the verge of war from the viewpoint of a culturally conflicted protagonist." On *Stalin's Ghost* (*EQMM*, December 2007): "A televised 'blitz' chess tournament is one of several memorable scenes in the sixth [Renko] novel....The investigation into some subway sightings of the ghost of Joseph Stalin centers on an ominous turn in Russian politics. The prose, the characters, the unpredictable plot, and especially the picture of post-Soviet life are all outstanding."

Mickey Spillane. Many whose opinions I respect (Otto Penzler, Max Allan Collins, William L. DeAndrea) have been fans of Spillane, but I've never gotten his work. Comparing the Mike Hammer short story "The Night I Died," in the Spillane-Collins anthology *Private Eyes* (*EQMM*, July 1998), to the narration of the "Girl Hunt" ballet in the 1953 Fred Astaire musical *The Band Wagon*, I explained my apparent blind spot: "With its stylized cityscapes and writ-large events and characters, a Spillane story is to most other private eye fiction as grand opera to a naturalistic play. Opera goers accept simplistic plotting, exaggerated emotions, and rudimentary acting for the beauty of the music, without which their devotion would be baffling. When it comes to Spillane, call me tone deaf."

Donald Thomas. Though he has somewhat flown under the radar, the author (as Francis Selwyn) of several novels in the 1970s and '80s about Victorian cop Sergeant Verity is arguably a major figure in the rise of the historical detective story. On *The Secret Cases of Sherlock Holmes* (*EQMM*, January 1999): "Between the preface, in which he assumes the voice of Dr. Watson with rare authority, and a concluding historical note, Thomas presents seven stories involving Holmes in such real life events as the disappearance of the Irish crown jewels, the Dreyfuss case, and the alleged morganatic marriage of George V. Thomas…may in this remarkable melding of fact and fiction have written the best volume of Holmes pastiches ever published." *The Execution of Sherlock Holmes* (*EQMM*, February 2008) reflects "respect for the canon, deep knowledge of Victorian and Edwardian Great Britain, and the writing chops to replicate the Watsonian style….These five novella-length cases begin with the remarkable title story's account of Holmes's imprisonment by his enemies in the recently deactivated Newgate Prison. Along with excellent detective work, a sense of the cultural, intellectual, and political scene gives the stories added distinction."

Paco Ignacio Taibo. The Mexican novelist's approach to crime fiction is uniquely quirky and always intriguing. On *Just Passing Through* (*EQMM*, July 2000): "An opening series of notes playfully dodges an obvious question: How much of this documentary novel recounting the…author's effort to track the life of '20s anarchist, labor activist, and left-wing hero Sebastian San Vicente is nonfiction and how much invention? A thriller, even a detective story in a way, it's unconventional as either, a time-jumping mix of politics, history, and journalism from a unique literary talent." On *Frontera Dreams* (*EQMM*, January 2003): "…[P]rivate eye Hector Belascoaran Shayne tracks a former school friend, now the beautiful movie star Natalia Smith-Corona (she also considered Olivetti and Remington for her stage name), who has fled to the northern border. Taibo's observations on the Mexican character, relations with the United States, and male-female interactions are stimulating as always. The mystery plot is best characterized by a Chestertonian paradox: 'Belascoaran, unlike the authors of crime novels, liked complex stories, but only those in which nothing happened'…."

Peter Tremayne. The scholarly author (real name Peter Beresford Ellis) writes some of the best historical mysteries, both at novel and short story length. On *The Haunted Abbot* (*EQMM*, January 2005): "In December 666, Irish advocate Sister Fidelma and her Watson/lover Eadulf, visit Aldred's Abbey in East Anglia, where Fidelma is accused of witchcraft by the pernicious abbot, plagued by the ghost of his late wife. This is a solid product in every respect, with impeccable scholarship (a six-page historical introduction and four-page pronunciation guide!), compelling narrative drive, details of law and ritual, including a seventh-century Christmas celebration, and real detection, with a fair-play clue to the main secret." On *A Prayer for the Damned* (*EQMM*, February 2008): "A much-hated bishop, who supports celibacy of the religious and protests the wedding of...Fidelma...[to] Eadulf, delays the ceremony by being murdered. A detailed background of seventh-century Ireland, including a description of a wild boar hunt, and a cast of characters vividly realized and well differentiated despite their unusual and sometimes similar names highlight a well-constructed, generously-clued whodunit."

John Wainwright. Once a four-book-a-year author of remarkably varied novels, the former English cop has fallen into unjustified obscurity. Summing him up in a review of *Brainwash* (*EQMM*, December 1979), I wrote, "He is constantly experimenting with structure and point of view, and his stories, though seeming to put forth a hard-line law-and-order stance, often leave the reader with a disquieting sense that it is not all that simple. Though Wainwright has his faults—he tends to overwrite and is never far from the border of the cornfield—his novels at their best *work* beautifully...[In *Brainwash*,] Detective Inspector Lyle interrogates a suspected child-rapist in a Yorkshire police station....The style is more hard-boiled American than subdued British, and the insights into police interviewing techniques are fascinating. The author brings the setting and characters vividly to life, making the reader feel the tension and genuinely care what will happen." His best may have been *Blayde, R.I.P.* (*EQMM*, November 1982), the "fictional biography of a policeman...[in which] Wainwright's prose is under better control than ever before. It is a tribute to his mastery that he can take one of the most hackneyed situations in crime fiction—two brothers, one a cop, one a crook—and create from it a crime novel of near classic proportions."

Donald E. Westlake. In a near fifty-year career, this Grand Master has written more great books in more mystery sub-categories than almost anyone. On *Don't Ask* (*EQMM*, November 1993): "That very capable but ill-starred crook John Dortmunder and his gang are back in another wild adventure from the mystery genre's premiere humorist. Only one of two Eastern European republics, Tsergovia and Votskojek, will be granted a United Nations seat. Which one gets it hinges on the possession of a religious relic: the femur bone of Saint Ferghana Karanovich (1200-1217?), whose story Westlake interpolates in mock-encyclopedic style (chapter 2A, designated optional and not for credit)." *Smoke* (*EQMM*, February 1996) "skewer[s] the hypocrisy of the tobacco industry in the course of offering his take on a classic science fiction situation: the Invisible Man. The story of thief Freddie Noon considers aspects of invisibility unexplored by H.G. Wells. While I believe 450+ pages is too long for most crime novels and comic novels of any sort are best kept brief, Westlake is exempt from both strictures." On *The Ax* (*EQMM*, December 1997): "Burke Devore is out of work, a victim of corporate downsizing. Exactly how and why he turns to murder to solve his problems I'll leave it to you to discover. In this extraordinary novel, Westlake captures some of the grimmer aspects of American life in the nineties without a single false note, including an ending that you probably won't predict but that is perfect for the theme of the book. Though not the usual semi-farcical Westlake comedy, it has an underlying vein of very, very dark humor." On *The Hook* (*EQMM*, August 2000): "There is little humor but great irony in the story of best-selling Manhattan novelist Bryce Proctorr, who aims to solve his problems of writer's block and an elongated messy divorce action by enlisting less successful author Wayne Prentice as both ghost writer and killer for hire. Closest comparisons to this grimly involving account are some works of Patricia Highsmith and James M. Cain, though (pardon the heresy) I'm not sure Cain ever wrote anything quite this good." On *Ask the Parrot*, as by Richard Stark (*EQMM*, March 2007): "On the run following a bank robbery, career criminal Parker first becomes part of the posse searching for him, then aids a disaffected racetrack employee in a plan to loot the track's take....[The author] can get a character in a couple of paragraphs better than many authors with a twenty-page dossier and can surmount any challenge, including writing one short chapter from the convincing viewpoint of a caged parrot."

Phyllis A. Whitney. She published into her nineties, died a centenarian, and continued to improve at an age when most writers are doing well not to regress. In both her adult novels and her juveniles, Whitney explored a new locale each time out. *Emerald* (*EQMM*, July 1983) is "set in a well-realized Palm Springs and involves both the afterglow of Forties movie glamour and the contemporary phenomenon of parental child-snatching. The final twist is so surprising, and yet so well prepared for, that most readers will grant the measure of artistic license necessary to believe it." On *The Ebony Swan* (*EQMM*, November 1992): "In a splendid romantic suspense novel set on Virginia's Northern Neck, the peninsula between the Rappahannock and Potomac rivers, Whitney departs from her usual pattern by writing in the third person and featuring two virtually co-equal heroines: 72-year-old former ballerina Alexandrina Montoro, widow of a Peruvian novelist haunted by the ostensibly accidental death of her daughter years before, and granddaughter Susan Prentice, who after witnessing at age six her mother's death (a memory she has repressed) was whisked away to the Southwest by her father....In her late eighties, Whitney remains a consummate master, bringing her characters and background to life and, scornful though she is of conventional detection, even providing a neat fair-play clue to the killer."

Laura Wilson. One of the most promising writers to emerge in the new century merits comparison with Dickinson, Cook, and Rendell. On *Little Death* (*EQMM*, May 2001): "This extraordinary first novel...traces the lives of a brother, sister, and servant from the early-century death of a five-year-old younger brother, through a celebrated 1928 murder trial of the sister for the murder of her husband, to a presumed double-murder-suicide in 1955. In a whodunit where the only detective is the reader, each of the three narrators has a distinctive and believable voice and a sense of the changing times enriches the mystery." On *My Best Friend* (*EQMM*, May 2003): "The author's ability to shift among multiple viewpoints and timeframes while keeping the reader guessing is evident once again in her third novel, the story of a World War II era murder of a teenage girl and a 1995 child-in-jeopardy situation. The three narrators are Gerald Haldane, now nearing retirement, first met via the diary he began as an eight-year-old in the war-threatened Britain of 1938; his co-worker Jo, who gave birth at 17 to her now-12-year-old daughter; and his aunt Tilly, an 87-year-old retired actress and bearer of secrets. A key figure in the plot is Gerald's mother, unsuccessful as a parent but famous as a writer of juvenile mystery/adventure fiction—some sample pages from her work are right on target."

Paula L. Woods. After making her mark on the mystery field with the landmark anthology *Spooks, Spies, and Private Eyes* (1995), Woods joined the ranks of novelists with *Inner City Blues* (*EQMM*, September 1999): "Los Angeles Homicide detective Charlotte Justice's first book-length case takes place during the 1992 Rodney King riots, allowing for a vivid depiction of a city and a police department in chaos as well as the subtle social levels of the black community." *Stormy Weather* (*EQMM*, February 2002) concerned "the hurried demise of a dying actor-director who had been working on a documentary about African Americans in Hollywood. The plot is nicely worked out, the characters involving, and best of all, though Justice comes equipped with the requisite tragic back story, large extended family, and complicated love life, she sticks to the case at hand with minimal personal tangents." On *Dirty Laundry* (*EQMM*, November 2003): "...[I]n March of 1993...a Korean-American aide to a Latino mayoral candidate is murdered and the subsequent investigation highlights all kinds of urban politics, whether ethnic, sexual, economic, or just plain dirty."

James Yaffe. The boy wonder who first published at age 15 in *EQMM* was a protégé of Fred Dannay, and his detective fiction invariably reflects the EQ influence. His 1950s short-story series about one of the great armchair detectives, a New York Jewish mother who solved her cop son's cases for him, was revived at novel-length decades later. On *Mom Doth Murder Sleep* (*EQMM*, October 1991): "When a Mesa Grande, Colorado, theatre company's production of 'the Scottish play' results in on-stage murder,...Mom helps her fiftyish son Dave, investigator for the Public Defender's office, and his young assistant Roger solve the case. The telling...demonstrates the author's customary low-key humor, and the...puzzle, featuring a delightfully elongated gathering-of-the-suspects scene, will please readers who still value ingenuity in the detective novel." On *Mom Among the Liars* (*EQMM*, April 1993): "A Korean madame's murder, of which a homeless intellectual has been accused, is resolved with the usual Queenian linking of fairly showcased clues and topped with an equally Queenian final surprise. The liars of the title are politicians, specifically those running for the office of district attorney, and the voting-booth decisions of Mom and Dave carry an interesting and arguable political message."

SECTION THREE

TOPICAL ESSAYS

MURDERING HISTORY

The Weekly Standard, January 3/10, 2005

The line between fact and fancy has always been blurred in tabloid newspapers, plays and movies *"based on a true story,"* biographies for schoolchildren, television commercials, political-campaign material, and other sources of popular entertainment. But in recent years, the confusion has spread even to reputably published novels written for adults. Consider, for example, the growing fictional practice of making detectives of historical celebrities.

In a small way, the phenomenon has been around for sixty years (or even longer, if you count the nineteenth-century fiction-alized exploits of such real-life investigators as Vidocq and Allan Pinkerton). The first author to write a detective series about a historical personage was probably Lillian de la Torre, who cast Dr. Samuel Johnson in the Sherlock Holmes role, with James Boswell as his Watson, for a 1943 short story in *Ellery Queen's Mystery Magazine*. First collected in book form in *Dr. Sam: Johnson, Detector* (1946), the series would eventually fill four volumes.

Frederic Dannay, the editorial half of the Ellery Queen team, liked the idea. After publishing mysteries featuring Charlemagne, King Arthur, and Socrates, he discovered and nurtured the versatile Theodore Mathieson, who beginning in 1959 made one-shot detectives of Leonardo da Vinci, Alexander the Great, Omar Khayyam, Hernando Cortez, Don Miguel de Cervantes, Daniel Defoe, Captain Cook, Dan'l Boone, Stanley and Livingstone, and Florence Nightingale. Mathieson followed his collected stories, *The Great "Detectives"* (1960), with one of the first novel-length examples, *The Devil and Ben Franklin* (1961).

Still, as recently as the 1970s, the practice was rare, involving only stray volumes like John Dickson Carr's final novel *The Hungry Goblin* (1972), with Wilkie Collins as detective, and Margaret Doody's *Aristotle Detective* (1978).

Then came the deluge. The ranks have included some whose real life roles made them plausible sleuths—British magistrate Sir John Fielding, Al Capone's nemesis Eliot Ness, onetime New York Police Commissioner Theodore Roosevelt—while others were more unlikely: Queen Elizabeth I; Edward VII while he was prince of Wales; First Lady Eleanor Roosevelt; and such entertainers as Groucho Marx, the team of Enrico Caruso and Geraldine Farrar (she being the brighter one), and Elvis Presley.

Most of the subjects have been writers, usually but not always those associated with fictional crime. The appearances in detective fiction of Arthur Conan Doyle, who actually had some experience investigating real-life mysteries, have varied from the young medical student playing Watson to his mentor Dr. Joseph Bell (the inspiration for Sherlock Holmes) to the latter-day apologist for spiritualism, often in tandem with Houdini, the debunker of spiritualist frauds rather than the believer. Dashiell Hammett, once a Pinkerton operative, was a natural as fictional sleuth. Also detecting have been writers outside or on the periphery of the field, including Mark Twain, Jack London, and Jane Austen.

Among recent entries, there's Philippa Morgan's first novel, *Chaucer and the House of Fame* (Carroll & Graf, 2004), about Geoffrey Chaucer on a 1370 mission to France for his patron John of Gaunt. The Comte de Guyac, whose loyalty to the English king Chaucer seeks to clarify, is colorfully murdered in the course of a boar hunt. Chaucer's diplomatic profession makes him at least marginally credible as detective, and Morgan spins a neat mystery plot. Chaucer has yet to write *Canterbury Tales*, and he gets the inspiration for the Miller's Tale in course of his adventures. Some readers may question the decision to insert modern idioms into the dialogue, but given that Chaucer and his contemporaries spoke nothing like we do now, Morgan manages to make them sound natural while avoiding the most jarring anachronisms. She includes no historical notes, but her knowledge of the poet and his time is convincing.

The one unpublished effort in Theodore Mathieson's series featured Shakespeare, who narrated his case in the first person. Editor Queen wrote, "Imagine a pure detective story written by Shakespeare himself—in authentic Shakespearean language! It is no discredit to Mr. Mathieson that this incredibly daring attempt failed." The first-person Shakespeare of Leonard Tourney's *Time's Fool* (Forge, 2004) might have attained Fred Dannay's editorial approval. Tourney, a longtime academic specialist in Shakespeare and his time, previously wrote eight Elizabethan-period mysteries about the husband and wife sleuthing team of Matthew and Joan Stock, who make a brief cameo appearance (though unnamed) in his new book. Tourney's complex Shakespeare displays no false modesty about his talents, bears the weight of grief over the death of his only son, rationalizes his double life as London party animal and Stratford husband and father, and often depicts himself in an unheroic light. The story begins in December 1603, when the prosperous Will is summoned to a meeting with the dark lady of his sonnets, now afflicted with the pox, who attempts to extort money from him. The novel is adequate as a mystery but more distinguished in its command of period style and detail. True, Will and the other characters are awfully eloquent in their everyday speech, but wouldn't Shakespeare have rewritten it that way had he recounted his experiences in the then-unknown genre of a detective novel?

Harold Schechter also dares to have his subject narrate in the first person in his third novel about Edgar Allan Poe, who invented the detective story and provided a fictional solution to a real-life murder in "The Mystery of Marie Roget." *The Mask of the Red Death* (Ballantine, 2004) gives us Eddie Poe, action hero, and plays the character largely (though not entirely) for laughs. The novel begins with the editor of the *Broadway Journal* considering the uninspiring review copies before him and bemoaning the lowly state of serious literature in 1840s New York. Every reference to literary works of others comes with a sting in the tail. At one point, Poe responds with ostensible modesty to an admirer of "The Raven," in an everyday speaking style as ornate as his prose: "You are altogether too kind....Both Shakespeare and Milton, after all, produced several works which—while not necessarily surpassing my poem in sheer originality of conception—may certainly be considered its near equal."

Comic egotism aside, Poe emerges as sympathetic, likeable, and personally responsible, with his alcoholism under control. Other real-life characters appearing in *The Mask of the Red Death* reflect their public images: P.T. Barnum speaks in advertising copy for his American Museum and Kit Carson is every bit the larger-than-life hero of the dime novels. Poe joins Carson's hunt for the mountain man, "Liver-Eating" Johnson, whose scalping proclivities are on display in a gruesome series of Manhattan murders. The whodunit part of the plot falls prey to a pitfall of mysteries featuring historical subjects: a shortage of fictional suspects to choose from. Some of the plot turns will elicit groans, but the background is fascinating and the language (apart from a sore-thumb appearance of the modern atrocity "as of yet") on the button.

Charles Dickens was intrigued by police work and some of his novels border on detective fiction. Most of the stories in the recent

anthology *Death by Dickens* (Berkley, 2004), edited by Anne
Perry, put his fictional characters in original mysteries, but two
present the man himself as sleuth. In Martin Edwards's "The
House of the Red Candle," Dickens, in the company of drinking
buddy and fellow novelist Wilkie Collins, solves the locked-room
murder of a prostitute's customer in a shabby Greenwich bordello.
The characters and the sordid atmosphere are nicely done, but the
mystery is simplistic and easily seen through by the alert reader. In
Peter Tremayne's "The Passing Shadow," an older Dickens, in the
company of son-in-law Charles Collins (Wilkie's brother), is
asked to investigate an unidentified body pulled from the Thames,
resulting in trumped-up "origins" story for both Dickens's *Our
Mutual Friend* and Wilkie Collins's *The Moonstone*.

San Francisco *Examiner* journalist Ambrose Bierce has as his
excuse for becoming a fictional detective his employer William
Randolph Hearst, who encourages investigation in competition
with the official police. The title of Oakley Hall's *Ambrose Bierce
and the Trey of Pearls* (Viking, 2004), his fourth novel about the
quotably cynical author of *The Devil's Dictionary*, refers to a trio
of women's suffrage activists in the San Francisco of 1892. The
narrator, Bierce's colleague Tom Redmond, seeks carnal knowledge of his cousin, the member of the trio who advocates Free
Love. The mystery, involving the murder of a philandering minister, turns on a clue that is fair at least to the linguistically knowledgeable reader. Hall came to mystery fiction with a mainstream
literary reputation, and his prose is finely honed—on the scene of
a suffrage parade, we read, "two mules stood in their mulish dejec-
tion with no gender to celebrate."

In the world of Beatrix Potter, those mules would have had
plenty to say. The creator of Peter Rabbit may have the least excuse of this group to be a fictional detective, but she fits right in
with the self-sufficient heroines of contemporary amateur-
detective cozies. In Susan Wittig Albert's *The Tale of Hill Top
Farm* (Berkley, 2004), Potter comes to England's Lake District
where she has purchased the titular farm and stays to solve possible murder and lesser crimes. While I normally draw the line at
talking animals in an adult mystery, in this context they seem unavoidable. The author, who writes a series of Victorian mysteries
with husband Bill Albert under the pseudonym Robin Paige, is one
of the most scrupulous in separating fact from fiction, including a
character list that asterisks the real people (and pets) in the novel,
along with a concluding historical note and bibliography, a glos-

sary of slang, and (this is a cozy after all) a selection of recipes. There is much charm to the writing and background, but the mystery plot is exceedingly thin, suggesting that Albert was merely using the genre as an excuse to write about Potter.

Of all the writers of historical mystery fiction, Max Allan Collins has the highest ratio of real people to invented characters. In his Nate Heller private eye series, which is systematically addressing virtually every real-life mystery of the twentieth century, only the detective Heller himself is fictitious. Collins's knack for making real people come to life in fiction is a rarer gift and a trickier task than it sounds. His paperback-original "disaster" series puts popular writers in the role of detective: Jacques Futrelle (who really did go down with the ship) in *The Titanic Murders*; Leslie Charteris in *The Hindenburg Murders*; Edgar Rice Burroughs in *The Pearl Harbor Murders*; and Willard Huntington Wright (a.k.a. S.S. Van Dine, the creator of Philo Vance) in *The Lusitania Murders*.

I was especially impressed with *The London Blitz Murders* (Berkley, 2004), in which Agatha Christie is the sleuth and Collins manages to plug a real-life crime into her style of classical detection. But when I passed it along with a recommendation, I got a surprising reaction from another reader who just didn't buy it. Would Agatha Christie at that time have these particular thoughts about how the detective-story genre was developing? Would Sir Bernard Spilsbury, a thorough forensic pathology professional, actually invite a detective novelist, however renowned, to visit crime scenes with him? This reader's disquiet found the use of real people for fictional entertainment, especially ones who lived relatively recently, a disturbing invasion of privacy.

Is that right? All of the novels considered above have something to offer as entertainment, but should the trend they represent be viewed with alarm? Maybe not if you assume an educated audience. Historical fiction involving real people implies an unwritten contract between writer and reader, hard to define but ideally clear in the minds of both. Obviously, the reader understands that the made-up dialogue was never spoken and some of the specific events and encounters never took place. But the reader has the right to expect that the hard facts of the historical person's life, the dates and places, the opinions and attitudes, the social and religious values, as far as possible the manner of speaking, are consistent with what is known about that person. When relatively little is known, as with Chaucer or Shakespeare, more can be invented than when much is known, as with Potter or Christie.

As cultural literacy declines, the everyday reader or viewer may have a harder and harder time making the needed distinctions between the real and the fanciful. Blurring the line in supposed nonfiction, as in Edmund Morris's semi-fictionalized Ronald Reagan biography, makes matters worse, as does the overly vague application of the useful neologism "docudrama," which should apply only to works which take their language from a printed record (a trial transcript, for example, or correspondence) but now often refers to any dramatic presentation ostensibly based on real events. So-called "reality" shows on television, the nonfiction equivalent of professional wrestling, may be passable entertainment if you know they are contrived but problematic if you think they are real.

True, this confusion is no new phenomenon. We have long heard of people writing advice to soap-opera characters or sending letters off to Sherlock Holmes at 221B Baker Street. Do we have to put aside our pleasures of mixing fact and fiction because some people are too ignorant or uninformed to tell the difference? Mystery novelists are not going to stop writing about real-life detectives, and I don't intend to stop enjoying them at least selectively.

But the current climate calls for a greater measure of care. One practice that should be encouraged is to provide a foreword or afterword, as Collins always does, spelling out exactly what is real and what invented. This is especially helpful when arcane events that sound the product of imagination turn out to have a basis in reality.

AMERICAN WOMEN MYSTERY WRITERS

(review of *The Dead Letter & The Figure Eight* by Metta
Fuller Victor and *That Affair Next Door & Lost Man's Lane* by
Anna Katharine Green, both Duke University Press, 2003; *Painted
for the Kill* and *Corpse de Ballet* by Lucy Cores, both Rue Morgue
Press, 2004; *In a Lonely Place* and *The Blackbirder* by Dorothy B.
Hughes, both Feminist Press, 2003 and 2004))

The Weekly Standard, July 5/12, 2004

Revisionist history sometimes becomes conventional wisdom.
Consider this proposition, now universally accepted as true: *While
British women long ruled the mystery roost, their American sisters
were a downtrodden underclass in a genre dominated by bullying
hardboiled males.* Or try this, which most of those who comment
on mystery fiction seem to believe: *American women pioneers in
the development of the detective novel have been ignored or marginalized by mostly masculine historians and scholars.* Or this:
*Strong, self-sufficient non-spinster female detectives were un-
known in fiction before the 1970s.* Or, finally, this: *Pulp fiction is
some kind of prestigious and mysterious old boys' club.*

As it happens, all of these are false. But the truth doesn't seem
to fit the story that people want to tell about the field of crime fiction, and so the facts go out the window. Introducing one of two
recent omnibus volumes by the American detective novel's two
most important 19th-Century pioneers, Catherine Ross Nickerson
asserts that most historians of the detective story begin with the
American Edgar Allan Poe but "go on to trace the development of
the detective novel in the work of British writers . . . [and] tend to
return to the American scene only with the arrival of the hardboiled style in the 1920s." While one of her subjects, Metta Fuller
Victor (1831-1885), has only recently been recognized for her historic role, the other, Anna Katharine Green (1846-1935), has long
been celebrated for her seminal status and renders the sweeping
statement inaccurate.

Victor, who wrote her two early novels under the name
"Seeley Regester," genuinely does deserve credit as the first
American detective novelist—but with an asterisk. *The Dead Let-
ter* (1867) begins with Richard Redfield, a postal employee in

Washington, finding a cryptic letter dated two years earlier that sheds light on a mystery that has virtually destroyed his life. By opening the story with the finding of the letter before introducing a flashback to the events leading up to it, Victor gives the reader the illusion of a story set in motion by an incredible coincidence (fictionally acceptable) rather than resolved by one (fictionally unacceptable).

Two years before, Redfield was a student in the offices of lawyer John Argyll and in love with his benefactor's daughter Eleanor, whose fiancé Henry Moreland is found stabbed to death while en route to the Argyll home. The novel has enough of the essential elements to qualify as a detective story. Burton, the Great Detective figure, introduced as taciturn but increasingly garrulous as the story goes on, "chooses such cases as demand...the benefit of his rare powers." The final revelation of the criminal (which can hardly have surprised the readers of its time much more than it will today's) comes in a gathering of the suspects. The novel keeps a consistent focus on the case, apart from romantic interludes. But in place of real detection, Victor resorts to parlor tricks and supernatural visions. When Burton makes Sherlock Holmes-like deductions from the handwriting of a letter, the reader must take his graphological acuity on faith, since no explanations are given. Some of Burton's detection comes via the gifts of his clairvoyant eleven-year-old daughter.

Though hard sledding for a reader of today, the novel is well enough written to show the author was good in her time, and the social and domestic details are instructive. The Irish servant class is stereotyped as superstitious and over-emotional, with their dialect presented in tiresome phonetic transcription. Modern marvels include train travel and photography to aid identification. A long sea voyage is needed to travel to California to track down a clue. The publisher's back-cover blurb claims "a background of post-Civil War politics," but nothing of the kind appears—indeed, the action takes place in the late 1850s, before the Civil War.

The Figure Eight (1869) includes the same brand of stock characters as its predecessor—the gallant but misunderstood narrator, his kind elderly benefactor, an evil rival in love, and women of beauty, innocence, and nobility—but it is a more successful novel. It begins with a body in the library: the uncle of the narrator Joe Meredith, a country doctor who had recently returned from California with $60,000 in gold bars intended to pay off a mortgage and retire from medical practice. The victim, poisoned by prussic acid in a glass of port, leaves a dying message: a scribble that includes the figure eight of the title. The gold has disappeared, and the narrator is accused of the crime. The characters, including a Mrs. Danvers-like governess and the victim's young Cuban wife, are more complex and less predictable than those in *The Dead Letter*, but the detection is no more advanced. Don't expect any great revelation on the meaning of that dying message. The novel exemplifies the mystery as social history, including the hero's resolve during his exile on the western frontier to make a killing in real estate.

For many years, before scholars unearthed Victor's work, Anna Katharine Green was regarded as the first woman to write a detective novel—indeed, as the first American mystery novelist of either sex. Her 1878 novel *The Leavenworth Case* has been almost universally recognized as a milestone, and all the early, mostly male historians of the form recognized her pioneering status. The two novels chosen for reprint exemplify one of Green's many innovations: the spinster sleuth, later to be explored by writers as various as Mary Roberts Rinehart, Agatha Christie, and Stuart Palmer.

In *That Affair Next Door* (1897), wealthy Manhattan resident Amelia Butterworth becomes suspicious late one evening when she sees a man take a young woman into the seemingly closed house next door and shortly leave without her. When the woman's body is found crushed under a heavy cabinet, Amelia ponders the eternal question of mystery fiction: Was it accident, suicide, or murder? A semi-comic figure who reveals herself more than she intends in her first-person narrative, Amelia enthusiastically probes the complicated relationships of her neighbors and offers help to Ebenezer Gryce, the elderly policeman of earlier Green novels. The novel is leisurely paced but not padded, and the detecting rivalry of amateur and professional is humorously and sensitively managed. Much of its careful plotting and attention to detail would be at home in a formal detective novel of decades later, though the final solution comes from a witness with an explanation anticipated by neither Gryce nor Butterworth. The surprise killer, though probably anticipated by latter-day readers, must have been a sensation in 1897.

Amelia gradually wins Gryce's grudging respect, to the extent of becoming involved at his invitation in *Lost Man's Lane* (1898), about a series of broad-daylight disappearances in a New York mountain village. With mysterious noises in a houseful of secrets and the legend of a phantom coach, the novel is much more in the gothic tradition than the superior *That Affair Next Door*. A frankly preposterous story, with a broadly painted least-suspected-person culprit and at one point a highly unlikely disguise for Gryce, it is a lesser book than its predecessor, though not devoid of interest.

Historical importance apart, has Green become merely a museum piece? Some 1940s commentators, including Howard Haycraft and Ellery Queen, would have said so on the basis of her florid Victorian style. But perhaps they were too close in time to appreciate what then was merely out of fashion. On the basis of these two novels, Green can be accessible and rewarding today to the right reader.

In the early years of the twentieth century, American women ceded none of their preeminence. Green continued producing into the 1920s and by the beginning of World War I had been joined by the hugely successful Mary Roberts Rinehart, who would remain a perennial bestseller into the 1950s, and the less well-remembered (but celebrated in her time) Carolyn Wells, among other female American detective novelists. By the 1930s, such writers as Leslie Ford, Mignon G. Eberhart, Elizabeth Sanxay Holding, and Phoebe Atwood Taylor had launched long and successful careers. In the 1940s came Craig Rice, Margaret Millar, Dorothy Salisbury Davis, Charlotte Armstrong, and Helen McCloy, among many others.

The prominence of women was not limited to the writers. Many, perhaps most, of the prominent mystery editors at midcentury were female: Lee Wright, Marie F. Rodell, Joan Kahn, Isabelle Taylor, Margaret Norton. By the early 1950s, women occupied the mystery reviewing chairs of major newspapers and magazines: Avis de Voto, Lenore Glen Offord, Dorothy B. Hughes, Frances Crane. The major tastemaker was a man—the *New York Times Book Review*'s Anthony Boucher—but he loved books by women.

And what about the characters these women wrote about? Strong independent women were non-starters in sleuthing roles until the private eyes, policewomen, pathologists, and trouble-prone amateurs of the 1970s and 1980s, right? Wrong. Rue Morgue Press, Tom and Enid Schantz's small Colorado publishing firm, has reprinted several writers of the 1940s who put the lie to such nonsense, most recently two novels by Lucy Cores.

Cores's *Painted for the Kill* (1943) introduces Toni Ney, physical trainer and jujitsu instructor at a posh Manhattan salon that will remind you of the setting for Claire Boothe Luce's *The Women*. When a French movie star is murdered during a mudpack treatment, Toni turns amateur sleuth, and her relationship with police detective Torrent parallels that of Butterworth and Gryce half a century earlier. The novel has all the elements of a present-day cozy mystery—specialized background, amateur sleuth with interesting job and independent nature, romantic misunderstandings, humor, suspense set-pieces, even a cat—but is miles better than most of today's product, mainly because of a better sense of pace, a lack of tangential soap-opera complications, and some genuinely clued detection. *Corpse de Ballet* (1944), with Toni working as a reporter covering a ballet production, is not quite as good, partly because of a tiresome romantic subplot, but it is still well written and deceptively plotted.

Macho resentment over women in the workforce is one motivation for the serial strangler who stalks post-war Los Angeles in the 1947 novel *In a Lonely Place* by Dorothy B. Hughes, one of the biggest names in mid-twentieth-century crime fiction, both as reviewer and novelist. Her earlier *The Blackbirder* (1943) is a pursuit novel with a vivid visual sense and a strong sense of faceless menace, with details of what is going on only gradually revealed. Juliet Marlebone, the American-born daughter of a naturalized French father, has fled wartime Europe with unofficial help. Following the murder in New York of a German acquaintance, she flees to Santa Fe in search of the shadowy title character, an illegal transporter of refugees from Mexico. In the course of her travels, several locales are economically captured, along with the details of wartime conditions on the home front.

The reprinting of these two excellent novels by Feminist Press is most welcome, but the editors do Hughes an unintentional disservice by the series title, "Femmes Fatale: Women Write Pulp." By any sensible definition, Hughes was not a pulp writer. "Pulp fiction" refers to material written for the pulp-paper magazines that flourished from the 1920s to the 1940s and died out in the 1950s. Some commentators, reasonably enough, extend the term to include material written for the digest-sized fiction magazines and paperback-original publishers that took the place of the pulps in the marketplace—or, as much of the marketplace as the rise of television left for them. For purposes of the Feminist Press series, though, pulp seems to be a synonym for mass-market paperback, which leads the editors and their consulting scholars into a morass

of misunderstanding, sweeping generalizations, and fuzzy thinking.

For example, the editors claim in their overall introduction,
"authorial name and persona were rarely linked to real-life identity." Pseudonyms were widespread in pulp magazine and paperback staples like mysteries, science fiction, and westerns, but they
were not the norm. In her afterword to *The Blackbirder*, Amy Vil-
larejo calls the early Pocket Books "among the first pulp novels."
Pocket Books, one recalls, specialized in cheap reprints of classics.
If Shakespeare, Emily Brontë, P.G. Wodehouse, Edgar Allan Poe,
and Jane Austen are now pulp writers, the designation has lost all
meaning.

In fact, pulp writer is not a dishonorable label. Dashiell
Hammett and Raymond Chandler came out of the pulps, as did
many other distinguished writers of popular fiction in various genres. But most pulp fiction, in its strictest definition, was disposable
product, written fast for low rates of pay, without the care or the
literary ambition of writings for slick magazines or for book publication. It's no accident that most anthologies of pulp fiction draw
on the more respectable and better-edited latter-day digests for
most of their material rather than the real pulps. Even in those
early pulps, there were women writers—notably Leigh Brackett,
who would become a prominent screenwriter best known for her
work on *The Big Sleep* and *The Empire Strikes Back*.

Regardless, pulp writer simply will not do as a description of
Dorothy B. Hughes. Her first book was a volume of poetry from
Yale University Press, her novels were written for the hardcover
book market from the beginning, she was inspired to fiction writing by the very un-pulpish Eric Ambler, and she received respectful reviews from distinguished publications throughout her career.

Quibbles about terminology aside, what remains is the work,
and it is good to have all these books available to readers. And
there are many other unjustly neglected woman deserving revival:
the wonderful Charlotte Armstrong, for just one example. But
there are many men who deserve reprinting, as well. There simply
isn't any truth in the story that women writers are especially ignored by readers and historians of mystery fiction. Time and for-
getfulness are equal-opportunity erasers.

CRIME FICTION FOR CHRISTMAS

(review of *A Crossworder's Holiday* by Nero Blanc, Berkley, 2002; *A Puzzle in a Pear Tree* by Parnell Hall, Bantam, 2002; and *The Christmas Garden Affair* by Ann Ripley, Kensington, 2002)

The Weekly Standard, December 23, 2002

The tradition of telling ghost stories at Christmas has a venerable history, reaching back well into the middle ages. Christmas detective stories have a shorter history. Arthur Conan Doyle's "The Adventure of the Blue Carbuncle" (1892) is an early example, but Yuletide mysteries remained relatively rare—until, in recent years, their commercial possibilities began to be exploited with a stack of new books every year. Though Doyle gave Sherlock Holmes only one holiday case, recent writers of Holmes parodies, imitations, and pastiches have filled two volumes with them: *Holmes for the Holidays* (1996) and *More Holmes for the Holidays* (1999).

Over the years, some long-running sleuths have followed Holmes in investigating Yuletide crime, including Nero Wolfe in Rex Stout's "Christmas Party" (1957) and Simenon's great police detective in "Maigret's Christmas" (1954). Several prominent British sleuths solve cases involving traditional Christmas pantomimes: Ngaio Marsh's Roderic Alleyn in *Tied Up in Tinsel* (1972), G.K. Chesterton's Father Brown in "The Flying Stars" (1911), and John Mortimer's Rumpole of the Bailey in "Rumpole and the Old Familiar Faces" (in this year's *Rumpole Rests His Case*). The best of James Yaffe's intricately plotted novels about a Jewish mother detective, *Mom Meets Her Maker* (1990), provides a non-Christian's view of the holiday.

Approaches vary with the authors' styles. Christmas mysteries in the classical tradition often take the favored sleuth to a deceptively cozy holiday house party, preferably snowed in, at which the family and friends gathered only pretend to be jolly—and sometimes they don't even pretend. By contrast, hardboiled private eyes and jaded big city cops live in a world of emaciated Santas, barroom wreaths, and other symbols of the grim loneliness of a mean street Noel.

The mystery writer who has turned most often to Christmas for inspiration is Ed McBain, whose 87th precinct cops pull holiday duty in *The Pusher* (1956), *Sadie When She Died* (1972), and *Money, Money, Money* (2001). *Ghost* (1980) admits in the Christmas season the only supernatural moment in McBain's long-running series. With the separately published short story *And All Through the House: Christmas Eve at the 87th Precinct* (1984), a station-house Nativity metaphor with an ironic final line to cut the sentimentality, McBain produced a Christmas novella—a cash-cow formula that has well served such bestselling crime writers as Mary Higgins Clark (several times), John Grisham, William Bernhardt, and Janet Evanovich.

Cozy writers are more likely than their noirish brethren to produce Yuletide mysteries, as shown in three examples from the 2002 crop. Two of these are from the highly specialized subgenre of crossword-puzzle mysteries, which dates back to Dorothy L. Sayers's Lord Peter Wimsey short story, "The Fascinating Problem of Uncle Meleager's Will" (collected in *Lord Peter Views the Body*, 1928). To make a crossword the key to the solution is a formidable challenge even in the context of formalist artifice. The husband-and-wife team (Cordelia Frances Biddle and Steve Zettler) who write as Nero Blanc manage it in *A Crossworder's Holiday*, gathering five agreeably written and trickily plotted short stories about their sleuthing team of puzzle designer Belle Graham and her private eye husband Rosco Polycrates. The last and best is "A Ghost of Christmas Past," about a Cotswold house with a history of vanishings.

The running joke of Parnell Hall's "Puzzle Lady" mysteries, continuing with *A Puzzle in a Pear Tree*, is that amateur sleuth Cora Felton is neither the master puzzle-setter nor the sweet little old lady her public image suggests. During rehearsal for a village Christmas pageant, in which Cora reluctantly plays one of the seven maids-a-milking, a threatening acrostic (to be followed by several more) is substituted for the partridge in a pear tree. Refreshingly in the current market, Hall is a pure entertainer, with no great themes or underlying seriousness. There is some sly social satire, as when the local PTA doesn't want actors in the village's "living manger" scene to change clothes in a local church—because they don't want the Nativity associated with organized religion. Hall has fun with hoary genre conventions, including the curare-tipped blowgun dart, the near-miss falling sandbag during a stage rehearsal, and the witness who fears talking to the amateur sleuth will mark him for murder as the Man Who Knew Too

Much. As one of the few active practitioners of the elaborate Golden Age-style detective novel, Hall should be cherished.

Ann Ripley's *The Christmas Garden Affair* is a more typical contemporary cozy in its emphasis on specialized background and disdain for fair-play clues. Louise Eldridge, PBS garden show host and heroine of several earlier Ripley novels, attends the new First Lady's garden party, designed to celebrate native American plants. Murder follows among a variety of horticultural hangers-on, many with reason to loathe rival TV host Bunny Bainfield, whose breasts are more notable than her botanical knowledge. All the elements of a classical detective story are here: a despicable murder victim, a large cast of potential suspects, an unusual weapon, even a half-baked locked room problem. But the reader has no shot at solving it, the amateur sleuth's relation with the police is absurd, and the climax is one of the sillier into-the-killer's-clutches sequences in the mystery genre. The holiday content is also slight until the feel-good final chapter at the Eldridge family feast.

For the best of the Christmas mysteries, turn to the classics. Agatha Christie's *Hercule Poirot's Christmas* (1938; U.S. title *Murder for Christmas*), in which a dying patriarch uses his Christmas gathering to gleefully announce plans to change his will, is widely admired as one of her finest puzzles. Be warned, though, that there is not nearly as much holiday trimming in the novel as occurs in the picturesque television adaptation with David Suchet as Poirot.

Ellery Queen's *The Finishing Stroke* (1958) was originally intended by the authors (Frederic Dannay and Manfred B. Lee) to be the last bow of detective Queen. They set the first chapter in 1905, the year of birth of Ellery and his creators; the main body in 1929, the year the first Queen novel was published; and the final section in 1957, when Ellery finally solves the case that had stumped him all those years before: a Christmas house party of theatrical, artistic, and publishing people disrupted by murder and the appearance of mysterious verses based on "The Twelve Days of Christmas." The nostalgia mystery, rich in period allusions, is commonplace now, but it was unusual when the book appeared. As with all Queen problems, the reader is given enough clues to work out the incredibly elaborate solution, provided (as Manfred Lee once observed) the reader is a genius.

Cyril Hare, pseudonym of English barrister and judge Alfred Alexander Gordon Clark (1900-1958), was less famous and prolific than Queen or Christie, but in *An English Murder* (1951), he produced one of the finest snowbound Christmas mysteries, notable both for its puzzle and its portrait of Britain's changing politics and social classes at mid-20th Century. The hideously ill-assorted "family" house party, containing enough social, political, and personal conflicts for a much larger group, consists of a dying peer, his neo-Nazi son, the Labour chancellor of the exchequer, the wife of a whiz kid who wants the latter's job, a Jewish history scholar from Eastern Europe, and a titled ingénue once romantically involved with the son. Also present are a Scotland Yard man guarding the chancellor and one of detective fiction's most fully realized butlers since Wilkie Collins's *The Moonstone* appeared in 1868. Hare keeps the reader guessing about everything: who will die, who will kill, and who will detect. The solution is ingenious, surprising, and perfectly fair if you follow the historical clues. There's not much Christmassy, apart from the snow, the cold, and the foreign scholar's name (Dr. Wenceslaus Bottwink), but the novel is an under-appreciated classic of detective fiction.

Gather up all of these, and you'll have plenty of good mysteries to see you through the twelve days of Christmas.

Postscript 2008: A flood of Christmas mysteries still comes each year, and Anne Perry has joined the club of bestselling writers turning out an annual Christmas novella.

THE GHOST AND MISS TRUMAN

(review of *Every Midget Has an Uncle Sam Costume: Writing for a Living* by Donald Bain, Barricade, 2002; and *Murder at Ford's Theatre* by Margaret Truman, Ballantine, 2002)

The Weekly Standard, November 18, 2002

In the waning decades of the Twentieth Century, a bizarre phenomenon first observed in the 1940s became a crime-fiction epidemic. Famous entertainers, athletes, and presidential relatives, longtime mystery buffs all, sat down at the old typewriter or word processor and started banging out their own novels—or so they would have us believe. In truth, in nearly every case, the celebrity made a deal through an agent or book packager, collected a nice advance for the use of the name, and left to a professional ghost all the actual writing.

Ghostwriting is a time-honored practice, and most readers surely realize that movie stars and baseball players have help with their memoirs, as do office holders and candidates with their speeches, campaign literature, and policy statements. But the dissemination of ghostwritten novels is more blatantly deceptive and ethically questionable. A new memoir by a veteran "silent partner" on both fiction and nonfiction provides a ghost's eye view of publishing.

Donald Bain has written, under his name or others, some 80 books. *Every Midget Has an Uncle Sam Costume* entertainingly describes his experiences as an officer in charge of censoring American Armed Forces Television in Saudi Arabia, as a jazz musician, and as an airline public relations flack in a happier and more free-wheeling era of air travel, but the most intriguing topic, especially for his colleagues in the writing trade, is ghostwriting. Bain's first major success, *Coffee, Tea, or Me* (1967), drew on the comical amatory adventures of two stewardesses who appeared in public as the authors, Trudy Baker and Rachel Jones. Three sequels followed, plus similar faux first-person accounts of nurses, office temps, teachers, and actresses, always with attractive young women recruited to front the books for publicity purposes. Bain also wrote the autobiography of actress Veronica Lake; crime fiction signed by actor David Toma and ex-cops Nick Vasile and Mike Lundy; and the *Murder, She Wrote* novels in ostensible collaboration with Jessica Fletcher, the character played on TV by Angela Lansbury.

Employing a ghost on a work of fiction is almost always dubious, but never more than when the putative author is really a writer. Brett Halliday, Leslie Charteris, and Ernest Tidyman all turned to ghosts to carry on the exploits of their famous characters (Mike Shayne, the Saint, and Shaft respectively), while the Ellery Queen team employed other writers to turn out paperback originals very different from the genuine Queen novels. According to Bain, one case of posthumous ghosting, *Chains of Command* (1999), credited on the cover to William Caunitz, who died in 1996, but almost entirely written by Christopher Newman, precipitated a class-action suit by readers who believed they had been defrauded.

Illustrating the lack of sophistication of some readers, Bain reports that one fan, regarding the cover photos on the *Murder, She Wrote* books, "found it amazing how much Angela Lansbury looked like Jessica Fletcher." While this is akin to the public naïveté exploited by celebrity mystery novels, thinking fictional characters are real requires a much greater level of gullibility than assuming the real person whose name appears on the cover actually wrote the book.

Celebrity mystery novels, like other ghostwritten books, differ in the way the actual writer is (or is not) credited. In the most honest method, arguably not technically ghostwriting at all, the celebrity makes the writing pro a full collaborator, as in the recent *Blue Moon* (Berkley), signed in equal-sized print by bandleader Peter Duchin and Edgar-Award-winning novelist John Morgan Wilson.

The second method doesn't admit the ghost's existence to the world at large but at least tips off others in the writing and publishing trade. Many of the novels attributed to *Star Trek*'s William Shatner credit in the acknowledgements the assistance of science-fiction humorist Ron Goulart. Actor George Kennedy's paperback mysteries offer thanks to Walter J. Sheldon. A more subtle variation is to dedicate the book to the real author, as actor George Sanders did for Craig Rice and Leigh Brackett in the two 1940s crime novels published under his name. (Bain used the same method to give himself credit on the *Coffee, Tea, or Me* books.)

Finally, presenting the most dubious ethics as well as the most tantalizing challenge to those who must know who done it, some celebrity mystery writers eschew the slightest hint of a ghostwriter's presence. Great pains were taken to suggest that the earliest successful example of a celebrity mystery novel, Gypsy Rose Lee's *The G-String Murders* (1941), was the stripper's own work, though it has long been attributed to Craig Rice. Helen Traubel's *The Metropolitan Opera Murders* (1951) was actually the work of Harold Q. Masur. Though the late TV personality and show-business all-rounder Steve Allen had a legitimate track record as a writer, his mystery novels of the 1980s and 1990s were all ghost-written, first by Walter J. Sheldon, later by Robert Westbrook.

The children of Presidents who have emerged as ostensible authors of mystery fiction neatly represent the three methods of dealing with the ghost. The most recent to enter the field, Susan Ford, credits a co-author, Laura Hayden, for *Double Exposure: A First Daughter Mystery* (St. Martins Minotaur, 2002).

Elliott Roosevelt, whose first novel featuring his mother Eleanor as sleuth was *Murder and the First Lady* (1984), didn't offer a shared byline but gave his ghost a nod via a note in his early books crediting William Harrington as "my mentor in the craft of mystery writing [who] has given me invaluable assistance with the First Lady mysteries." After Roosevelt died in 1990, his publishers added to his jacket biography for *A First Class Murder* (1991) this disingenuous claim: "A hard-working and prolific writer, he left behind a number of already-completed Eleanor Roosevelt mysteries." By 1998's *Murder in the Maproom*, they were still touting "a number of unpublished manuscripts to be enjoyed by readers in the years to come." One *Booklist* reviewer ironically called Roosevelt "one of the mystery genre's most prolific dead authors." Harrington, ironically, would finally be credited as author of a Roosevelt book, *Murder at the President's Door* (2001), only after his own death.

Margaret Truman, the longest running and most commercially successful of the Presidential offspring fronting mysteries, offers no hint in any of her books, beginning with *Murder in the White House* (1980), that she has a ghost, a collaborator, or even a literary mentor. Her Capital Crimes novels, which usually use as background Washington, D.C. landmarks (Kennedy Center, National Cathedral, Pentagon, National Gallery, Watergate, Library of Congress, Potomac) or government branches and agencies (CIA, FBI, Supreme Court), while providing plenty of historical tidbits and tourist information, are far from distinguished detective fiction but above average celebrity mysteries.

The latest, *Murder at Ford's Theatre*, is soundly crafted and professionally paced. The headline-inspired plot concerns the murder of a senatorial intern evocatively named Nadia Zarinsky. The stock characterizations sound like casting notes, but at least it's easy to tell the people apart. The author employs familiar strategies to puff up the page count: potted biographies (often irrelevant) of characters major and minor, and repetitious dialogue, as when the cops report to their superior investigative details that are still fresh in the reader's mind. Truman's amateur sleuthing team of law professor Mackensie Smith and his gallery-owner wife Annabel (sometimes likened by generous reviewers to Nick and Nora Charles) share the stage with an odd-couple police team, a Jewish Lincoln buff and his African-American partner. The latter's desire to argue who had it worse, Jews in the Holocaust or blacks under slavery, doesn't ring true.

The prose and dialogue are efficient but flavorless, occasionally demanding quotation for their clunky archaism ("Klayman had proved his mettle on more than one occasion, facing down dangerous situations with steely resolve and audacious fearlessness"); clumsy genre references ("The strange case of the murdering midget. Sounds like a Holmes novel"); ponderous banality ("Sunday, as everyone knows, is a day of rest, except for those in jobs demanding their presence"); or faulty syntax ("Seemingly social brunches offer both eggs Benedict as well as the scrambled eggs of negotiation").

Arbor House's Donald Fine, Truman's publisher at the time of her first mystery, swore she had no ghostwriter, but there was a clue from the very beginning: though widely and favorably reviewed, the novel was not nominated for the Edgar Award for best first novel by an American author, nor, according to Allen J. Hubin, a member of the committee, was it even submitted by the publisher.

Hubin's *Crime Fiction III: A Comprehensive Bibliography, 1749-1995*, the most authoritative source on mystery authorship, identifies Donald Bain as Margaret Truman's ghost, based on intelligence from reliable publishing community sources. Bain has flatly denied it, both to Hubin and in an e-mail to me: "I do not ghostwrite Margaret Truman's murder mysteries." But what does Bain's autobiography have to say?

A note at the end of the bibliography claims that "[c]ontractual obligations prohibit Donald Bain from publicly taking credit for an additional 20 novels ghosted by him...." Elsewhere in the book, he partially contradicts this, writing that "some of my best work appears in an 18-book series ghostwritten over the past 20 years for a well-known person. It would be professionally inappropriate for me to take public credit for this series, although I'm not under contractual obligation to conceal my involvement." (*Murder at Ford's Theatre* brings the total of Truman's novels to 19.) Obligatory or not, Bain's denial fulfills his duty as an honorable ghostwriter. In the same chapter, he excoriates the ghostly unprofessionalism of Lucianne Goldberg, who publicly claimed credit for the novel *Washington Wives* (1987) out of anger over putative author Maureen Dean's interviews.

If Bain is Truman's ghost, he clearly won't admit it, but he provides enough clues to support a strong circumstantial case. He states his involvement with the series "for a well-known person" began in 1980 and continues, "I've been writing novels in this series ever since, a book a year, most of them well reviewed and appearing on many bestseller lists throughout the country." How many other candidates for a frequently bestselling book-a-year mystery series beginning around 1980 are there?

Bain writes that he disagreed with a young editor over "a husband-and-wife team of characters [created] for a book in a series I was ghosting. My characters were in their 50s, erudite, physically fit, and madly in love." Though the editor thought them too old, "The characters stayed and went on to become particular favorites of critics and readers of the series." That sounds very much like Mackensie and Annabel Smith.

In researching the coffee-table book *Caviar, Caviar, Caviar* (1981), Bain learned of the underground trade in Iranian caviar, smuggled into the United States via Copenhagen. He writes, "I later used what I'd learned as the basis for a crime novel I went on to ghost for a well-known person." The plot of Truman's *Murder on Embassy Row* (1984) involves caviar smuggling.

Recognizing that the ghosting of fiction presents a greater ethical dilemma than nonfiction, Bain asks, "Is a book buyer cheated when buying a novel not written by the person whose name appears on the cover? Is it fraud? I don't think so, though my bias is understandable." Understandable, yes, but try to follow the logic of his next statement: "In most cases, the consumer gets a lot better book than if the nonwriting collaborator had tried to do it solo." Okay, but so what? The book is still being sold on the premise that a celebrity wrote it, and there is no excuse for such a pretense other than deceiving the consumer.

Still, one might ask, where's the harm? The journeyman pros doing the actual writing undoubtedly realize more profit from being celebrity ghosts than they could from books under their own names. While one might claim the inflated money the celebrity and the ghost get would otherwise go to more deserving but less famous professional writers, that is specious logic along the lines of, if NASA didn't spend so much money on the space program, we could wipe out world hunger. The deceptiveness of attributing a book to a person who didn't write it is minor next to the credits for doing nothing on many major motion pictures. And what does the deceived reader care, if the novel is a good read that draws on (or even appears to draw on) the celebrity's area of expertise?

There are several harms. The books, more even than most commercial fiction driven by the marketplace rather than the artistic impulse, are rarely very good mystery fiction. The celebrity publicity machine attracts readers that might otherwise be drawn to better books. While the big money advance might not have gone elsewhere, some of the bookstore display space, public library buying, and newspaper or magazine review attention certainly would. The public impression that anybody can write a book erodes the professional respect accorded to real writers. And finally, in the unlikely event a celebrity author actually writes a novel, no one in the cynical book world will believe it.

Bain writes, "I'm often asked when talking to groups about my career: 'How can you stand to see someone else's name on a book that you've written?'" He finds it easy to answer: he makes a good living writing for others, and he takes pride in doing the best work he can on every project. Most professional writers would agree. Writing is such a hard way to make a living, it's tough to blame the ghost for going where the money is. The question for the ostensible celebrity novelist should be harder to answer, but in this time of rampant classroom cheating, falsified resumés, and corporate malfeasance, it probably isn't: how can you stand to see your name on a book somebody else wrote?

Postscript 2008: While the obituaries of Margaret Truman referred to her mystery writing, none that I saw suggested it was ghostwritten, though the fact has been well-known in the publishing community for years.

TOO MANY COOKS

(review of *Yeats is Dead*, edited by Joseph O'Connor, Knopf, 2001; *Naked Came the Phoenix*, edited by Marcia Talley, St. Martin's Minotaur, 2001; *Natural Suspect*, devised by William Bernhardt, Ballantine, 2001)

The Weekly Standard, December 17, 2001

Multiple-author novels are the equivalent of the old-time theatrical benefit. Though they are not directly lucrative to the performers, it's an honor to be chosen to participate. Usually, it's all in a good cause, whether a charity or the treasury of a professional organization. While the end product is ephemeral, especially when compared to individual projects more vital to the author's living and more worthy of the reader's attention, a sense of professional pride demands the best possible performance under the existing constraints.

Passing the baton among a relay of storytellers holds an irresistible lure for the participants. What a challenge to take the stage with your colleagues and outshine them all with the brilliance of your prose. What a wicked pleasure to saddle the next writer on the list with enigmatic characters and impenetrable plot complications. Though literary writers as high-toned as Henry James, among the dozen authors of *The Whole Family* (1908), have participated in group novels, the mystery and detective genre has produced most of them. Since such stories are inevitably driven by plot more than character or theme, their attraction to puzzle-spinners is obvious.

The earliest example may be "Behind the Screen" (1930), a six-part serial written as a listener contest for the BBC by members of Great Britain's Detection Club. At a time midway through the Golden Age of Detection, the pure clues-on-the-table detective story was at its apex. The first three writers (Hugh Walpole, Agatha Christie, and Dorothy L. Sayers) set the problem (the murder of a family's sinister boarder), while the last three (Anthony Berkeley, E.C. Bentley, and Ronald Knox) jointly worked out a solution. In 1931 came a longer non-contest serial, "The Scoop," with the plotting done in committee by its half dozen contributors (Sayers, Christie, Bentley, Berkeley, Freeman Wills Crofts, and

Clemence Dane). First printed in the BBC journal *The Listener*, the two serials were brought together in book form in 1983.

The Detection Club took on a greater challenge in their first book-length effort. *The Floating Admiral* (1932) removes the safety net of collaborative plotting and consultation for pure authorial wing walking. Following an atmospheric prologue by the Club's president, G.K. Chesterton, Canon Victor L. Whitechurch's opening chapter sets the murdered Admiral Penistone adrift on the River Whyn in the local vicar's boat. Eleven chapters follow by major British detective writers of the day, including Christie, Sayers, Crofts, Knox, and (with a necessarily lengthy windup chapter called "Clearing Up the Mess") Berkeley, who should be but isn't as celebrated as Christie and Sayers. In the serial novel, your heaviest hitter bats not fourth but last.

The rules of the *Admiral*'s game were daunting. While each contributor had the fun of adding complications for subsequent writers to deal with, each one from the third chapter on also had to have a specific, reasoned solution in mind. In a 45-page appendix, a fascinating exposition of classical detective writers' minds at work, they explained their conclusions in sections ranging from 22 pages (Sayers) to a short paragraph (Edgar Jepson).

The next Detection Club collaboration, *Ask a Policeman* (1933), plays a different and more humorous game. John Rhode propounds a puzzle, which is presented to four writers for their respective sleuths to solve. By an "awkward blunder" that is obviously deliberate, each writer is asked for the conclusions of another writer's character—thus Berkeley writes of Lord Peter Wimsey, Sayers of Berkeley's Roger Sheringham, Helen Simpson of Gladys Mitchell's Mrs. Bradley, and Mitchell of Simpson's Sir John Saumarez. When each comes up with a different murderer, Milward Kennedy provides a fifth solution, through the admittedly unfair course of inventing facts not in evidence.

Subsequent Detection Club group efforts appeared as newspaper serials in 1953 and 1954 and in British hardcover as *Crime on the Coast and No Flowers by Request* (1984). John Dickson Carr led off the former serial, while the latter included a chapter by Sayers, though she had long since deserted Lord Peter for religious drama and Dante translation.

The first American group mystery, *The President's Mystery Story* (1935), addresses a problem posed by President Franklin D. Roosevelt to *Liberty* magazine editor Fulton Oursler: "How can a man disappear with five million dollars in any negotiable form and not be traced?" Oursler, later famed as author of *The Greatest Story Ever Told*, wrote a synopsis with an elaborate solution and asked six popular writers (one of them himself under his mystery-writing pseudonym Anthony Abbot) to turn it into a group novel. The set framework took away the fun of laying booby traps for the next performer, but they could still compete on style, with the poorest writer of the group, Rupert Hughes, leading off. One of his sillier ideas, that the vanishing millionaire wanted to establish a University of Sports and Sportsmanship, is wisely ignored by the others, most well remembered of whom is S.S. Van Dine (Willard Huntington Wright), the creator of Philo Vance. The entertaining and ingeniously plotted book was adapted into a 1936 film, *The President's Mystery*, one of whose screenwriters was Nathanael West. A 1967 reprint substitutes for Oursler's preface a more informative and analytical introduction by Arthur Schlesinger, Jr. and adds an exceedingly clever chapter in which Erle Stanley Gardner adds Perry Mason and Paul Drake to the mix.

In *The Perfect Crime* (1991), Jack Hitt introduces an unhappy husband named Tim who asks five mystery writers (Lawrence Block, Sarah Caudwell, Tony Hillerman, Peter Lovesey, and Donald E. Westlake) for advice on how to murder his wife. Though at least one feminist critic found a wife-murdering manual in questionable taste, it remains one of the best group mystery novels.

Coincidentally, no fewer than three new multi-author mysteries have appeared in 2001. All are from major publishers; all boast well-known contributors; and all at least partially benefit non-profit organizations. The first is the work mostly of mainstream Irish literary figures, the second of cozy female mystery writers, the third of American specialists in the legal thriller. One celebrates the diversity of its styles and approaches; another aims for a more uniform style but at least identifies who wrote which chapter; and the third withholds who wrote what and takes pride in *not* reading like a "various hands" work.

First to appear was *Yeats is Dead*, whose 15 Irish authors, most from outside the crime fiction specialty, were chosen for their variety, with fiction writers both "literary" and popular, dramatists, screenwriters, a stand-up comedian, and even an *Irish Times* sportswriter among them. Their primary aim is humor, ranging from sophisticated wordplay and literary allusion to broad parody and outright slapstick. Roddy Doyle, a Booker Award-winning novelist, begins well with a pair of enforcers reminiscent of the movie *Pulp Fiction*, and many pages later Frank McCourt, bestselling author of *Angela's Ashes*, ties up the loose ends like a Restoration dramatist.

The MacGuffin (that sought-after object that propels the plot) is the manuscript of an unpublished novel by James Joyce. In editor O'Connor's Chapter Nine, a character named Mrs. Blixen (partner to Mrs. Bloom) describes the lost work: "It is beyond language...It has no story, no character development, no purpose at all....The novel released from the narrow cage of meaning. Abstract art in literary form. A new literature for the new world."

One of the most memorable characters is a senior policewoman, reminiscent of the one played by Helen Mirren on TV's *Prime Suspect*, who makes Holmesian observations based on suspects' wardrobe. The whole enterprise, though, is more like an Elmore Leonard crime caper than either classical detection or police procedural. The level of carnage is high. Though the book's proceeds benefit Amnesty International, one of whose tenets is the eradication of capital punishment, the Irish authors have no compunction about applying the death penalty to their characters.

The *Yeats is Dead* collaborators did not work without a safety net. According to a note from editor O'Connor, included with publicity materials but unfortunately not in the book itself, the participants "allow[ed] their individual contributions to be tampered with, moved around, generally tweaked, massaged, and sometimes mercilessly kicked into the shape of a readable novel."

The 13 authors of *Naked Came the Phoenix* claim they took their rules from *The Floating Admiral*: 1) writing with a definite solution in mind, and 2) not changing or ignoring any of the preceding writers' clues or plot elements. However, the first must be taken on faith: in an era of less rigorous puzzle construction, they are not required to provide individual solutions.

The book, part of whose proceeds benefit breast cancer research, takes its title pattern from the best-known (though far from best) 20th-Century group novel, *Naked Came the Stranger* (1969), a tale of suburban sexuality written under the group pseudonym Penelope Asch by 25 journalists who sought bestsellerdom with a deliberately meretricious piece of soft-core porn. The years since have brought homage in the form of *Naked Came the Manatee* (1996), a Floridian thriller whose contributors included Elmore Leonard, Edna Buchanan, and Carl Hiaasen; and such small press products as *Naked Came the Farmer* (1998) and *Naked Came the Plowman* (1999).

The most recent naked coming has its humorous touches but plays the story relatively straight. Nevada Barr's opening chapter efficiently introduces a large cast of characters at a luxurious Virginia health spa, centering on Caroline Blessing, a Congressman's wife, and her recently widowed mother Hilda Finch. Subsequent writers add crimes, beginning with the mud-bath murder of the spa's owner, and other complications. Laurie R. King does wrap-up honors, a harder job than McCourt's: the whodunit format makes flying blind tougher than Leonard-style crime comedy. Though she ties the loose ends, the recourse to multiple murderers renders the novel less than satisfactory as a detective puzzle, at least to classical purists.

Entertainment value is high, however, and the characters remain remarkably consistent given how many are putting thoughts in their heads and words in their mouths. Some abrupt changes of direction are to be expected. In a humorous early touch, most of the suspects refuse to talk to the police without counsel present, but later writers lose the lawyers and let the suspects speak more freely. One writer arranges to allow the young heroine and amateur sleuth to accompany the police pro on his interrogations, but later writers want no part of this artificial situation. (That's not to imply they eschew other artificial situations.)

Like those theatrical benefits, group novels have an advertising function. Which of these performers would you come back to enjoy at greater length in her own show? The only real loser in this regard is J.D. Robb, whose second chapter offers miniseries prose and tin-eared dialogue. Writers like Nancy Pickard, Faye Kellerman, and Anne Perry prove as readable and professional as one would expect, but two contributors outshine the rest in seeking repeat business: Lisa Scottoline, whose introduction of police detective Vince Toscana in chapter four allows the book to achieve belated lift-off, and Val McDermid, whose penultimate chapter provides a great line for the female medical examiner, looking over a corpse found in a pool of nail polish: "Bodies, I don't mind. But I've always thought cosmetics were more trouble than they were worth."

Natural Suspect is like the other two in benefiting a charity (the Nature Conservancy) but unlike them in not identifying which authors wrote which chapters. The only precedent I can find, apart from *Naked Came the Stranger*, which was not the work of brand-name authors, is the 1951 novel *The Marble Forest*, written under the group pseudonym Theo Durrant by a dozen members of the

Mystery Writers of America's Northern California chapter, best known of whom was longtime N.Y. *Times* mystery critic Anthony Boucher.

Though left to guess at the contributions of John Katzenbach, John Lescroart, Philip Margolin, Michael Palmer, Lisa Scottoline, and the rest, we know William Bernhardt wrote the first chapter, introducing in comic style an extremely dysfunctional family. When patriarch Arthur Hightower's body is found in the family freezer, alcoholic widow Julia goes on trial in a New York court for his blunt-instrument murder. In a typical trial novel complication, defense attorney Devin Gail McGee opposes her former lover Trent Ballard, appearing for the prosecution. Presiding, in a joke for old movie fans, is Judge Hardy. Disappointingly for trial buffs, the novel plays out its farcical complications without returning to court, save for a brief scene in which McGee offers a unique excuse for requiring a recess: the explosion of her car has rendered her temporarily deaf. The more outlandish characters include a giant pet rabbit who is taken for walks like a dog and a literate villain who variously disguises himself as a clown and a female Foot Locker employee.

In the end, though it lacks the highbrow literary touches of *Yeats is Dead* and the straight-faced effort at pure detection of *Naked Came the Phoenix*, *Natural Suspect* with its consistent comic tone is the best of the 2001 crop. Maybe the semi-anonymity of the authors facilitated teamwork over upstaging. In his afterword, Bernhardt states none of three friends who read the book in manuscript guessed it was the work of more than one author.

What generalizations can we make about these group novels? At their best, they provide sophisticated insights into the art and craft of storytelling. They are fiercely complicated, depending on chapter-ending cliffhangers (encouraged in *Natural Suspect*, ostensibly discouraged in *Naked Came the Phoenix*) and coincidental interlocking of the characters' lives, often including impersonation and surprises of parentage and kinship. But it is paradoxically easy to keep track of the plots since so many of the contributors feel obliged to clear their heads and get their bearings by reprising for the reader what has gone before. The challenges the writers present each other recall a short-lived 1939-40 radio show called *Author, Author*, in which writer and performer became one: a group of literary panelists (anchored each week by the Ellery Queen collaborators) would be presented with an incongruous situation (e.g., "Why does the jewelry store owner sell a $500 watch to an unfa-

miliar customer for a dollar?") and draw on their structural wiz-
ardry to explain it.

Maybe the best theatrical comparison is the English Christmas
pantomime: not Shakespeare, not Shaw, but ideal for its season.
Though fun is had by all, the actors may be having an even better
time than the audience.

*Postscript 2008: Other examples of the group novel have fol-
lowed. To suggest how tough this kind of this is to bring off, consider my review of* The Sunken Sailor, *edited by Elizabeth Fox-
well, in the January 2005 "Jury Box": "Simon Brett begins this
multi-author homage to...* The Floating Admiral *beautifully, introducing a colorful cast of characters at an English country house
party between World Wars and finishing chapter one with the
fishpond murder of an annoying American admiral. The next seven
contributors—Newman Sharan , Francine Mathews, Walter
Satterthwait, Margaret Coel, Carolyn Hart, Carolyn Wheat, and
Dorothy Cannell—follow his lead, adding not-too-outrageous plot
complications while balancing a straight-faced period style with
satirical touches. But beginning in chapter nine and accelerating
in chapter ten, things fall apart rapidly, becoming progressively
sillier and more strained. The finished product is best avoided by
anyone who values Golden Age detection."*

REGIONAL MYSTERIES

(review of *The American Regional Mystery* by Marvin Lachman,
Crossover, 2000)

The Weekly Standard, February 5, 2001

Detective fiction was born in the Paris of Edgar Allan Poe's C.
Auguste Dupin and reared in the London of Arthur Conan Doyle's
Sherlock Holmes. These pioneers influenced their successors not
only in narrative conventions and structural techniques but also in
the use of contemporary urban backdrops. There were notable exceptions—Melville Davisson Post set his Uncle Abner tales in rural 19th-century Virginia—but for most practitioners, fictional detection remained a city game, and even the choice of cities offered
little variety.

For many years, the vast majority of American mystery novels
were set in a handful of major cities: usually New York or Los
Angeles, occasionally Chicago or San Francisco, Boston or Miami. Indianapolis? Seattle? Cleveland? Not likely. For the most
part, even the few cities that did appear proved interchangeable,
with little distinctive information provided—the action and the
puzzle, the plot and the pace, the snappy dialogue and interplay of
character were the important things. That body decorously laid out
in the library or bleeding in the back alley could be found in the
posh or impoverished sections of any metropolis. The 1920s and
'30s New York of S.S. Van Dine and early Ellery Queen lacked
much specific local detail. The characters in Dashiell Hammett's
The Maltese Falcon (1930), though surrounded by creeping fog
and San Francisco street names, could have played out their quest
for the Black Bird anywhere. George Harmon Coxe's Boston and
Brett Halliday's Miami were also relatively anonymous, in contrast to later and fuller depictions of those cities by Robert B.
Parker and Edna Buchanan.

Often the mysteries that were not set in that small group of
approved cities were given purely fictitious locales, with even the
state kept vague. There were good reasons for this: you could
make up the laws and procedures and lessen the chance of offending someone's civic pride. When Ed McBain created the 87th Precinct in 1956, he put them in a fictional city, though one obviously
based on New York, so he would not have to keep track of every

change in Manhattan police procedure. Though that series is still going strong, few writers beginning today would choose a similar route. The locations of early small-town whodunits may have had shared characteristics but usually lacked distinctive regional character. Even today small towns are often fictitious or pseudonymous, presumably out of fear of lawsuits, but are more likely to be given the characteristics associated with their part of the country. However, representing the older style, Lilian Jackson Braun says that Pickax, the locale of her cat mysteries, though assumed to be Midwestern, is "anywhere you want it to be."

The increase in regional detail in mysteries came gradually. Beginning with *The Big Sleep* in 1939, Raymond Chandler's novels about private eye Philip Marlowe gave a vivid portrait, first admiring and later jaded, of Los Angeles, while the mature Ellery Queen team brought a terrorized New York to life in the serial-killer classic *Cat of Many Tails* (1949). A.B. Cunningham's Sheriff Jess Roden series, published throughout the '40s, was firmly set in rural Kentucky, while Phoebe Atwood Taylor made distinctive use of her Cape Cod background in the series of '30s and '40s novels about Asey Mayo. Dorothy Salisbury Davis's *The Clay Hand* (1950) memorably depicted the West Virginia coal-mining country. Introducing a 1963 reprint of the Davis novel, the New York *Times'* influential mystery critic Anthony Boucher expressed a desire for "more regionalism in the American suspense novel," inspiring detective story enthusiast Marvin Lachman to a study of American regional mysteries.

Boucher, before his death in 1968, also encouraged the emergence of mystery fan publications that would provide a forum for buffs like Lachman to share their enthusiasms. Between 1970 and 1977, first in *The Mystery Reader's Newsletter* and later in *The Armchair Detective*, Lachman wrote a series of 14 articles about those relatively few American mysteries that provided a true sense of their locales' distinctiveness. Eleven years later, when he contemplated turning the articles into a book, Lachman "realized that it would not be possible merely to use [his] articles with only minor additions. The number of regional mysteries had increased dramatically...." Another dozen years having passed, Lachman's book has finally appeared and goes immediately to an honored place on the serious mystery reader's reference shelf.

The book is a tour of the United States via its crime fiction, beginning with New England and moving westward with sections on New York, the Middle Atlantic States, the South, Florida and the Caribbean, the Middle West, the Southwest, the Rocky Mountain States, the Pacific Northwest, California, and finally Alaska and Hawaii. Borderline decisions about what state goes in what section are fully explained. Every state is represented, plus Puerto Rico and the Virgin Islands. Those states with the most entries, unsurprisingly, are New York and California; those with the least, Delaware and North Dakota. I don't know how many pages those original 14 articles would have occupied, but thanks to the explosion of regional mystery fiction of the past few decades, Lachman's tome runs 542 pages including the index.

For the most part Lachman sticks to fictional crime, though there are often references to real-life murder cases that took place in the various locales and occasional references to true-crime books, such as Edward D. Radin's *Lizzie Borden: The Untold Story* (1961), about a Fall River, Massachusetts, case that (like Jack the Ripper) has achieved honorary fictional status.

Though names like Joyce Carol Oates and Shelby Foote turn up in the index, Lachman primarily confines himself to the mainstream mystery. For example, the chapter on Maine has no reference to horror specialist Stephen King, most of whose works are at least borderline crime fiction.

Few commentators on crime fiction have the breadth of knowledge, soundness of judgment, and sheer writing talent of Lachman, whose reference book I read with enjoyment from cover to cover. His choice of facts and quotations gives a strong impression of the locale under discussion as well as the quality of writing of the subject authors. I can even imagine someone who never intended to read a crime novel profiting from the observations about the various regions' characteristics.

In crime fiction references that cover so many authors and titles and dates, I can usually find a multitude of errors, but Lachman's are frustratingly rare. (This is the best I could do at nit-picking: actor George Sanders is the detective in only one of the ghost-written novels credited to him, not both; and I'm pretty sure Lachman's claim, also made by Stuart M. Kaminsky, that L.A. smog was a common butt of radio jokes in 1940 is almost a decade too early.)

Frankly, it's easy for a detective story traditionalist to be cynical about the current regionalist explosion. At a time when writers and would-be writers sometimes seem to outnumber readers, newcomers to the field need a special niche to set themselves apart, whether it's an unusual occupation for the detective or a previously untapped geographical background. As the major publishing conglomerates continue to favor potential bestsellers over bread-and-butter mid-list titles, the market is also demanding longer and longer books. You have to fill all those extra pages with something, don't you? Unnecessary recurring characters, repetition of plot points, irrelevant personal details, and columns of sentence-fragment dialogue can only get you so far. So why not throw in some local color, to invoke the name of a 19th-Century school of American fiction?

Ironically, this increased emphasis on regionalism has come at a time when regional differences in the United States are growing smaller and smaller. The local color school of American fiction, among whose major practitioners were Bret Harte, Kate Chopin, Joel Chandler Harris, Hamlin Garland, Sarah Orne Jewett, Mary E. Wilkins Freeman, and Charles W. Chesnutt, was at its peak in the years after the Civil War. At that time, Americans did not have motion pictures or radio or television or cookie-cutter shopping malls or fast cross-country travel to eradicate our regional differences.

To be precise, local color and regionalism are related but not synonymous terms. *The Oxford Companion to American Literature* (6th edition, 1995) distinguishes them thus: Local color "emphasizes its setting, being concerned with the character of a district or of an era, as marked by its customs, dialect, costumes, landscape, or other peculiarities that have escaped standardizing cultural influences." Regionalism, on the other hand, "emphasizes a special geographical setting and concentrates upon the history, manners, and folkways of the area as these help to shape the lives and behavior of the characters. It generally differs from local color in that it lays less stress upon quaint oddities of dialect, mannerism, and custom and more on basic philosophical or sociological distinctions...."

If as this definition implies, local color is superficial and regionalism organic, most of the titles discussed by Lachman are probably closer to local color. A true regional mystery could only happen in its particular locale, either because of a local institution or industry or legal quirk or attitude, the kinds of differences that occur less and less frequently in the increasingly homogenized U.S.A. While Tony Hillerman's novels of the Navajo country are closely involved with the unique beliefs and attitudes of the characters and thus could take place nowhere else, and the Salt Lake City mysteries of Robert Irvine take their uniqueness from the pervasive influence of the L.D.S. Church on Utah life, most contemporary big-city police and private-eye novels could happen in any big city, and just as certainly most small-town whodunits could happen in any small town.

There is one other oddity in the definition of regionalism. As Lachman notes, some critics, "especially of mainstream fiction, had too narrow a definition of 'regional.' They considered only books set in rural areas—for example, the Ozarks or the William Faulkner country of Mississippi." As the emphasis on cities suggests, Lachman's "definition is broader, encompassing stories that tell important things about any portion of the United States. American regional mystery writing can occur anywhere, be it the South Bronx, Miami, Cleveland, South Dakota, or San Diego."

That leads to an obvious question: which are the ones to read and which the ones to avoid? Lachman's comments for the most part are descriptive rather than critical, but he includes enough expressed or implied evaluation to give some added zest to the enterprise as well as advice to the potential reader. His favorable comments are much more plentiful than his unfavorable ones. Phyllis A. Whitney, still active in the field in her late nineties, is perhaps the most conscientious and certainly the widest ranging American mystery regionalist. Lachman repeatedly lauds her impeccable research into such locales as Palm Springs (in *Emerald*), Monterey-Carmel (*The Flaming Tree*), East Hampton (*The Golden Unicorn*), Palm Beach (*Poinciana*), the Blue Ridge Mountains (*Rainbow in the Mist*), Hawaii (*Silversword*), Newport, Rhode Island (*Spindrift*), historic San Francisco (*The Trembling Hills*), and Sedona, Arizona (*Vermilion*).

Besides celebrating many contemporaries, Lachman's book may revive interest in some once-famous writers of the past, such as the often devalued old-timer Leslie Ford, whose variety of locales may be second only to Whitney's. Ford's racial attitudes don't always please Lachman, but she provided solid regional detail of Washington D.C. and environs (*The Murder of a Fifth Columnist* and other novels), rural Tennessee (*Burn Forever*), Chesapeake Bay (*Ill Met by Moonlight*), Baltimore (*The Girl from the Mimosa Club*), Hawaii (*Honolulu Story*), Mississippi (*Murder with Southern Hospitality*), Philadelphia (*The Philadelphia Murder Story*), Reno (*Reno Rendezvous*), Yellowstone National Park (*Old Lover's Ghost*), and San Francisco (*Siren in the Night*). Two other past writers winning praise from Lachman are Doris Miles Disney (Connecticut) and Juanita Sheridan (Hawaii).

Among the contemporaries Lachman most values are Archer Mayor (Vermont), John Dunning (Amish country in Pennsylvania and Denver), Bill Crider (Texas), Margaret Maron (North Carolina), the late Robert Campbell (Chicago), and Carl Hiaasen (Florida). These, of course, are expected recommendations. Many knowledgeable readers could come up with them, as well as Nevada Barr (national parks), John D. MacDonald (Florida), Loren D. Estleman (Detroit), or Sharyn McCrumb (Tennessee). The greatest benefit of Lachman's work may be the relatively obscure writers he commends, such as Richard Hilary, whose series about an African-American Newark private eye is proclaimed as good as Walter Mosley's Easy Rawlins series. Margaret Page Hood is credited with "the first good contemporary series about Maine"; John Billheimer's *The Contrary Blues* (1998) is "West Virginia's best mystery"; and Thomas Lipinski's private eye series "may prove to be the best of all about Pittsburgh."

To many purists, the short story is the natural vehicle for fictional detection—indeed the first great writer of regional mysteries, Melville Davisson Post, invariably wrote in that form. Lachman values the mystery short more than most commentators, and he recommends a group of writers for *Alfred Hitchcock's Mystery Magazine* unlikely to be familiar to most readers: David K. Harford on the Allegheny National Forest; William T. Lowe on the Mohawk reservation that borders Quebec; Marianne Strong on the Pennsylvania coal country; and Kenneth Gavrell on Puerto Rico.

Negative critical comments are less frequent but often pointed. Lachman was a longtime resident of the Bronx, and he is most critical of mysteries set in his former home. Bob Reiss and Jerome Charyn are charged with exaggerating the borough's unattractive aspects, while Richard Fliegel is faulted for lack of regional detail. (Lachman is also freer with praise of Bronx mysteries, citing favorably works of S.J. Rozan and Tom Philbin.) One of the most negative assessments in the book is reserved for Caleb Carr's 1994 bestseller about Theodore Roosevelt and 1890s New York, *The Alienist*, in which Lachman finds anachronisms and "unnecessary history lessons [that] pad the novel to 597 pages." Richard Parrish, author of a series set in mid-century Arizona Indian country, is also faulted for anachronisms, while Richard Ellington is charged with racist attitudes toward Puerto Ricans in a 1950 novel and Elliot Paul with stereotyped Indians circa 1940. The authors of more recent books, Stephen Wright and Tom Tolnay, are both charged with questionable taste in their use of real-life Hollywood celebrities in fiction.

Even the cynical traditionalist can see the entertainment and informational value of a well-realized geographical setting, however incidental to the mystery plot it might be. Still, real and potential pitfalls cannot be denied. Lachman, himself something of a traditionalist, makes the last point in his introduction to *The American Regional Mystery* a cautionary one: "By the 1990s, settings were sometimes described in such great detail as to become intrusive and were poor substitutes for strong plotting and story telling. There is a danger that if detective fiction continues to emphasize lengthy description and depressingly serious subject matter, readers who originally chose the genre for intelligent escape may desert it."

Still, even the traditionalist will admit a well-realized geographical setting can add entertainment value to a mystery novel. It can also educate and enlighten. The most respected of contemporary American regionalists, Tony Hillerman, whose books have been used as school texts on the Navajo country, achieved this stature without padding his books with irrelevant information and without retreating from the features that make detective fiction a unique genre. Writers of regional mysteries could not find a better model.

Postscript 2008: This was my first piece for The Weekly Standard *and was more heavily edited than any of those to follow. While the published version may have read more snappily, I have reverted to my original, which includes some added points I wanted to make. Lachman's book, a natural for an Edgar award in the biographical-critical category, was unaccountably denied even a nomination.*

ADVICE TO WRITERS

Criminal Brief (criminalbrief.com), July 28, 2007

In the last five years before retirement, my day job was teaching English composition at a community college. Of the courses I taught, I believe I did the poorest job with creative writing. The classes filled, and the students and I had a good time, but I don't know how much I conveyed to them that was useful. Recently in this space, Robert Lopresti quoted Gore Vidal as having nothing to say but plenty to add. Similarly, I can't tell anyone how to write but I can talk around the subject all day.

While it's an exaggeration to say there are no rules in writing, certainly there are exceptions to nearly every rule. Take the following familiar writing truisms.

First, write what you know. Yeah, I guess so, but for most of my professional career I was a librarian, and all my attempts at creating a librarian detective proved unsuccessful. The only one to be published was a short private eye parody called "The Dewey Damsel System," which appeared in somewhat altered form in the April, 1971 issue of the late, lamented periodical *Wilson Library Bulletin*. (It's also in my out-of-print 1982 parody collection *Hair of the Sleuthhound*.) The protagonist was a private eye working for a public library system, and I wanted to call him Mel Dewey. Melvil Dewey, said the editors, was too sacred a figure to be kidded in this way, so I used an anagram instead and called him Ev Millweedy. The punishment for the perp ("When somebody's defacing library books, sweetheart, a librarian's expected to do something about it," Ev tells her) was to be revoking her library card—permanently. But no, the editors said their readers took the right to a library card too seriously to make fun of, so I had to consign her to licking labels in the library basement instead.

Second, never discuss work in progress. Again, generally wise, though as great a writer as Elmore Leonard blows it to smithereens in an interview in the current issue of *The Strand Magazine*. Asked what he's working on, he tells interviewer Andrew Gulli the whole plot of his current project right up to the point he has reached in the writing. On the other hand, my only anecdote about discussing work in progress provides a cautionary note. At a mystery writers' gathering in the 1970s, I shared with a well-known novelist and a prominent mystery scholar my idea for a ghost story in which a used book dealer discovers a talent for authentically signing the names of dead authors to first editions of their books. When the story reached fruition in my 1984 novel *The Gathering Place*, the novelist (who was also a reviewer, a fine and generous man but one given to embellishing the truth to make a better story) shared with me a review of the book in which he recalled our discussion. In his version, however, there was a whole roomful of prominent writers kicking the idea around, and I was the one out of this group of informal collaborators who actually decided to write it. In other words, not necessarily my original idea at all. I wouldn't have stopped him from running the review, but the magazine it was written for folded before it appeared.

Third, always go the second mile in doing research. How could I argue with this one, right? But I sold eight stories in a period of about three years to *Ellery Queen's Mystery Magazine* about baseball umpire Ed Gorgon without ever actually meeting an umpire or going behind the scenes at a ballpark. After I wangled press credentials to Anaheim Stadium for one game and actually talked to some umps, I found I was unable to write another Ed Gorgon for about four years. (In fairness, when I finally did return to him, I used some of what I picked up that day at the ballpark.) Then there was my short story "The Auteur Theory." It had a courtroom scene, and it occurred to me I should run it by my friend Mike (writing name Francis M.) Nevins, a law professor at St. Louis University. But no, I just sent it off as it was. It sold to *Alfred Hitchcock's Mystery Magazine* and appeared in the January 1978 issue. When it appeared in print, Mike assured me, "No judge in the world would have allowed that testimony!" The lesson? If I'd shown it to him first, I might have lost the sale. And, of course, my defense is that there are plenty of nutty judges around who might allow any kind of nonsense in their courtrooms, whatever might happen on appeal.

Fourth, use plenty of details. This is more of a general composition rule than one applied specifically to creative writing; we drummed it into our students writing their freshman English essays: "Details and examples! Details and examples!" But it's quite possible to overdo it. I had a student who took the advice to heart in writing about a fishing trip. We learned when he got up in the morning, how the weather looked, what he had for breakfast, how he dressed to go fishing, what time his friend arrived, what kind of car they drove in, what route they took to the lake, what the traffic was like, what they'd packed for lunch, and so forth. By the time he got around to the actual fishing, though, my student had run out of both time and space, and the conclusion amounted to "I caught two fish, my friend caught one, and we went home." While a writer of mystery fiction is unlikely to commit the second half of this blunder, many novelists are constantly committing the first, filling page upon page with irrelevant detail. If it's well done, we might enjoy it anyway; if it isn't, it's deadly to the reader.

Fifth, in a detective story, play fair with the reader. This is one that is still at least given lip service, but its meaning has undergone a subtle change over the years. It used to mean, provide some clues along the way that will permit the very sharp reader to logically figure out the solution before the detective elucidates it. Now, many seem to think it means telling the reader everything the same time as the detective learns it. Thus, if the detective finds an old diary in chapter 37 that reveals who the murderer is, and the reader finds this out at the same time, the author has played fair with the reader. Well, maybe. But it should mean more than that. In the current market, I'm apt to applaud any novel that provides even one fair-play clue to the reader; the kind of intricate edifices the Golden Age masters routinely provided is too much to expect.

Did I wander off the point? Now you know what my creative writing classes were like.

AMERICAN MYSTERIES

Introduction, *A Modern Treasury of Great Detective and Murder Mysteries*, edited by Ed Gorman (Carroll & Graf, 1994)

Some people will always insist, first, that the good old days were better, and second, that there is nothing new under the sun. If you claim that the last twenty-five years have brought an unprecedented renaissance to the field of crime and mystery fiction, that the real Golden Age is right now, they will haul out some heavy ammunition to challenge you. And as long as consideration is confined to individual titles and authors, the advocate of the past will be able to make a case.

There is probably no single book so original in its theme, approach, or subject matter that an enthusiast with a pack-rat memory can't reach back to the twenties or thirties or forties to cite something roughly comparable. And if someone asks you, where is there a writer today who is the equal of Hammett or Chandler or Sayers or Christie or Queen or Carr or Stout or Tey or Allingham or Armstrong or any of the other crime/mystery/ suspense icons, you might have to grudgingly admit that in their particular specialties, those great individuals will never be equaled. But as soon as you start comparing the whole field of the last couple of decades with that of any other period of time, the amazing breadth and depth of the present-day output is overwhelming.

What has happened to transform the field of crime and suspense fiction in the last quarter century? Though the old traditions are still honored where appropriate, the old constraints have broken down. There is much less emphasis on what can and can't be done in a mystery novel.

In years gone by, even in most mysteries considered tough, violence and gore were muted, as if, in the tradition of Hollywood movies before the sixties, bullets could politely, antiseptically kill without drawing blood or making a hole in the fabric of the victim's clothes. Today, even in some books considered cozy, the odd *fuck* may creep into the dialogue, corpses may evacuate their bowels, and the sleuth may be seen coping with all the same bodily functions as the reader.

We hear a lot today about political correctness, which supposedly constrains writers and others from statements that offend members of an ethnic, religious, or racial group, a gender, or a sexual orientation. Though the phenomenon exists, its pervasiveness has been exaggerated. Compared to any other period, writers of today are more free to depict members of all classes and categories of people as fully human individuals with good features and bad. Would we really like to return to a time when an African American could never be a hero, could never be a villain, could only be comic relief, a bit player, or (in the odd brave liberal offering) a symbol of suffering nobility? Would we prefer a climate where gay people only exist as objects of derisive humor, disgust, or suspicion? Would we be more comfortable if a character's Native American blood could be cited as a proud touch of exoticism but no connection to any kind of tribal culture was suggested? Would we prefer a world where Della Street and Mme. Maigret, admirable as they were, defined the limits of a woman's aspirations?

In the crime fiction field of a quarter century ago, the spy was king—indeed, some claimed that the international espionage thriller, with its determination to hang the fate of the world by a thread in every outing, had forever displaced the musty old detective novel with its quaint focus on single crimes, single deaths. How can a crime against one or two people engage our interest, asked the spy proponents, when we've developed weapons that can take out whole cities with a single push of a button? (It shouldn't take the O.J. Simpson case to tell us what a misreading of human nature that theory was.)

At the same time, the romantic suspense novel or modern gothic was approaching its peak—it was a form that could be magical when practiced by its masters but tired and formulaic in the hands of their imitators. And one of its prime characteristics was an avoidance of clues and detection.

True, many of the great names of the pure detective story were still practicing twenty-five years ago—Ellery Queen, Agatha Christie, John Dickson Carr, Ngaio Marsh, Michael Innes, Helen McCloy, Rex Stout—but most were past their prime and only a few new classicists (Emma Lathen and John Ball among the American ones) had been recruited to join them. Similarly, though Ross Macdonald was the object of critical acclaim and other established private-eye bylines like Brett Halliday, Richard S. Prather, and Mickey Spillane continued to command a market share, the shamus seemed to be an endangered species. (One of the few major ones to debut in the sixties was Michael Collins's Dan Fortune.)

When the first general mystery fanzines, *The Armchair Detective* and *The Mystery Lover's* [later *Reader's*] *Newsletter* began to appear in the late sixties, the emphasis of the articles, letters, and even book reviews was on the old classics, with relatively little attention paid a somewhat depressed current market. When I conducted a poll on the ten favorite novels and twelve favorite authors for *TAD* (results published in the February 1973 issue), the most recent novel among the top vote-getters (Josephine Tey's *The Daughter of Time*) was over twenty years old and the living writers in the top sixteen had all debuted in the forties or earlier, with John D. MacDonald the contemporary having least seniority. Freeman Wills Crofts, now forgotten by all but a few long-memoried specialists, had seven different book titles nominated by participants.

Though it may have seemed both classical and hardboiled detection were on the ropes in the '60s and early '70s, there was at last one strong clue to their continued viability. With their last books, Agatha Christie and Ross Macdonald began to join spy specialists like John Le Carré, Ian Fleming, and Len Deighton on the bestseller lists. The growing preponderance of crime fiction writers on such lists, which has steadily increased right up to the present, demonstrates both the strength of genre fiction and the relative weakness of mainstream fiction. Many writers of considerable literary talent, turned off by the lessened reader interest and the decreased emphasis on pure storytelling in so-called serious fiction, have turned to popular genres where they could deliver an intriguing plot and still make serious statements about humanity and society.

Through the '70s, '80s, and early '90s, these were some of the developments in American crime fiction:

1) The private eye made a strong comeback with the introduction of such characters as Bill Pronzini's Nameless, Loren D. Estleman's Amos Walker, Robert B. Parker's Spenser, Joe Gores' Daniel Kearny Associates, and Lawrence Block's Matt Scudder, plus a new group of female operatives—Maxine O'Callaghan's Delilah West, Marcia Muller's Sharon McCone, Sue Grafton's Kinsey Millhone, Sara Paretsky's V.I. Warchawski, and Linda Barnes's Carlotta Carlyle.

2) The pure detective story was given a new lease on life by writers who could observe its rules of fair play while satisfying the other demands of the market. Some of them were William L. DeAndrea, James Yaffe, Herbert Resnicow, Susan Dunlap, Sharyn

McCrumb, Nancy Pickard, and Jane Haddam (Orania Popa-
zoglou).

3) Women writers, always a strong presence in the field,
seized a share of the market more closely proportional to their rep-
resentation among the readership.

4) Crime fiction, once a contemporary form almost by defini-
tion, began to mine the past for fresh backgrounds and viewpoints.
Prominent American writers of historical mysteries included
Elizabeth Peters (a.k.a. Barbara Michaels), Max Allan Collins, and
James Sherburne.

5) A field whose gestures toward multiculturalism hadn't extended much beyond Earl Derr Biggers's well-intended but much-
maligned Charlie Chan now had more and more sleuths of varied
ethnicity and, even more amazingly, sexual preference. See, for
example, the works of Barbara Neely, Walter Mosley, Joseph
Hansen, Katherine V. Forrest, Eleanor Taylor Bland, Manuel
Ramos, and Tony Hillerman.

6) Mystery-story elements were used more and more frequently by mainstream writers, even those who did not enter the
field overtly, among them Joyce Carol Oates, Don DeLillo, E.L.
Doctorow, Norman Mailer, and Diane Johnson.

5) Social, sexual, religious, and political issues, once considered outside the realm of escapist popular fiction, were explored in
a way previously unprecedented.

6) Lines dividing popular genres were crossed, as bestselling
writers like Stephen King, Peter Straub, Dean R. Koontz, William
Peter Blatty, and Michael Crichton drew elements from various
categories.

7) Through conventions like the annual Bouchercon and its
specialized or regional equivalents, periodicals like *The Armchair
Detective* and *Mystery Scene*, and a growing number of fan publications, the American mystery field developed an expanded sense
of community coincident with the unprecedented volume of new
titles being published.

In the early 1980s, I took a hiatus from regular book reviewing, partly because I felt I was becoming a slave to the new, that I
didn't have enough chance to delve into the vintage mysteries that
lined my walls. They are still there; I still rediscover them periodically; and if you ask me to name the greatest mystery byline of
them all, I will still say Ellery Queen without the slightest hesita-
tion. But as the new books pour in at a delightful if overwhelming
rate, in a volume no mortal could possibly keep up with, nearly all

of them better written and more readable than the average standard of the '30s or '40s, I realize I may never retreat again. Present-day crime fiction is where I want to be as a writer and a reader.

Postscript 2008: A lot of the above I still agree with, but I'm not as sanguine about the field as I was in 1994. The blockbuster-happy state of commercial publishing, and the increasing standardization of categories—cat cozies, conspiracy thrillers—have made the market a much less happy place than it was in 1994. But there is still much good material being published.

FOUR UNDERVALUED WRITERS

Mystery Scene, Summer 2005

That more and more mysteries are being published through more and more channels is both good news and bad news for the writer. The good news: more ways to get published. The bad news: more ways to be lost in the shuffle. All four writers discussed below have achieved a measure of success but are less highly valued than they should be. They represent, respectively, 1) the paperback original writer who gets less prestige and attention than the hardcover writer, 2) the successful British writer who for whatever reason has not gained a foothold in the American market, 3) the writer who switches from a New York "major" to a small regional publisher, and 4) the writer who returns to the field after an absence of a decade or more.

1. Deborah Donnelly

Do mystery reviewers (male ones especially) have it in for the so-called cozy mystery, so much so that they have made the phrase itself a kind of slur? Not this reviewer. As a descriptive term, cozy is no more pejorative than hardboiled, and if I were forced to divide the whole of detective fiction into the toughs and the cozies, the classical figures I most revere (Queen, Christie, Carr, Marsh) would inevitably land in the cozy column. However, I do get impatient with the current crop of cozies when they are unconscionably padded and/or neglect the basic requirement of a good plot.

Cozy mystery heroines have all sorts of occupations—caterer, book dealer, tea-shop proprietor, domestic, animal breeder, journalist, landscape architect, teacher, librarian, ghostwriter, tour leader—but one of the most promising is that practiced by Deborah Donnelly's Carnegie Kincaid: wedding planner. Weddings are as sure-fire a background for murder as for comedy or romance. The Kincaid series has won a following but, since paperbacks continue to get less review attention than hardcovers, it might have missed some of its potential audience.

A self-described "skinny five-foot-eleven redhead," Carnegie (named for Andrew Carnegie because her father appreciated the public libraries he funded) was launched in *Veiled Threats* (2002), but I first made her acquaintance in *Died to Match* (2002), in which the nuptials are planned for an unusual venue: the Seattle Aquarium. Aside from the humorous narrative style, the inside details of wedding planning, and the fresh background, I was impressed by an element often absent from present-day cozies: real detection from fairly offered clues.

Following *May the Best Man Die* (2003), Carnegie has her fourth case in *Death Takes a Honeymoon* (2005), in which she goes to the wedding of an old college friend as a reluctant guest but winds up running the show when the bride's family can't get along with the designated planner. Meanwhile, she becomes involved in investigating the recent death of her cousin, a firefighter, in an apparent smoke-jumping accident. The two plot elements come together in an exciting forest-fire climax. There's no clued detection in this one, unless it was too subtle for me, but the plot is nicely involved and the humor on target. A couple of samples that could have come from Ron Goulart's joke file: the bride, Tracy Kane, has become famous starring as a professional dogwalker on a TV sitcom called *Tails of the City*, and the characters imbibe a local brew called Moose Drool Ale. (For all I know, that last may be authentic!)

While Donnelly follows the dubious current practice of having a large cast of continuing characters—Carnegie's journalist boyfriend, elderly business partner, obnoxious professional rival, Russian floral consultant—they are never dragged in for no reason or allowed to bring plot movement to a grinding halt so they can perform. The rocky romantic subplot is nicely integrated with the mystery. I'm less sanguine about Donnelly's use of cliffhanger endings, particularly annoying in the latest book since it's so incongruous with the light overall tone. But the general quality of the product disarms gripes.

2. Ben Elton

If *Mystery Scene* were a British publication, calling Ben Elton an undervalued writer would be laughable. Though famed in the UK as stand-up comic, actor, playwright, and bestselling novelist, he has not gained the audience he deserves in the US. A couple of his novels, including the Gold Dagger-winning *Popcorn* (1996), have found American publishers, but his most recent work is distributed here in its original British editions by Trafalgar Square. Elton has a satirist's eye for contemporary lunacy, a fine novelist's ability to create individual and involving characters, and a respect for the traditions of crime fiction.

Popcorn is a searing satire on contemporary society as viewed and influenced by its entertainment and information media. On the evening he wins an Oscar for his over-the-top violent *Ordinary Americans*, writer/director Bruce Delamitri (clearly inspired at least in his professional persona by Quentin Tarantino) is taken hostage by the notorious Mall Murderers who were inspired to their killing spree by his film. Along with the Oscar ceremony and general Hollywood hypocrisy (the cynical director's acceptance speech is remarkable for its knee-jerk insincerity), Elton touches on racial politics, cosmetic surgery, rampant litigation, campus political correctness, television news and talk shows, commercials, and numerous other targets in service of his overarching theme: that everybody blames somebody else for everything and nobody takes responsibility for anything. In his spot-on rendering of American settings and dialogue, Elton slips only occasionally: Americans would call a lounge a living room; our TV personalities are rarely called presenters; and California has Highway Patrol officers, not State Troopers.

Elton's later books continue to explore various crime/mystery subgenres while keeping a satirical focus. The stalker novel *Blast from the Past* (1997) is a riff on sexual politics, describing a re-kindled romance between two comic extremists, a conservative American career Army officer and a left-wing British woman. *Dead Famous* (2001) targets a uniquely unsavory current phe-nomenon (the TV reality show), applies a contemporary frankness in language and sexual explicitness, and uses all this in service of an Agatha Christie-style closed circle whodunit as complexly and fairly plotted as a choice specimen from the Golden Age of Detec-tion. *High Society* (2002), about an effort to legalize recreational drugs in Britain, shows that personalities more than serious argu-ment determine political decision-making. *Past Mortem* (2004), a police procedural about an online reunion service and a serial kil-ler of bullies, returns to fair-play detection and is entertaining as ever, but the murderer is too obvious too early.

What could be more welcome in the current market than a writer with a 21st-Century sensibility and range of references (in-cluding the ability to look back on 1980s musical groups I've barely heard of as nostalgia!) coupled with a classical command of mystery plotting?

3. Kathy Lynn Emerson

In her series about Susanna, Lady Appleton, Elizabethan gentlewoman and herbalist, Kathy Lynn Emerson offers a remarkable range of vivid and telling details, whether domestic, scientific, political, social, legal, or religious. She also manages to create dialogue that achieves a period sound without being stilted or unnatural.

In her first appearance, *Face Down in the Marrow-Bone Pie* (1997), Susanna is living at Leigh Abbey in Kent, where she has a prickly but not completely unhappy relationship with her husband Sir Robert, a serial philanderer. The steward at Appleton Manor has died suddenly while inappropriately dining on the elaborate concoction of the title, a delicacy usually enjoyed only by the very rich. Reports that he was frightened to death by the ghost of a young woman have scared off all the other servants. Against the wishes of Sir Robert, who has gone on a diplomatic mission to France, Susanna travels to Lancashire to clear up the mystery.

Like any heroine of a contemporary historical, Susanna is awfully independent and liberated for a woman of her time, but Emerson makes her attitudes and impulses believable. From the first book, the point is made that a widow's position in Elizabethan society is far preferable to a wife's, but Susanna doesn't actually achieve widowhood until the fourth entry, *Face Down Beneath the Eleanor Cross* (2000), in which she is accused of bringing it on prematurely. Her trial in the Old Bailey for the murder of her husband is quite different from contemporary proceedings: the same jury are asked to bring verdicts on multiple felonies in a single day and are denied food and heat until they reach a decision.

The eighth novel, *Face Down Below the Banqueting House* (Perseverance Press, 2005), describes the elaborate cooking facilities at Greenwich, the Maundy Thursday ceremony in which the Queen washes the feet of the poor (after three functionaries have washed them first), and the odd traveling arrangements which allow the Queen to commandeer any house that suits her and banish the inhabitants during her visit—unless they are of sufficiently elevated rank to be kept around. One of the houses selected for a royal visit is Susanna's, and her exchange with the Queen's self-important advance man is choice. A banqueting house, described as "a place where a considerable number of people could consume sweets and delicacies following the main part of their meal," is built in a tree at Leigh Abbey in anticipation of the Queen's visit, and from it a servant falls to his death. Accident, suicide, or murder?

Perseverance Press is one of the classiest of the regional publishers, producing a well-edited and beautifully packaged product. Still, when an established series becomes a victim of the find-me-a-blockbuster shakeout and moves from a New York publisher to a small specialty house, readers must wonder if this book is to be a bittersweet curtain call. But Emerson reports that another in the series is coming from Perseverance in 2006, and she also turned to a small publisher in launching a series about 1880s New York journalist Diana Spaulding with *Deadlier Than the Pen* (Pemberley, 2004).

Ideally, historical mysteries should provide something on the real history, with a clear delineation of what is real and what imagined. Not until *Face Down Beneath the Eleanor Cross* did Emerson append a very brief historical note. Beginning with the sixth novel, *Face Down Before Rebel Hooves* (2001), Emerson has provided a character list with real people in the cast helpfully asterisked, and the notes have become more extensive. *Face Down Across the Western Sea* (2002), seventh in the series and last to be published by St. Martin's, adds a map and a referral to her website for a full bibliography. The short story collection *Murders and Other Confusions* (Crippen & Landru, 2004) has a six-page introduction plus a concluding note to each story placing it in the context of the overall series.

Only one question remains: what if Lady Susanna finds a murder victim lying face up?

4. Joseph Telushkin

Like Ben Elton, Rabbi Joseph Telushkin has more on his mind than pure entertainment, and that may make his work problematic for some readers. If you've heard nationally syndicated radio talk show host Dennis Prager, a longtime friend and sometime nonfiction collaborator of Telushkin, you'll recognize the very traditional religious and social views espoused on such issues as abortion, homosexuality, capital punishment, feminism, and the distinct roles of men and women in worship. Telushkin's first novel even includes a reference to one of Prager's favorite ethical conundrums: "If you saw your dog and a stranger, both drowning, and you could only save one, which one would you save?"

The Unorthodox Murder of Rabbi Wahl (1987) introduced Rabbi Daniel Winter, the second major rabbi detective in fiction, following Harry Kemelman's David Small. It would be followed by two more, *The Final Analysis of Dr. Stark* (1988) and *An Eye for an Eye* (1991). While Kemelman's purpose was to explain the tenets of Judaism to Jews and non-Jews alike, Telushkin has a broader agenda. Even those who least share Telushkin's views will find him a skilled writer of fiction, whose prose and character building are fine and whose plotting (much rarer in the current market) recalls the clues-on-the-table puzzle spinning of the Golden Age formalists.

In his essay "Is This Any Job for a Nice Jewish Boy?" (in *Synod of Sleuths* [1990]), James Yaffe wrote disparagingly of Rabbi Winter's first appearance, calling him less a character than "a collection of wish-fulfillment fantasies that belong to the vulgarest contemporary notions about success and glamour." While there may be some merit to Yaffe's assessment, I believe he's too harsh: Winter admits to too many human foibles and uncertainties to be charged with "intolerably smug superiority." Even Yaffe admitted that Telushkin produced "an interesting puzzle, with good clues and a genuinely surprising solution that is also logical."

Victim in the first novel is a female rabbi, murdered shortly after she appears on Winter's radio program, seemingly patterned on Prager's first Los Angeles program, "Religion on the Line."

The Last Analysis of Dr. Stark, about the murder of a Los Angeles psychiatrist, is less impressive because of a problem similar to Ben Elton's in *Past Mortem*: the main clue is just too obvious. *An Eye for an Eye* is perhaps the best of the three Winter novels, if also the one with the clearest agenda. When a man who killed his girlfriend gets off with a conviction for voluntary manslaughter, the victim's incensed father kills the defendant and is released on bail as a result of Rabbi Winter's arguments. But then the defense attorney is murdered, the father accused, and the rabbi faced with a crisis of conscience. As before, the puzzle spinning is expert, but in his eagerness to denounce the liberal courts, the author stacks the cards a little too neatly.

By contrast, Telushkin's most recent novel, *Heaven's Witness* (2004), written with Allen Estrin, gives full measure to all points of view in a novel with a theme of reincarnation, generally (to put it mildly) not a part of mainstream Christian or Jewish theology. The villain is a serial killer known as the Messenger, the amateur detective psychoanalyst-in-training Dr. Jordan Geller. With multiple suspects and expert mystery construction, the book struck me as one of the best of its year, and I hope Telushkin is back in the field to stay.

These four quite different writers represent scores of gifted practitioners, past and present, who have done better work than many regulars of the bestseller lists. Read them to see if you agree with me, and then look for more of crime fiction's hidden treasures.

HOW TO WRITE MYSTERIES IN SIX DIFFICULT LESSONS

Mystery Scene, Summer 2006

In 1913, the Home Correspondence School published Carolyn Wells's *The Technique of the Mystery Story*, the first how-to manual for prospective writers of detective and mystery fiction. Today its value is purely historical, giving a detailed account of the kind of mystery Wells and her contemporaries were producing in the years before World War I. In subsequent years, Wells would be joined at the lectern by such mystery practitioners as Nigel Morland, Marie F. Rodell, Patricia Highsmith, Robert Turner, Joan Lowery Nixon, H.R.F. Keating, Shannon OCork, Larry Beinhart, Dean R. Koontz, William G. Tapply, and Carolyn Wheat.

Approaches have been as varied as the writers doing the instructing. One who maps out every move in advance might stress the nuts and bolts of the writing process, while one who sits down at the keyboard and lets fly with no idea where the story is going might take a more inspirational or cheerleading stance. The best how-to books provide a measure of both elements. Early technical manuals concentrated strictly on literary concerns (plotting, style, characterization, research), but those written for the contemporary market are expected also to deal with the business aspects of writing (getting published, finding an agent, promoting the work).

These how-to books have a wider audience than wannabe writers. Apart from biographical and critical insights into their authors, they often can be read purely for entertainment. Lawrence Block's *Write For Your Life*, self-published to accompany seminars he conducted in the 1980s and something of a rarity because of its limited distribution, will soon be made available as an e-book by HarperCollins. It will undoubtedly be sought by Block collectors and fans who never intend to write a word for publication.

Certain pieces of advice recur in manuals on fiction writing—avoid substitutes for "said"; don't worry about a bad first draft; avoid agents who charge reading fees; include plenty of conflict; don't overdo dialect; show, don't tell; write what you know; research what you don't know; cultivate booksellers—but the modes of delivery vary tremendously, as the six in-print volumes considered below demonstrate.

G. Miki Hayden begins *Writing the Mystery: A Start-to-Finish Guide for Both Novice and Professional* (2001; revised edition 2004) provocatively, telling new writers what a good time it is to break in. Publishers are dumping established authors in their quest for the next blockbuster and looking for newcomers who will work cheap. Hayden pays more attention to e-books, independent presses, and the short-story market than most competing works. But her meandering style needs editing; her descriptions of cozy and hardboiled fiction are exaggerated; and her carelessness with names (John D. and Ross "McDonald"; Jane "Austin") and dubious statements do not inspire confidence. Most stories in *Ellery Queen's Mystery Magazine* and *Alfred Hitchcock's Mystery Magazine* do not "verge on novella length" as she believes, and both magazines are more receptive to new talent than she suggests.

Hayden also gives some questionable advice. Sure, go ahead and send out simultaneous submissions without informing the recipients. Murmur, mumble, and mutter instead of say? Go for it. Tom Swifty adverbial dialogue tags? No problem. While Hayden is a skilled writer of short stories, reading her instruction manual would not be likely to attract anyone to her fiction. (Comments are based on the first edition.)

Jean Hager is an expert crafter of traditional mystery puzzles, but *How to Write & Market Your Mystery Novel: A Step-by-Step Guide From Idea to Final Rewrite and Marketing* (1998) wouldn't necessarily make me want to read her novels. She offers good advice, but her approach is more simplistic and mechanical than most of the others. However, her brief book gathers strength as it goes along. To prove old tricks are not necessarily useless to the contemporary writer, Hager reprints Lester Dent's 1936 Master Fiction Plot, which Dale Furutani used to develop his award-winning debut, *Death in Little Tokyo*.

Though I haven't read one of Gillian Roberts's novels about schoolteacher sleuth Amanda Pepper in some years, the charm and humor of *You Can Write a Mystery* (1999) made me want to seek one out. Her example of awful dialogue is especially choice: "Ever since my treacherous fiancé, Humphrey, tried to force himself on you, my sister, and in a fit of anger I killed him and we buried him near the roses, I can't sleep or eat because I'm so afraid that the gardener will dig Humphrey up and our secret will be revealed." She is also good on style and the eternal question "Where do you get your ideas?" Her stress on the puzzle element is heartening to those of us who believe fair-play clueing is becoming a lost art.

These strengths are enough to forgive the misapprehension that Sherlock Holmes, like Nero Wolfe, is "pathologically sedentary."

If I didn't already know I enjoyed Roberts's style, her how-to would attract me to her work. With Elizabeth George, the opposite is the case. Through some blind spot no doubt, I don't care for her novels, and *Write Away: One Novelist's Approach to Fiction and the Writing Life* (2004) struck me the same way, overlong and over-elaborated. Still, she is an experienced writing teacher and certainly provides helpful encouragement and sound practical advice. She stresses character to the extreme: her exhaustive system requires full character analyses before the novel is even plotted, let alone written. Her allusions are as likely to come from general literature as from mystery fiction, and her sample quotations, both from her own and the work of others, tend to substantial length. George's admirers will appreciate the grueling and traumatic process she goes through to create her bestselling novels, reflected in the amazingly insecure and self-doubting journal excerpts used as chapter epigraphs.

Like George, Loren D. Estleman seeks a larger audience than would-be mystery writers in *Writing the Popular Novel: A Comprehensive Guide to Crafting Fiction That Sells* (2004). Estleman, who looms as large in western as in crime fiction, is one of the finest stylists in any popular genre, and he has written the most entertaining of the six manuals under review, while also providing useful advice. He has strong views on the English language. Sample opinions: it's okay to split infinitives, end a sentence with a preposition, and use *contact* as a verb (no other single word does the job); but it's not OK to confuse *imply* and *infer*, use *lay* when you mean *lie*, or make *impact* into a verb (it means the same as *affect*). He joins Nero Wolfe in excoriating *Webster's Third*. His chapter titles give an idea of the book's pleasures: "The Rapture of Research"; "How to Ignore an Outline"; "Wyatt Earp and Me"; "Ten Things You Can Do to Avoid Success" (e.g. "End each chapter with a cliffhanger" and "Join a writer's group"); and "Five Things Your Teacher Never Told You" (e.g. "Believe good reviews, ignore bad reviews" and "If you can't do it right, do it wrong").

Hallie Ephron's *Writing and Selling Your Mystery Novel: How to Knock 'Em Dead with Style* (2005) is the first technical manual to be nominated for the biographical-critical Edgar since that award was instituted in 1977. Purely as a textbook, it is much the best of this group. Ephron never talks around a particular writing problem but gives specific step-by-step guidance on every aspect of the process, from schedule and workspace through submitting and selling, complete with focused student exercises. Any reader who conscientiously followed her program would finish a mystery novel—not necessarily a publishable one, but the next try might be.

Suggestions are appropriately given with the current market in mind, but contemporary methods are not necessarily the best. Ephron gives terrible advice to Conan Doyle: "If [he] were writing the Sherlock Holmes stories today, he surely would have made Holmes the point-of-view character....Because Holmes is at the center of the action. He should be telling the story." Sorry, Dr. Watson. Elsewhere she expresses a requirement that some (okay, I) believe represents what is wrong with much current series mystery fiction: "You have to keep coming up with new catastrophes and life-changing crises to throw at the main character." If the detective must be the protagonist and must go through devastating trauma, write stand-alones, not series, lest you wind up with soap opera.

Under the joint pseudonym G.H. Ephron, Hallie Ephron writes novels with Donald Davidoff about forensic neuropsychologist Dr. Peter Zak. I have not read them, but her lively style, her sense of humor (wryly countering a writer cliché, she notes, "My characters never take over. How I wish they would"), her stress on the role of clues, and the professionalism she evinces in this guide make me want to try one.

Whether read for enjoyment or instruction, most how-to-write-a-mystery volumes reflect a commendable professional generosity. Any mystery writer who found producing a technical manual a more lucrative use of working hours than writing another novel probably wouldn't be worth reading in either format.

BRITISH MYSTERIES IN THE TWENTIETH CENTURY

Foreword, *A Century of British Mystery and Suspense*, edited by
Anne Perry (Mystery Guild, 2000)

The year is 1900. Depending on how you choose to count, it is either the first year of the 20th Century or the last of the 19th. Technology is running rampant. The telegraph and telephone with their revolution in instantaneous communication have been joined by automobiles and moving pictures, with more wonders on the horizon. Life seems to move ever faster, grow more complex, produce new sources of stress. Spare time is rare and precious.

In your leisure reading, you have developed an appetite for detective stories, a well-established genre of popular literature. Tales of detection are thrilling and suspenseful but, you tell yourself, more than mere light entertainment. Indeed, they are improving; they test the intellect, hone the reader's reasoning skills, educate about social problems. While giving pleasure, they also equip you to deal with the increasing pressures of modern times. But can there ever be enough good detective fiction to satisfy your craving? You anxiously scan the pages of magazines and the shelves of bookshops. As each new practitioner appears, you eagerly pounce. As a turn-of-the-century mystery buff, what are your options?

To begin with, the American Edgar Allan Poe's founding fatherhood notwithstanding, the British stand at the top of the mystery food chain. Sherlock Holmes, the most famous detective in fiction, is officially dead, his impatient and ungrateful creator Sir Arthur Conan Doyle having killed him off in the final story of *The Memoirs of Sherlock Holmes* (1893). (The Baker Street sleuth won't be revived provisionally until *The Hound of the Baskervilles* [1902] or permanently until *The Return of Sherlock Holmes* [1905].) Still, his influence continues to be pervasive. Most of the other well-known detectives follow his lead: preternaturally gifted, supplied with a full panoply or a pointed lack of eccentricities, able to pursue their investigations unencumbered by police procedures and red tape, concentrating their activities in the short-story form to take advantage of the lucrative magazine market. Arthur Morrison's Martin Hewitt, perhaps the best-known of them, finished his magazine career in the waning years of the century. (The final collection of his cases, *The Red Triangle*, will appear in 1903.)

Burglar A.J. Raffles, the anti-Holmes figure created by Doyle's brother-in-law E.W. Hornung, is at his peak, having been collected last year in *The Amateur Cracksman*, with a second group coming next year in *The Black Mask* (American title, *Raffles: Further Adventures of the Amateur Cracksman*). Old Dick Donovan is still at it: his 1900 collection is *The Adventures of Tyler Tatlock, Private Detective*.

Various professions are represented by fictional detectives, and not only the physicians and lawyers whose connections to criminal investigation seem obvious. The cases of reporter sleuth Beverley Gretton have been gathered this year in Herbert Cadett's *The Adventures of a Journalist*. All manner of crime solvers are plying their trade, even (would you believe it?) *female* ones: the cases of George R. Sims's *Dorcas Dene, Detective* were collected three years ago, in 1897, and this year the adventures of M. McDonnell Bodkin's *Dora Myrl, the Lady Detective* have appeared in book form. Female *writers* of detective stories are not quite as unusual: L.T. Meade (Elizabeth Thomasina Meade Smith) has been writing in the field for nearly a decade. This year her collection is *The Sanctuary Club*, written in collaboration with Robert Eustace.

With the short fiction market so bullish, detective novels have taken a back seat, but there have been a few milestones since Wilkie Collins's classic *The Moonstone* (1868). In 1892, Israel Zangwill produced the first great locked-room novel, *The Big Bow Mystery*, which also pioneered a classic whodunit surprise gimmick, one that was turned up a notch by Marie and Robert Leighton in last year's *Michael Dred, Detective*. Fergus Hume, who made such a splash with *The Mystery of a Hansom Cab* (1886), will have half a dozen new novels in the shops this year. Surely no future detective novelist will ever be so prolific.

Yes, there's plenty of interesting stuff around for the mystery reader of 1900. But what new wonders does the century to come hold in store?

The Short Story Tradition Continues

Between 1900 and the beginning of World War I, most of the best British writers of detective fiction continued to specialize in the short form. The first great sleuth to be introduced in the twentieth century was Baroness Orczy's Old Man in the Corner, the armchair detective whose cases were first collected in *The Case of Miss Elliott* (1905). He lives only in short stories, as does Orczy's memorable female sleuth, *Lady Molly of Scotland Yard* (1910). Contemporaries like Robert Barr in *The Triumphs of Eugene Valmont* (1906), with its satirical contrast of British and French police methods, also kept it short. Although one of the most famous sleuths of the era, R. Austin Freeman's scientific detective Dr. John Thorndyke, first appeared in the novel *The Red Thumb Mark* (1907) and would have many other book-length cases, his short-story appearances, first collected in *John Thorndyke's Cases* (1909), have generally been more highly valued. Similarly, though Ernest Bramah's pioneering blind detective Max Carrados would appear in a single novel, *The Bravo of London* (1934), his most notable work is in short stories, first collected in *Max Carrados* (1914).

As Hugh Greene pointed out in introducing his 1970 anthology *The Rivals of Sherlock Holmes*, much of this pre-war British detective fiction had been grittier and in some ways more realistic than the work that would follow: "The setting of most of these stories is much closer to Raymond Chandler's 'mean streets' down which Philip Marlowe walked than to the unreal country house, ye old English village, world of the English detective story in the years between the wars...."

The greatest British sleuth to be introduced between 1900 and World War I did not belong to this tradition of urban realism, however. G.K. Chesterton's Father Brown solved bizarre, sometimes impossible, crimes while coining paradoxes and making subtle theological points. More than any other writer, he foreshadowed the games-playing and puzzle-spinning of post-war detective fiction. The brilliant though unobtrusive amateur sleuth, first of a long line of Roman Catholic religious detectives, never appeared at greater than short-story length in a career that spanned a quarter of a century.

There were a few key novels in the period before the Great War. *Trent's Last Case* (1913), by Chesterton's friend E.C. Bentley, was credited with augmenting the realism of detective fiction by stressing the humanity of the sleuth. Ironically, journalist Philip Trent's purported last case was actually his first, and despite his failure (a reversal of the normal infallibility of fictional detectives) became popular enough to be revived in a series of short stories. A.E.W. Mason's *At the Villa Rose* (1910) introduced, at a time when most fictional sleuths were amateurs or private enquiry agents, the French police detective Hanaud, who would have another notable case in *The House of the Arrow* (1924) and whose career would extend into the forties, concluding with *The House in Lordship Lane* (1946). Mrs. Belloc Lowndes' *The Lodger* (1912) fictionalized the Jack the Ripper murders, a frequent ploy of crime fiction writers ever since, and in its psychological approach foreshadowed the modern crime novel.

The trauma of World War I brought British detective fiction to a virtual halt. In the new wave of fiction after the war, emphasis would shift to the novel, though short stories remained popular. The early stories about Agatha Christie's Hercule Poirot, narrated by Captain Hastings, are solidly Holmesian in structure and atmosphere, and most of the other great sleuths of the period appeared at least occasionally in short stories. (The same is true of the leading series sleuths, as well as non-series writers, today.)

The Golden Age of the Twenties

Post-war Britain, a generation of its male population decimated (through death or disability) by the conflict, returned to relative peacetime stability, though in a society markedly changed in attitudes, standards of moral behavior, and worldly experience. The populace was ready for some light relief, some of which was provided by the amusing, artificial, but intellectually rigorous detective fiction of what would be called the Golden Age of Detection. To some readers, the detective story became a game more than a literary form, a brain teaser as surely as the crossword puzzles that gained popularity around the same time. But the Golden Age detective story's remoteness from real life and real humanity has been exaggerated: the work of its best writers was always rooted in character and, while its plots and situations may have been unlikely, they were usually no more so than those of the allegedly more realistic crime fiction of later decades.

The year 1920 is considered a milestone in British (and thus all) detective fiction, largely but not entirely because of the debut of Agatha Christie. *The Mysterious Affair at Styles* introduced her great detective Hercule Poirot with an early example of the audacious reader bamboozlement that would reach its peak in the controversial *The Murder of Roger Ackroyd* (1926). Christie was a pioneer in establishing the concept of fair play to the reader, offering all the clues a clever reader needed to beat the great detective to the solution. Fair clues had *sometimes* been presented in detective stories extending all the way back to Poe, but they were far from the rule. It had been more common for Sherlock Holmes and his imitators to conceal the clues until explaining them in the denouement. The greater space for expanding the plot and hiding the clues in plain sight afforded by the novel length may have helped to account for the rise of fair play, but the best of the post-1920 practitioners practiced it in short stories as rigorously as in novels.

Decades after her death, Christie is still among the most famous and most widely reprinted writers of detective fiction. She has been so successful, so influential, so maddeningly persistent in her dominance of the paperback shelves that an inevitable backlash has occurred. Nothing better demonstrates the dominance of Christie than the way later writers fall over themselves asserting how unlike her they are, dutifully saluting her plot spinning while exaggerating the flatness of her characters and underestimating the subtle charm of her style.

Freeman Wills Crofts, master of the time-table puzzle, also appeared for the first time in 1920 with *The Cask*, while H.C. Bailey, harking back to the short story emphasis of an earlier era, published his first collection of stories, *Call Mr. Fortune*.

Three years later, the second great female British writer of the period, Dorothy L. Sayers, introduced Lord Peter Wimsey in *Whose Body?* (1923). Christie and Sayers have been the most written about Golden Age practitioners, the former for her mastery of puzzle making and reader misdirection, the latter for her fusion of the detective novel with the mainstream novel. Ironically, the early Sayers was as committed to the detective story's game elements as anyone, even incorporating a crossword puzzle into one of her short stories. But by the time Sayers left detective fiction for other literary pursuits in the late '30s, she had shown how a detective character can grow and deepen over a series of novels and how romance (scorned by the rules-makers of the '20s) could be integrated into the detective story. With the romance came a feminist icon, detective novelist Harriet Vane, who over the course of several books is saved from the gallows, pursued, and finally married by Lord Peter Wimsey.

A figure whose historical importance equals that of Christie and Sayers has been relatively neglected. Journalist and humorist A.B. Cox had two distinctive authorial identities: as Anthony Berkeley, he created an intentionally offensive detective in Roger Sheringham and produced the classic traditional detective novel

The Poisoned Chocolates Case (1929); as Francis Iles, he pioneered the modern crime novel that stresses psychology over detection in two classics, *Malice Aforethought* (1931) and *Before the Fact* (1932).

Though he is not usually regarded as a writer of detective fiction, humorist P.G. Wodehouse merits at least a mention. The perfect butler Jeeves often acted very much like a detective in bailing his employer Bertie Wooster out of trouble, and the relationship of the pair influenced Sayers in her creation of Wimsey and his ever-reliable manservant Bunter. The upper-class, amusedly observed milieu of Wodehouse's stories helped set the tone for other mystery writers of the era, and in his prolific provision of jacket quotes over the years he constantly revealed his enthusiasm for the form.

Like Elizabethan drama and any other literary school, British detective fiction is defined in terms of its giants. But many writers of the period kept to a high standard. Other major practitioners to debut in the twenties included John Rhode, the creator of the irascible Dr. Priestley, whose career extended from 1926 to 1961; Philip MacDonald, whose great contributions may have been overshadowed by a couple of American writers with the same surname; and Margery Allingham, whose Albert Campion changed and developed as interestingly as Lord Peter Wimsey. Gladys Mitchell, whose Beatrice Lestrange Bradley, first appeared in 1929's *Speedy Death*, gave her sleuth a 55-year run matched only by Hercule Poirot. Even some of the lesser writers of the period—names like Anthony Wynne, J.J. Connington, and R.A.J. Walling—produced work that is still enjoyable for present-day readers, if they can find it.

The Golden Age Tradition Continues

The mystery reader of 1930 was well adapted to the idea of detective fiction as a game. The narratives were often accompanied by character lists, maps and floor plans, and the clues had better be there. A number of writers, notably the American S.S. Van Dine and the Briton Ronald A. Knox, had drawn up sometimes facetious but essentially serious lists of rules. Aside from fair play, they added seemingly arbitrary strictures. In his "Detective Story Decalogue," Knox insisted the story contain no Chinaman (a term that is now deemed racist but may not have been intentionally offensive at the time), no "more than one secret room or passage," no poison unknown to science, no accident or sixth sense that helps the detective. In his "Twenty Rules for Writing Detective Fiction," Van Dine insisted there could be no love interest, no extended descriptions or literary flourishes; there must be one murderer and he or she can't be a servant. Members of the Detection Club, of which Chesterton, Sayers, and Berkeley were prominent members, had to swear they would shun solutions by "Divine Revelation, Feminine Intuition, Mumbo-Jumbo, Jiggery-Pokery, Coincidence, or the Act of God." New writers in the field flouted the rules at their peril—but often to the great advantage of their work.

In the thirties, more writers in the tradition of the twenties appeared, most notably Ngaio Marsh, Michael Innes, and Nicholas Blake. They held to the tradition of fair play to the reader while helping effect a steady rise in the general literary quality of the field. Marsh and Innes used police detectives, Roderic Alleyn and John Appleby respectively, but very unusual ones—well-educated, intellectual, even aristocratic—that had more resemblance to the gentleman sleuths of the Wimsey school than to the police procedural heroes of later years. Innes matched or surpassed Sayers in loading his dialogue up with literary allusions and quotations.

The beginning of World War II is generally taken to mark the end of the Golden Age of Detection. Unlike the previous global war, it did not have the effect of shutting down production of detective stories in Great Britain, though paper shortages limited the number of books that could be published. In his essay "The Whodunit in World War II and After," Howard Haycraft noted, "At the height of the Nazi blitz of London in 1940 special 'raid libraries' were set up at the reeking entrances of the underground shelters to supply, by popular demand, detective stories and nothing else." The category had become a staple of the population's leisure reading, a literary comfort food in a time of increasing stress. The war inspired some writers of classical detection to introduce elements of espionage and thriller fiction into their plots—see for example, Michael Innes's *The Secret Vanguard* (1940) and Margery Allingham's *Traitor's Purse* (1941).

After the war, fashions in crime fiction changed, and new subgenres rose to prominence. But at no time since has there been a lack of British writers in the classical tradition, including in rough chronological order Christianna Brand, Elizabeth (known in the U.S. as E.X.) Ferrars, Edmund Crispin, Patricia Moyes, Catherine Aird, Robert Barnard, Colin Dexter, and other traditionalists. The two most celebrated contemporary icons of British detection, P.D.

James and Ruth Rendell, for all their ambition and success in increasing the depth and literary interest of their works, began with classical detection and still observe its standards and conventions in at least some of their novels.

Confusions of Nationality

Mutual attraction, whether geographically or stylistically, has sometimes blurred the distinction between American and British writers of crime fiction. Though John Dickson Carr, master of the locked room puzzle, was not of British nationality, he lived in England for much of his life, usually employed a British setting and British detectives (Dr. Gideon Fell and, under his pseudonym Carter Dickson, Sir Henry Merrivale), stayed put in his adopted homeland in the dangerous days of World War II, and earned a place in British mystery fiction by being more British than the British. In later years, American novelists Patricia Highsmith and Michael Z. Lewin achieved similar honorary British status. Some writers moved in the other direction, born British but gravitating to America: Leslie Charteris, creator of the Saint who occasionally functioned as a detective but usually as a Robin Hood-ish criminal, and the Q. Patrick/Patrick Quentin collaborators, Richard Webb and Hugh Wheeler, who were born British but lived and set most of their work in the United States.

Apart from the Anglo-Americans, there is some ambiguity about Down Under crime writers. Ngaio Marsh, a New Zealander, set most of her novels in Great Britain and is generally claimed by the British, while Arthur W. Upfield, whose series about Inspector Napoleon Bonaparte is probably the most notable series of Australian detective novels, was born an Englishman.

The Broadening of the Crime Story

Early histories of mystery fiction, notably H. Douglas Thomson's *Masters of Mystery* (1931) and Howard Haycraft's *Murder for Pleasure* (1941), focused on detection, and to many readers the solidly-clued whodunit remains crime fiction's Main Street (or in British terms High Street). Still there are many other subgenres under the broad crime-mystery umbrella, and British writers have been prominent in most of them.

The Crime Novel: As noted earlier, Anthony Berkeley writing as Francis Iles was a pioneer of the transition from detective to crime novel traced by Julian Symons in his history *Bloody Murder* (1972; third revised edition 1992). Some of the ways the crime novel differs from the detective story as summed up by Symons: "Based on psychology of characters...or an intolerable situation that must end in violence. No deceptions of the locked-room or faked-print kind, no obscure poisons...Often no detective...Quite often no clues in the detective story sense...The lives of characters are shown continuing after the crime...[O]ften radical in the sense of questioning some aspect of law, justice or the way society is run." The modern crime story began in the thirties as a trend paralleling the continuation of classical detection. Among Iles' fellow crime writers of the thirties were the satirist C.E. Vulliamy (a.k.a. Anthony Rolls) and F. Tennyson Jesse. Later came the transplanted American Highsmith, Symons himself, and such present-day writers as Minette Walters and Frances Fyfield.

The Thriller: Though sometimes used in Britain as a term for the whole field of crime fiction, it properly describes stories where the stress is on action, adventure, and intrigue more than detection. In its lowbrow form (and don't take that necessarily as pejorative), examples include writers like William LeQueux, a spy and future-war specialist who debuted in the 1890s; E. Phillips Oppenheim, author of the classic *The Great Impersonation* (1920); the extremely prolific Edgar Wallace; "Sapper" (H.C. McNeile), creator of the celebrated and reviled Bulldog Drummond; Sax Rohmer, whose creation of the sinister villain Fu Manchu may have been a factor in Father Knox's ban on "Chinamen"; and of course Ian Fleming, whose super-agent James Bond spawned nearly as many imitators as Sherlock Holmes. The higher browed thriller encompasses the work of Somerset Maugham (in *Ashenden*), Graham Greene, Eric Ambler, John Le Carré, Len Deighton, and Frederick Forsyth. Operating somewhere between the brows, and overlapping traditional detection, is the jockey-turned-novelist Dick Francis.

The Police Procedural: Though many fictional detectives have always been police, their cases were not usually police procedurals, a relatively recent form in which much of the interest lies in the everyday workings of a law enforcement agency. John Creasey, whose output surpassed that of Fergus Hume and Edgar Wallace by a considerable margin, made his greatest contribution to crime fiction with the police procedural novels he wrote under the name J.J. Marric, beginning with *Gideon's Day* (1955). Among other important British practitioners were two who drew on their own experience as police, Maurice Procter and John Wainwright. Many of the major contemporary British sleuths are official police, including P.D. James's Adam Dalgliesh, Ruth Rendell's Wexford, H.R.F. Keating's Inspector Ghote, Peter Lovesey's Peter Diamond, and Reginald Hill's Dalziel and Pascoe. Some of their more prominent colleagues are defined by their musical interests, including John Harvey's Charlie Resnick (jazz), Colin Dexter's Inspector Morse (choral music and classics), Peter Robinson's Alan Banks (opera), and Ian Rankin's John Rebus (rock).

Romantic Suspense: Since the romantic suspense novel (or modern gothic) can be traced to Charlotte Brontë's *Jane Eyre* (1847), as well as the original gothic novels of writers like Ann Radcliffe and Matthew G. (Monk) Lewis, it should be no surprise British influence has continued strong. Daphne DuMaurier's *Rebecca* (1938) is a twentieth-century classic of the form. Among the successful later practitioners have been Victoria Holt, Mary Stewart, and the less-well-known but outstanding Anna Gilbert.

The Historical Mystery: Though the detective story was once contemporary almost by definition, in recent years historical crime stories have become more and more popular. Agatha Christie was again a pioneer, with the ancient Egyptian whodunit *Death Comes as the End* (1944). After a false start in 1934, *Devil Kinsmere* (as by Roger Fairbairn), John Dickson Carr produced much historical detection through the fifties, including *The Bride of Newgate* (1950) and the time-travel fantasy *Fire, Burn!* (1957). But historical mysteries didn't catch on in a big way until the '70s when various British writers were mining the past for story material, notably Peter Lovesey in his series about Victorian-era police detectives Sergeant Cribb and Constable Thackeray, beginning with *Wobble to Death* (1970), and Francis Selwyn (pseudonym of Donald Thomas), whose slightly-earlier Victorian Sergeant Verity first appeared in *Cracksman on Velvet* (1974). Ellis Peters' introduction of Brother Cadfael in *A Morbid Taste for Bones* (1977) started a vogue for medieval sleuths, while Anne Perry achieved great success with backgrounds of Victorian England, introducing Charlotte and Thomas Pitt in *The Cater Street Hangman* (1979), and beginning a second series about amnesiac private detective Thomas Monk and Crimean War nurse Hester Latterly in *The Face of a Stranger* (1990). Also of note are Gillian Linscott, whose novels trace the feminist movement of the early twentieth century through the adventures of suffragette Nell Bray, beginning with *Sister Be-*

neath the Sheet (1991), and the incredibly prolific (if not *quite* to a John Creasey level) P.C. Doherty, who writes novels of various historical periods under various names. Sherlock Holmes pastiches have been appearing at a dizzying rate since the 1970s. While much of the impetus has come surprisingly from Americans, much of the best work has been done by British writers like Michael Hardwick (*Prisoner of the Devil* [1980] and *Revenge of the Hound* [1987]), June Thomson (several short story collections beginning with *The Secret Files of Sherlock Holmes* [1990]), and Donald Thomas (*The Secret Cases of Sherlock Holmes* [1997]).

Courtroom Novels: There have been relatively few British legal thrillers in the tradition of John Grisham, but there are an abundance of courtroom crime novels, including such classics as Edgar Lustgarten's *A Case to Answer* (1947; American title *One More Unfortunate*), Cyril Hare's *Tragedy at Law* (1942), Gerald Bullett's *The Jury* (1935), Raymond Postgate's *Verdict of Twelve* (1940), and Anthony Berkeley's *Trial and Error* (1937). Sara Woods's Antony Maitland laid claim to the title of British Perry Mason in a long series of novels beginning with *Bloody Instructions* (1962). Henry Cecil mined a Wodehouse-like vein of legal humor in novels beginning with *The Painswick Line* (1951). Many of solicitor Michael Gilbert's novels, notably *Death Has Deep Roots* (1951) and *Blood and Judgement* (1959) display his legal expertise in outstanding courtroom scenes. (Gilbert has written almost every type of crime fiction, which made it hard to decide where to insert his name in this survey.) The most famous British lawyer and sometime detective is probably John Mortimer's Rumpole of the Bailey, created for television but in book form since 1978.

The Hardboiled: The one area at which the British have not traditionally excelled is the hardboiled novel of American writers like Dashiell Hammett, Raymond Chandler, and James M. Cain, not that they haven't tried. British who have practiced it have usually used American backgrounds and characters. Hartley Howard and Basil Copper wrote about American private eyes in a way convincing to British readers if not to Americans. James Hadley Chase, who rarely visited the United States, had a major success with the gangster epic *No Orchids for Miss Blandish* (1939) and followed it up with many more American-based thrillers. Peter Cheyney sometimes used American settings and characters, introducing G-man Lemmy Caution in *This Man is Dangerous* (1936) but also created a British equivalent of the American private eye in

Slim Callaghan, who first appeared in *The Urgent Hangman* (1938). The recent rise of the Brit Noir school shows them still trying and with greater success. Writers like John Harvey, whose Charlie Resnick novels beginning with *Lonely Hearts* (1989) were inspired by Elmore Leonard, Ross Thomas, and TV's *Hill Street Blues*, and Liza Cody, who introduced British female private eye Anna Lee in *Dupe* (1980), show a strong influence of the American tough school. A whole new generation of down-and-dirty British writers has been represented in the *Fresh Blood* anthology series edited by Maxim Jakubowski and Mike Ripley. Prominent names apart from the editors themselves include Derek Raymond, Mark Timlin, Denise Danks, Russell James, Ken Bruen, and Phil Lovesey.

Why the British?

How have the British compiled such a remarkable record in the field of crime fiction? One measure of the high British standard of quality in the field is seen in how many of its practitioners, both one-shots and specialists, also distinguished themselves in other areas of writing. Victorian novelists Charles Dickens and Wilkie Collins set the pattern. Conan Doyle created a vast body of work, both historical fiction and nonfiction, that had nothing to do with crime and detection. Chesterton, of course, was a celebrated essayist, journalist, and critic. Father Ronald Knox produced a huge body of theological writings. G.D.H. Cole, a Golden Age staple writing with wife Margaret Cole, was a noted economist. Eden Phillpotts, a respected mainstream writer, entered the field in 1921 with *The Grey Room*. A.A. Milne, whose one-shot *The Red House Mystery* (1922) was hailed an instant classic, was most famous as a writer of children's books like *Winnie the Pooh*. Peter Dickinson, quite possibly the finest crime fiction writer on the contemporary scene, also is noted for his children's books. Sayers would become a distinguished translator of Dante and a religious playwright after abandoning detective fiction, while Nicholas Blake (C. Day Lewis) became poet laureate. Both John Harvey and Peter Robinson have produced volumes of poetry. C.P. Snow, who started and ended his novelistic career with detective fiction, became a respected mainstream literary figure with his *Strangers and Brothers* series of novels. Lady Antonia Fraser was a distinguished popular biographer of British royalty before she began recounting the adventures of Jemima Shore. Julian Symons was a formidable critic, poet, and historian outside his crime fiction specialty. Detective fiction may have been seen as a recreational activity, but serious writers have taken its creation seriously.

Another reason for British leadership in this particular mode may lie in the national character. The detective story from its beginnings has been a very moral form, one that has assumed (or at least sought after) a norm of stability. If crime upsets the order, the order must be restored, not by the force of dictatorship but by the rationality and common sense of democracy. What nation is more historically stable, traditional, and orderly than Great Britain? What nation with such a low murder rate can boast such a long history of colorful and memorable crimes? What country has more faithfully preserved its traditions, its great buildings, its landmarks?

What is to Come?

The year is now 2000. Depending on how you count, the first year of the 21st Century and third millennium or the last year of the 20th and second. Technology is sweeping us ahead in a way the citizen of a hundred years ago could not have imagined. There is no problem whatsoever finding enough good mysteries to read. Every crime writer could shut down production tomorrow, and you would never run out of reading matter, even if you were a speed reader and medical science found a way to grant you a second century of life. A concerted effort to read even all the *good* mysteries of the past would prove an insurmountable folly. A less ambitious program of reading all the good *new* mystery fiction being published, even confining yourself to the good new *British* mysteries, would leave you little time for anything else.

The crime story shows no signs of flagging, in the English-speaking world or elsewhere. There may be changes in delivery modes (downloaded a good e-book lately?), but it is still safe to say that all the variants of the crime-mystery-detective story will continue into the foreseeable future. And while no one country or even one language can lay claim to the whole field, continued British leadership is at least arguable.

NANCY DREW AND THE HARDY BOYS

"The Jury Box," *EQMM*, January 1993

When I was growing up in the 1950s, it was a firm rule (unwritten, unspoken, but nonetheless honored) that boys did not read girls' books. Thus, though I read the Hardy Boys with appreciation, I never cracked a Nancy Drew mystery, much as I was intrigued by their great titles. Now, all these years later, a reprinter has given me an excuse not just to revisit the Hardys but for the first time to see what a Drew book was like.

Applewood Press has published facsimile editions of the first three books in each of the classic series. The three Hardys, all first published in 1927, are *The Tower Treasure*, *The House on the Cliff*, and *The Secret of the Old Mill*. The first two have introductions by Leslie McFarlane, who wrote the early volumes in the series under the house name Franklin W. Dixon, while the third is introduced by William Tapply. The Drews, all 1930 and signed by Carolyn Keene, are (introducers in parentheses) *The Secret of the Old Clock* (Sara Paretsky), *The Hidden Staircase* (Nancy Pickard), and *The Bungalow Mystery* (P.M. Carlson). In later years, these books were revised and updated, toning down or eliminating some of the offensive racial and social views while also (say critics) rendering them rather bland and colorless. Applewood leaves the originals intact, with an appropriate disclaimer.

It's easy to see why today's mystery-writing feminists so love Nancy Drew. Despite the conventions of her time, she functions as a totally liberated woman (family wealth helps), who is always free to follow a mysterious scent and invariably survives unscathed her sometimes dubious judgment, typified by a tendency to drive her roadster or motorboat into gathering storms. Class-consciousness is rampant: in *The Bungalow Mystery*, one clue that a young woman's new guardian is a baddy is that he doesn't employ a single servant! And it's axiomatic in all these books that anyone who is less than impeccably groomed, looks or sounds foreign, or has bad taste in interior decoration is a villain.

Realizing there may be a gender bias at work here, I find the Hardy Boy books markedly superior to the Drews, with some of the same formulaic faults but much more humor and somewhat more complex plots. Though nowhere near reality, they come a

little closer than the Drews: at least the teenage Hardys still have
the burden of going to school, while Nancy is free as a bird at age
sixteen.

Perhaps the most incredible element in both series is the will-
ingness of the detecting fathers (Carson Drew and Fenton Hardy)
to let their offspring wade into dangerous situations with only the
mildest of admonitions—lawyer Drew even gives teenage Nancy a
loaded handgun for protection in one of the cases, which by present-day standards seems totally irresponsible. It's interesting from
a gender-role standpoint that the Hardy Boys are permitted to re-
ceive monetary rewards for their work, getting $1000 for rounding
up the counterfeiters at the end of *Old Mill*, while Nancy accepts
only keepsakes (e.g., the titular old clock). Is she preserving her
amateur standing for the 1932 Detection Olympics?

No amount of adult analysis can completely erase the pre-
adolescent enthusiasm these books evoked. The scriveners behind
the house names wrote with a strong sense of pace and atmosphere. If you loved these books growing up, you'll enjoy revisiting
them.

AN OBSERVER'S HISTORY OF MYSTERY SCENE

Mystery Scene, holiday issue, 2002 (#77)

As surely as every person, every magazine is unique. But *Mystery Scene*, which has ranged far more widely in the genres of popular fiction than its title suggests, has been more unique than most. It has had the combativeness of a war novel, the lover's quarrels of a romance, the shootouts on Main Street of a western, the huge cast of a multi-generational epic, the unpredictability of a lost-continent adventure, the intrigue of a spy novel, the reverence for the past of a historical, the fascination with possible futures of science fiction, the hidden but fairly clued secrets of a Golden Age whodunit, the in-your-face impact of a private eye novel, and sometimes even the sense of organization of a police procedural. The first 75 issues of *Mystery Scene* form an extraordinary documentary record of developments, concerns, and controversies the field went through over a period of seventeen years, a time of unprecedented growth, ferment, and change.

It all began with a phone conversation some time in the mid-1980s between a couple of versatile, prolific, and very busy writers, Ed Gorman and Robert J. Randisi. Either Ed or Bob noted how useful the periodicals *Locus* and *Science Fiction Chronicle* were in providing information to both fans and pros in the science fiction community. Lamenting the lack of a comparable newszine for the mystery field, either Bob or Ed expressed the wish to create one, a sort of criminous *Publisher's Weekly*. Fortunately, they decided to do more than talk about it.

The first issue of *Mystery Scene*, four pages long, was sent to subscribers with the October 1985 issue of *Mystery & Detective Monthly*, a letterzine published (then and now) by Tacoma, Washington, fan Robert "Cap'n Bob" Napier. That pilot issue was not quite a two-man operation: Randisi contributed an editorial and news notes (including in some cases dollar amounts of writers' contracts—Loren D. Estleman was doing especially well); Gorman surveyed half a dozen mystery editors and interviewed one of them, Michael Seidman (then of Tor), at greater length; and Ray Puechner inaugurated a "Mysteries of Publishing" column with a piece on how to find an agent.

Though the first issue gave only a slight hint of what was to come, *MDM* readers who commented in the November issue were positive and encouraging. The second issue, now grown to 24 pages, appeared with the December 1985 *MDM*. The founders now had titles: Gorman was Executive Editor, Randisi Managing Editor, and they'd been joined on the masthead by four Contributing Editors, i.e., columnists: Max Allan Collins (as tough-to-please movie critic), Ellen Nehr (on cozy mysteries to counterbalance the editors' perceived hardboiled bias), Seidman (mostly on publishing), and Warren Murphy (on whatever was annoying or amusing him at the moment). Also included were the reminiscences of private eye elder statesman William Campbell Gault; articles on Jim Thompson, cover subject Barbara Michaels (with no reference to alter ego Elizabeth Peters), and Bill Pronzini; an interview with editor Knox Burger; and Gorman's Dean Koontz profile, part of a three-page "Horror Scene" section that also included Karen Lansdale's report on the World Fantasy Convention. In the periodical's first published letter to the editor, Nehr ironically noted that the Real Men of the Private Eye Writers of America had been served quiche (!) at their Bouchercon luncheon. The magazine also had its first advertising (rates were $100 full page, $75 ¾ page, $50 half page). Clearly, the hatchling was ready to fly on its own. The second issue was the last to be distributed with *MDM*.

By the 52-page issue #3 (1986), the familiar mix of interviews, profiles, news notes, obituaries, reviews, letters, columns, and opinion pieces was established. A feature in which first novelists introduced their works would eventually be extended to veteran writers hawking their latest. Regional coverage, beginning with Barbara D'Amato on the Chicago scene and Marilyn Wallace on the West Coast, would gradually expand to include other sections of the United States and finally to international coverage, with Maxim Jakubowski reporting on the London scene. *Mystery Scene* would pick up and lay down reviewers and columnists in numbers too dizzying to keep track of.

Though ostensibly bimonthly, the periodical actually averaged about 4.4 issues per year. Because of the occasional lack of regularity, some issues carried a month and year, others only an issue number and year of copyright.

Apart from its news function *Mystery Scene* encouraged from the first a feisty and outspoken iconoclasm that was standard in the science fiction field but found only occasionally in such publications as the Mystery Writers of America's *The Third Degree* or the pioneering fanzine *The Armchair Detective.*

The early issues set the tone. Seidman's criticism of MWA in issue #2 was rebutted by Franklin Bandy in #3. In #4 (August 1986), Murphy challenged the cooking abilities of Robert B. Parker's Spenser. Randisi and Michaels crossed swords over the perceived lack of recognition to women in the Edgar Awards. Joe R. Lansdale and Barry Gifford tussled over regional stereotypes, Gorman and Estleman on the reality level of *Hill Street Blues.* In #16 (1988), Jo Ann Viceral compared Elizabeth George's heavily promoted first novel, *The Great Deliverance,* to the work of Dorothy L. Sayers, P.D. James, and Ruth Rendell; in #17, Joe R. Lansdale wrote as devastating a pan of George's highly touted effort as could be imagined; in #18, Viceral fired back, charging Lansdale with a personal attack on George; in #19 (January/February 1989), Seidman weighed in on Lansdale's side, defending his work as fair literary criticism.

Mystery Scene owed its unquenchable vitality in part to the editors' compulsive honesty. It often seemed they just couldn't bear to sweep dust under the rug—disagreements and misunderstandings were dealt with on the table, before the world. The editors admitted proofreading was sadly lacking and promised to do better. They openly discussed the practical considerations that led them to their frequent changes in content and format. (The actual page size changed only twice, to and from the tabloid newspaper format of #5 and 6.) Columnists and reviewers were obviously free to let fly with often outrageous, even embarrassing opinions. The magazine published letters (subscriber complaints, subscription cancellations, sometimes vicious denunciations of the editors and contributors) of a kind that few editors would have allowed to see print.

If the above paragraphs suggest a permanent war zone between covers, the impression is mistaken. The combativeness was tempered by the editors' enthusiasm for their fellow writers and desire to promote the whole genre. The quarrels were not between gangs competing for turf but, for the most part, disagreements within the family.

Early readers who questioned the inclusion of horror under the mystery rubric would see the nets cast even further. Kevin D. Randle began writing about the action/adventure genre in issue #3. Subsequent issues added coverage of westerns, comics, and, for a few issues beginning with #20 (March/April 1989), even science fiction.

Though the emphasis was on the current field, early issues included pieces on well-known past writers like David Goodis, Constance and Gwenyth Little, and Charles Williams. Pronzini celebrated such comparatively obscure ones as J.M. Flynn, Bryce Walton, and Robert Martin. Reminiscences by oldtimers like Gault, William R. Cox, Ryerson Johnson, and Dwight V. Swain became regular features.

The *Mystery Scene* logo extended to other publications. A single issue of *Mystery Scene Reader*, originally intended to be a quarterly, appeared in 1987 in trade paper format with tributes to the recently deceased John D. MacDonald; five short stories, including Harlan Ellison's Edgar-winner-to-be "Soft Monkey"; seven interviews; and a reprinted autobiographical piece by Todhunter Ballard. The anthology *Under the Gun: Mystery Scene Presents the Best Suspense and Mystery* (NAL, 1990), edited by Gorman, Randisi, and Martin H. Greenberg, was intended as the first in a best-of-the-year series. The concept re-emerged in *The Year's 25 Finest Crime and Mystery Stories* (Carroll & Graf, 1992), which would appear annually until replaced in 2000 by *The World's Finest Mystery and Crime Stories* (Forge). *Mystery Scene* joined Pulphouse in publishing a series of short story collections and separate publications of single short stories or pairs of stories between 1991 and 1993. Around the same time, a line of Mystery Scene paperbacks was being distributed by Carroll & Graf.

By issue #25 (March 1990), the pagination had grown to 120; the ad rates to $450 full page, $225 half page, $150 third page; and the two founders had adjusted their titles: Randisi was now listed as publisher, Gorman as editor. The masthead continued to adjust periodically. With #27 (October 1990), anthology king Greenberg, who had appeared on the masthead for the first time as an editorial consultant to Mystery Scene Books in issue #20 (March 1989), become publisher, which he would remain through #75 (2002), and the other two founding publishers. With #29 (April 1991), Gorman was again editor, Greenberg publisher, and Randisi, whose participation had gradually decreased, publisher emeritus. With issue #35 (July/August 1992), Joe Gorman became editor, with Ed disappearing from the masthead; from issue #53 (May/June 1996), Ed was Editorial Director, and Joe was Managing Editor.

In an editorial in #31 (October 1991), Ed Gorman sounded an ominous note for readers who had grown to love *Mystery Scene*'s eccentric eclecticism, reporting that consultant Scott Winnette "felt, and correctly, that *MS* wasn't so much a magazine as a grab bag of pieces that happened to interest Ed Gorman." Many readers undoubtedly muttered, "Yeah, that's why we like it." But the changes that came, primarily reducing the space devoted to genres outside the mystery, didn't affect the magazine's vitality or its position as a lightning rod for controversy.

There were, however, indications the magazine was pulling back from its free-for-all policy of publishing every letter received and every vitriolic attack. In #37 (1992), the letters column disappeared completely for an issue, and it became smaller and more sporadic thereafter. In responding to a letter in #41 (1993), Ed Gorman offered his rules of reviewing: "I will never use the magazine to criticize anybody with whom I've had a previous dispute. My opinion is just too skewed to be fair. Nor will I ever run a review that feels like a personal grudge match."

If the main things *Mystery Scene* had to offer were news, opinion, and promotion, where did fiction fit into the mix? Short stories appeared occasionally as early as John Lutz's "On Guard" in #5 (September 1986), but they were never a regular feature. Two issues after Dean Koontz's 20,000-word "Black River" in #63 (1999), undoubtedly the longest piece of fiction to appear in *Mystery Scene*, issue #65 devoted 47 pages, over half the issue, to first chapters of current mystery novels, temporarily expanding the magazine's promotional function. Issue #66 (2000) included a separate 40-page "Mystery Scene Extra" devoted entirely to first chapters. Occasional first chapters would appear in subsequent issues, but never again in such volume.

Issue #70 (2001) introduced a feature in which other writers would pay tribute to an especially prominent and significant living mystery practitioner. The first to be honored was Evan Hunter/Ed McBain; subsequent subjects included Elizabeth Peters (#71), Sue Grafton (#72), Mary Higgins Clark (#73), Lawrence Block (#74), and Joan Hess (#75). In #76, the first issue after Gorman and Greenberg passed the reins to Kate Stine and Brian Skupin, beginning a new era of *Mystery Scene*, the subject was Ed Gorman.

(Author's note: Since it was impossible to mention all the columnists, reviewers, and editors of *Mystery Scene* over its first seventeen years, and in order to avoid hurt feelings, I deliberately left out the six most important contributors apart from the founders and publisher Greenberg. So if your name doesn't appear in the piece above, you must be one of the six. If your name does appear there, my apologies.)

ON PLAGIARISM

Ed Gorman's blog, date uncertain

When I was teaching English composition at the community college level, my students may not have learned much, but one thing I did my best to impress on them was the importance of avoiding plagiarism, of which there seems to be an epidemic on the professional level recently, though more in nonfiction and scholarship than in fiction.

Plagiarism in fiction is a hard thing to pin down. Writers have always recycled old plots, Shakespeare being a prime example. In the early seventies, I reviewed a book for *Library Journal* that followed the story of Conan Doyle's *The Lost World* so closely that I didn't know whether to call the result plagiarism or homage. I'm still not sure. Roy Lewis's novel *A Fool for a Client* (1972), though quite different in setting, seemed to me to follow the plot of Patrick Quentin's *Black Widow* (1952) point for point, and I wrote to surviving Quentin collaborator Hugh Wheeler to alert him. Could it have been a coincidence? I doubted it, but even if it wasn't, was the similarity great enough to constitute plagiarism? Maybe not.

When you can compare passages side by side, you're on safer ground in charging plagiarism. As famous an author as Theodore Dreiser blatantly plagiarized the humorist George Ade, whose surprising response was that he felt honored to assist so great a novelist. There have been a few acknowledged plagiarisms in the mystery field, of one of John D. MacDonald's Travis McGee novels in a paperback original from a major publisher, of Dashiell Hammett in a 1940s novel by Raymond Marshall (a.k.a. James Hadley Chase) and the 1933 British novel *Death in the Dark* by Cecil Henderson, a direct theft of *The Maltese Falcon*.

Most of the recent plagiarism stories deal with nonfiction. Several eminent scholars have been guilty of the kind of sloppy attribution (or sometimes lack of attribution) that would have been unacceptable from my composition students—if I found them out, of course, which I'm sure I didn't some of the time. Most recent to be pinned to the wall is the famed Harvard law professor Lawrence Tribe who, according to a well-documented article by Joseph Bottum in *The Weekly Standard*, based parts of his 1985 book *God Save This Honorable Court* on Henry Abraham's 1974 book *Justices and Presidents* with no attribution. In defending Tribe's admitted "unacceptable" behavior, colleague Alan Dershowitz countered that the attack was politically motivated and that right-wing legal writers were undoubtedly guilty of similar offenses. While that is no doubt true, it is a lame response. Every child knows that two wrongs don't make a right.

Most plagiarism charges we hear about come when big money is on the line. The Harry Potter books were a target, as is M. Night Shyamalan's latest film *The Village*, which has been accused of plagiarizing the 1995 children's book *Running Out of Time* by Margaret Peterson Haddix. But what about cases where no money is on the line? Is plagiarism taken too lightly in cyberspace? Recently a writer in an online mystery fiction group pointed out that a well-known professional writer had lifted a whole paragraph virtually word for word from his website. What surprised me was not that this would happen but that the other members of the group seemed to take the theft rather lightly. Was there any money on the line here? No. Was it fodder for a lawsuit? No. But it was still plagiarism, and the offended party was due an apology and an online retraction. To my knowledge, these have not materialized.

If the public world, whether at Harvard or on the web, takes plagiarism lightly, what hope is there for those composition students of mine?

FRAGMENTS FROM
A LOST INTRODUCTION

Previously unpublished

Beginning with the first volume of The Year's 25 Finest Crime and Mystery Stories *(1992), I have contributed an annual year-in-review article to best-of anthologies edited by Ed Gorman and Martin H. Greenberg. The series has changed its name and publisher several times. The most recent version is* A Prisoner of Memory and 24 of the Year's Finest Crime and Mystery Stories *(Pegasus, 2008). Between its original incarnation at Carroll & Graf and its several-year life at Forge, where it was known as* The World's Finest Mystery and Crime Stories *for five volumes, one collection for which I wrote an introduction, covering the year 1998, fell through the cracks and has never been published, though it was long announced as forthcoming by Subterranean Press. The following are a couple of snippets from that introduction.*

English Teacher Gripes

Whatever happened to the fine arts of proof reading and copy editing? While writers commonly complain about copy editors undermining their precious prose, probably justly at least some of the time, they have never done me anything but good. But in too many recent cases, they seem to have vanished from the scene. I suspect the practice of submitting books online or on computer disk, which paradoxically makes correction both easier to accomplish and less likely to happen, hasn't helped.

In at least two recent crime novels, the phrase "just desserts" is used (without apparent irony) instead of "just deserts." Has what was once a pun (and used as such as a book title by Tim Heald in 1977, Roderic Jeffries in 1980, and Mary Daheim in 1991) now become standard usage? I've also seen more than one case where the traditional shout of approval is given as "Here, here" rather than "Hear, hear." These are easy mistakes for a writer to make, but surely someone in the editorial process should have caught the blunder and saved the writer from embarrassment. (Don't even think about a grimmer possibility: that the writer had it right to begin with and the copy editor "corrected" it.)

I'm tempted to say every time I see "just desserts" or "here, here," I experience *déjà vu* all over again, but that would be perpetuating another joke-turned-standard-usage.

Recipe for a Late-'90s Mystery Series

So many mystery books come with a collection of recipes these days, here are the ingredients for a successful series in the current market:

1 strong central character, an independent female sleuth (professional or amateur) with a first name either androgynous or out-and-out masculine sounding (recent examples: Vic, Nick, Benni, Charlie, Campbell, Micky, Sutton, Taylor, Morgan, Marti);

1 interesting occupation for the lead character (caterer, landscape gardener, teacher, librarian, cop, lawyer, private eye, reporter, forest ranger, computer programmer, firefighter, animal trainer, longshoreperson, gandy dancer);

1 continuing actual or potential love interest for the lead character, male or female depending on the lead character's sexual preference; may conveniently be a police officer—especially if the lead character isn't;

2 pages of acknowledgements per book to everyone the author is grateful to, from parents to first-grade teacher to spouse to best friend to agent to expert source who provided all the correct information and none of the wrong to copy editor who spotted "just desserts" (if you're really grateful, make it three pages; if your gratitude erodes as the series expands, reduce it to one but shrink it further at your peril);

5-6 or more genuine real-life miseries the lead character must cope with over the course of several books, including illness and injury, betrayal and divorce, sexual harassment, employment discrimination, sick or missing children and pets, post-traumatic stress syndrome, drug, tobacco, or alcohol addiction (1 full-scale tragedy may be substituted for a half dozen lesser misfortunes, but it must be a severe one—the loss of a husband or a child or a whole family, say—and it must be dwelt upon book after book);

7 or 8 regular associates (neighbors, co-workers, friends, present and former lovers) who will appear regularly in each book whether they have anything to do with the story or not;

10 or 12 full-life histories for minor characters who appear in one scene and are never seen again;

1 to 2 pages of padding for each page of forward movement.

Now, you ask, how do you blend these ingredients and in what order do you put them in the pot? Well, I know the last one is achieved by gradually stirring in the previous three, but beyond that, I'll evoke the cookbook cop-out: Do it to taste.

REVIEWERS' RATING SYSTEMS

Ed Gorman blog, date unknown

Reviewers' numerical ratings of movies or books or restaurants or whatever can serve as a handy shorthand for the consumer, but they come with inevitable problems. For example, as a lover of old whodunits from the thirties, I came across a very cheap DVD of the (no doubt) public domain film *The Death Kiss* (1933), a low-budget mystery with Bela Lugosi in his frequent post-*Dracula* role of red-herring suspect and an interesting background of a movie studio, where the star is shot to death with real bullets during filming. Looking the book up in Leonard Maltin's *2005 Movie Guide*, I was encouraged to see he'd given it a 3-star rating, so I bought one. The picture was a lot of fun. Typically of the time, there was no semblance of accurate police procedure. The acting was okay, though 1933 seemed late for the overly deliberate style, with pauses between speeches, that you often see in very early talkies. But there was some amusing dialogue and some gentle satire on the movie business. On the whole, I was happy and not at all mad at Maltin. At the same time I got a copy of *Murder by Television*, another Lugosi-as-red-herring-suspect (I assume—I've only watched half of it) from the same era. Maltin gave that one a star and a half (just north of a bomb), and it is truly awful, albeit interesting for the background. Thus, Maltin had put me onto to something worth watching and tried to warn me off something that wasn't, so I should be grateful. But still, what about that 3-star rating for *The Death Kiss*? One of my favorite films, *True Confessions* (1981), gets only 2 and a half stars in his rating system. Would Maltin really say that *The Death Kiss*, even judged in relation to other pictures of its time, was a better picture than *True Confessions*?

I doubt that he would, but of course I'm in no position to criticize somebody's use of a star system. When I took over "The Jury Box" review column in *Ellery Queen's Mystery Magazine* back in the '70s, I might not have used a star-rating system, but editor Fred Dannay suggested I do so. (Back in the early '30s, the Queen cousins had used an incredibly complicated 100-point scale to rate detective novels, so he obviously was fond of them. I guess he had a baseball fan's love of statistical measures.) So I adopted the scale previously used in *EQMM* by Anthony Boucher. It ran one to five stars. While the ratings were never explained, the attentive reader could figure out that 5 represented a classic, 4 a superior effort, 3 a good solid recommended bread-and-butter work, and as for the 2 and the 1, they never appeared, understandably since Boucher's column was called "The Best Mysteries of the Month" and he was plucking out the books he could recommend that he'd already reviewed in the *New York Times Book Review*. Boucher usually had only 3- and 4-star reviews, with the 5 coming up so rarely few readers probably realized there was a 5.

I followed the same pattern, very rarely trotting out the 5, but I did use the 2 (which essentially means some good points but some problems, too) and very rarely even the 1 (which means I don't understand why the book was ever published). Because I choose things for review I expect to like, the solid 3-star rating is the most frequent. If I were actually to read to the finish everything that comes to me (for which I would have to be a speed reader like Boucher), the 2-star rating would be the most common. Both of these ratings represent a fairly wide band, especially the 2. While I wouldn't want readers to think one 2 was absolutely equivalent to another 2, it is surely fair for the reader to conclude that in my opinion, any 3 is better than any 2 and so on up the line.

Guess what. The system isn't perfect. I'll give some examples, with names withheld to protect the guilty (i.e., me). At one point in my first stint as "Jury Box" reviewer, I was disappointed with the weak plot in an otherwise charmingly written book by one of my favorite writers, call him Writer A, and gave it a 2-star rating. Within a couple of months, a very prolific writer of paperback gothics, call her Writer B, produced a book that seemed to me unusually strong in comparison with her usual output, and I gave it 3 stars. Then I asked myself: do I really consider the best by Writer B superior to a below-par work of Writer A? Probably not.

Another factor is the first-book-read syndrome. When you read an author's work for the first time, you might tend to overrate it because it represents a fresh voice or underrate it because it irritates you in some way. I gave a 4 to the first novel I read by one of today's best known writers and 3's to books by that writer since. Was the first one I read really better than the subsequent ones? Not necessarily. I once criticized (and gave a 2 rating to) a detective novel for dragging in a science-fictional solution to the mystery, which seemed to me a cheat on the reader if not sufficiently foreshadowed. When I read later books by the same author, I knew what to expect; the mixing in of paranormal and science fictional elements didn't bother me as much; and I found myself handing out 3 ratings and even on one occasion a 4. Was that first book really inferior to the later books? Maybe not.

I once heard (or read?) a defense of his star rating system by Roger Ebert, in which he implied that the ratings were useful in comparing his opinion of a film against other films he reviewed in that particular column or that particular year but not necessarily for comparing his opinion of a film reviewed in 1990 to one in 2005. That sounds like a fair and honest way to look at it, but I don't know if I'll adopt his stance. We reviewers need to nurture that air of superiority and omniscience we've so carefully cultivated.

TRUE CONFESSIONS: NOVEL VS. FILM

The Big Book of Noir, edited by Ed Gorman, Lee Server, and Martin H. Greenberg (Carroll & Graf, 1998)

Does this dialogue sound familiar?

"I saw this great movie—"

"Yeah, but the book was better."

In one sense, a book—assuming it's a good book—almost has to be better than the movie. Novels provide depth of character and detail that is hard to duplicate in an adaptation. On the other hand, the two media are so different, comparisons are unfair. Only in relatively short, objectively written, and dialogue-driven novels that can be filmed scene-for-scene—*The Maltese Falcon*, say—can a virtual equivalent be achieved, and even then there are as many differences as similarities.

John Gregory Dunne's 1977 novel *True Confessions* is a rare example of a very good book that was made into an even better film. Scripted by Dunne and wife Joan Didion and directed by Ulu Grosbard, the screen version was released in 1981 to decidedly mixed reviews. In an unusually strong year—the Oscar nominees for best picture were *Reds, Chariots of Fire, Raiders of the Lost Ark, On Golden Pond,* and *Atlantic City*—it got no awards attention and fared only modestly at the box office. Still, to some observers it is one of the great films of the '80s, a classic of latter day film noir that provides almost a textbook of effective print-to-film adaptation. Comparing the film to the novel, I didn't so much feel regret at what had to be left out as marvel at how what was left was conveyed more briefly and pointedly.

Some writers hate the idea of trying to adapt their own work for the screen, perhaps for good reasons. In most cases, it may be better for the adaptor not to be too close to the original source material. But the presence of the original author as one of the co-adaptors is one key to the artistic success of *True Confessions*—obviously what Dunne wanted to say about L.A. and Catholic Church politics didn't change, so the two versions are thematically of a piece. Also, when favorite snippets of dialogue and character points didn't work where they appeared in the original novel, Dunne and Didion were able to use them in other contexts.

Why is the story so firmly in the noir/dark suspense tradition? With one exception, every single character, whether crook or cop or whore or priest, is corrupt. This does not mean the characters are unsympathetic—certainly both Spellacy brothers, cop Tom and priest Des, especially in the film, are very believably human and likeable. The single exception to the corruption in both versions is Monsignor Seamus Fargo, a crotchety old priest who plays irritating conscience for the other Catholic clergy. He tells Des, "You have a mind like an abacus. You do everything, in fact, but feel. And it's the unfeeling ones that bring the Church into disrepute."

The present-day chapters that begin and end *True Confessions* are narrated in the first person by retired L.A. cop Tom Spellacy, with the main part of the book set in the mid-forties told by an omniscient third-person narrator. As the novel opens, Tom is having lunch with his old partner Frank Crotty. The pair reflect on the changes in the city—for one thing their old colleague, black cop Lorenzo Jones, is now the Mayor. (Jones, based on long-time L.A. Mayor Thomas Bradley, does not appear in the film.) The chapter flashes back to memories of finding the body of Lois Fazenda, dubbed in the papers "The Virgin Tramp," a nickname Tom comes up with himself to get irritating *Herald-Express* reporter Howard Terkel off his back. Fazenda, a young woman whose oddly bloodless body is found in two pieces on a vacant lot, is clearly based on the Black Dahlia, a notorious '40s murder case.

Tom and brother Des grew up in the Boyle Heights section of Los Angeles, a tough Irish Catholic enclave at the time. Tom, the elder, had been a Navy boxer who joined the police force following a failed pro career. He also once worked as a car thief for a finance company, demonstrating the thin dividing line that sometimes separates law enforcers and law breakers. His wife, Mary Margaret, who talks to an imaginary saint, Saint Barnabas of Luca, is in a state mental institution in Camarillo. Their daughter Moira, who weighed 161 pounds at age 13, became a nun. They also have a son Kev, who is in the religious supply business and has both a wife and a girlfriend.

Monsignor Desmond Spellacy, the younger brother, is pastor of Saint Mary's of the Desert in Twenty-nine Palms in the present-day story. He has been there for 28 years. During the period of the novel's main action, he was chancellor of the archdiocese, a mover and shaker in the community, right hand man to Hugh Cardinal Danaher, "a combination lightning rod, hatchet man, and accountant." His tactlessness as a chancellor causes pastors to complain about how much time he spent "in country-club locker rooms buttering up the fat cats of the archdiocese." During World War II, he had gained fame (and star spot on a War Bond tour) as the Parachuting Padre.

The Cardinal and the Monsignor had real-life models. According to a June 22, 1997, Los Angeles *Times* review of Msgr. Francis J. Weber's *His Eminence of Los Angeles* by California State Librarian Kevin Starr, Danaher is a "thinly disguised" version of James Francis Cardinal McIntyre, "with McIntyre's chancellor and priest-of-all-work, Msgr. Benjamin G. Hawkes appearing as Msgr Spellacy..., whose priestly vocation had long been lost in his rise up the ecclesiastical ladder and in his toadying to the wealthy and the prominent."

The novel is more of a procedural than the film—a police procedural, with departmental politics a prominent feature, and a Catholic Church procedural, with archdiocese politics closely examined. As the police try to solve the Virgin Tramp case, the Church's problem is what to do about Jack Amsterdam, "[c]hief construction contractor for the archdiocese and pillar of the community," whose shady business practices and dubious associations are beginning to make him an embarrassment, leading to a decision to phase him out.

Tom also has an Amsterdam connection. Before coming to the Robbery-Homicide division, Tom had been a member of Wilshire Vice, where he was the bagman for Amsterdam's prostitution sideline, collecting payoffs in exchange for laying off the houses. When Tom shot and wounded a robber who held him up while he was sitting in a parked car registered to Brenda Samuels, a madame working for Amsterdam, his recovered wallet proved to have $1100 in it. The resultant cover-up brought a jail sentence for Brenda but a transfer for Tom. The novel suggests Des was involved in covering Tom's part, but Tom is uncertain Des was aware of Amsterdam's involvement.

In both the book and film versions, Tom eventually solves the Virgin Tramp murder, though the solutions are entirely different. Though Amsterdam is not the murderer, there is an Amsterdam *connection*, real in the film, manufactured in the novel. Out of his hatred for Amsterdam, who has brought on Brenda's suicide, Tom is determined to charge the builder for the crime, satisfied to ruin him even if he knows the charges can't stick. In doing so, he brings multiple scandals to light—though not involved in the crime, Des had known the girl—and effectively ruins his brother's ecclesiastical career.

It's the same story with the same ending, but the different ways of getting there on the page and on the screen are fascinating. That the film is finally a more effective telling of the story is due not just to the skill of the screenwriters and director Grosbard but to the extraordinary cast that was assembled. Robert DeNiro and Robert Duvall, arguably the best and most versatile screen actors of their generation, play Des and Tom respectively. Charles Durning plays Jack Amsterdam, a somewhat shadowy figure in the novel, who appears in many more scenes and is a much more striking and fully developed figure in the film. Kenneth McMillan as Tom's partner, Frank Crotty; Cyril Cusack as the somewhat ruthless and cynical Cardinal; Burgess Meredith as the non-corrupt Monsignor Fargo; Ed Flanders as slick lawyer Dan Campion; and Rose Gregorio as Brenda are all perfect choices.

All of the detail about Tom's family life in the book's prologue is jettisoned in the film, with the action beginning with him driving to the desert church, summoned there by Des. The dialogue at the church is truncated considerably, but Des's anecdote about the daughter of a parishioner leaving the nunnery to become a professional bowler is reproduced in the film almost word for word. In an example of reusing favorite lines in different contexts, Des of the film refers to the Irish having more hemorrhoids than other people—in the novel, another character credits *Mexicans* with having more hemorrhoids. Both versions segue from past to present with Des's revelation to Tom that he is terminally ill.

The screenwriters' choices reflect not just the need to compress but to provide interesting visuals. The funeral scene of the novel's second chapter becomes a much more pictorially interesting wedding. Film scenes of the Cardinal attending a Mexican fiesta, feeling "such a fool" while wearing a huge sombrero, and playing croquet are not in the novel. The Virgin Tramp's tattoo, on her lower abdomen in the book, is moved to her hip in the film so that it can be used as a visual clue without incurring an X rating. The stag film in which the tattoo appears leads to the movie's solution, not necessarily more ingenious or plausible than the book's but more interesting in motion picture terms.

Though the theme and the basic story line remain the same, some of the elements are interestingly reshuffled. In the novel, there are at least three women in Tom's life—in the film, there is only Brenda. The wife of the screen Tom is not hospitalized in

Camarillo but has simply left him, taking along her tuna casserole recipe ("her one dish!"). The mental failings of Tom's wife Mary Margaret in the book are attributed to his elderly mother in the film. The "let's-play-carnival" joke ("You sit on my face and I try to guess your weight") comes from a crank caller to the police in the book, from a prostitute in Brenda's employ in the film. A crack about mistrusting a priest whose eyes twinkle is made by Monsignor Fargo in the film but by the Cardinal *about* Fargo (whose eyes never twinkle) in the novel. The name Leland K. Standard is used in both versions, but the characters are entirely different. The banquet that provides an important scene late in both versions is Monsignor Fargo's retirement party in the book, the awarding of Catholic Layman of the Year to Jack Amsterdam in the film. The latter scene and the opening wedding of Amsterdam's daughter in the film show how the character's role was wisely expanded for the film, resulting in Durning's memorable performance—some of the dialogue about the pregnant bride comes from a scene much later in the book about the daughter of lawyer Dan Campion.

While most scenes from the book are shortened for the film, on at least one occasion the opposite happens: an argument at the crime scene over how many stretchers are needed for a body that has been cut in half, only a passing allusion in the book, becomes a memorable comic scene in the film.

On repeated viewings, the film version seems a virtually perfect piece of storytelling, aided by the focus and compression of a careful and faithful adaptation. The more rambling novel is a splendid work itself, though marred by two anachronisms. Des could not have won an exacta at Del Mar, since that exotic form of wagering was not available at California race tracks in the '40s. While only racing buffs might have noticed that gaffe, many more surely would do a double-take at Tom's appearance on a radio call-in talk show, complete with seven-second delay, a genre and a technology that did not exist in '40s radio.

In either version, *True Confessions* is a remarkable work of crime fiction, with an intriguing plot, deeply involving characters, and insights into the workings of two disparate institutions: the police and the Catholic Church. Both reward the consumer with a memorable experience. But if you had to choose only one of them, I'd head for the video store.

DON'T THRILL ME

(review of *Red Cat* by Peter Spiegelman, Knopf, 2007;
The War Against Miss Winter by Kathryn Miller Haines, Harper,
2007; *Chain of Evidence* by Garry Disher, Soho, 2007)

The Weekly Standard, September 10, 2007

Thriller is the label-de-jour for commercial crime fiction, favored over mystery or novel of suspense. There is absolutely nothing new in the novels being advanced as thrillers, though some
would have you believe otherwise. Promotional copy for a Manhattan bookstore event during the ThrillerFest convention in July
included the following absurdity: "In the wake of the runaway
success of such titles as *The DaVinci Code*, a new genre of popular fiction was embraced by millions of Americans." In fact, Dan
Brown's novel works best as an old-fashioned clued detective
puzzle, albeit an unusually badly written one.

Far from being a new genre, thrillers can trace their lineage at
least as far as 19th-century dime novels, which offered fast pace,
physical action, danger, pursuit, and clear good-guy-bad-guy de-
marcations. In the 20th century, the term was used in Britain to
denote the whole broad field of crime fiction, but more pointedly,
it was usually applied to intrigue and espionage fiction and was
given added literary credibility by writers like Eric Ambler and
John Le Carré. The rather vague definition of thriller today has
been expanded to include serial killer novels, some police procedural and private eye sagas, romantic suspense, tales of medical
menace and legal maneuvering, and supernatural horror.

The only 21st-Century thriller elements that could be counted
as remotely innovative are the least salutary ones: increasingly
higher page counts, cruelly severe and repeated trauma and soap-
opera travails visited on series characters, increasingly explicit
violence, cinematically choreographed action scenes, and hyped-
up suspense designed to artificially elevate reader anxiety. All the
worthwhile elements contained in contemporary thrillers have
been present in crime or espionage or detective fiction for a very
long time with varying degrees of emphasis.

Many excellent writers produce books that are called thrillers
by publishers or critics. But the celebration of the thriller and its
implicit denigration of the mystery, though essentially a matter of

commercial labeling, should concern anyone who takes crime fiction seriously as a literary genre. Very few of the classics of the
past emphasize the kind of "thrills" that seem to activate the present market. Their most important attributes always lay elsewhere:
in the evocation of time and place, in the illumination of character
and society, in the challenge of problem solving, in the sheer joy
of language, in all the other literary values that characterize good
fiction whatever the genre. To put it even more baldly, the whole
idea of thriller centrality serves to trivialize crime fiction, whether
hard, uncompromising mean-streets noir or sophisticated intellectual puzzle.

In 2004, some thriller writers who felt their vital genre needed
differentiating from the tired old mystery, including of course a
new set of annual awards, formed the International Thriller Writers, Inc. Their ranks include many talented and distinguished writers, and the effort to advance the careers of their members is laudable. But the organization put their commitment to quality in
doubt when, out of all the distinguished veteran writers they could
have given lifetime achievement awards, they chose two of the
most literarily undistinguished denizens of the bestseller lists,
writers who, for all their page-turning prowess, studious research,
and other sterling qualities, turn out numbingly flavorless prose
and dialogue: Clive Cussler and James Patterson.

Three recent books—a private eye novel, an amateur-detective
historical, and a police procedural set in Australia—demonstrate
the attributes of first-rate mystery fiction that are sometimes overlooked in today's rush for thrills.

Peter Spiegelman's *Red Cat* is the third novel about New York
private detective John March. His brother and client David, so
abrasive and annoying that only ties of blood could explain March
taking his case, is being stalked by a woman he knows only as
Wren, a meant-to-be-casual sex partner he met online. March is an
old-style private eye in a present-day setting. He uses the Internet
as a prime investigative tool, and the plot concerns a sick variation
on the video art that has so many contemporary galleries in its
thrall.

Spiegelman demands to be read for the same qualities that
marked his hardboiled predecessors. In questioning a witness,
March paraphrases a line from Dashiell Hammett's *The Maltese
Falcon*: "I wasn't sure if it was my story he believed, or my fifty
dollars." Like Raymond Chandler and Ross Macdonald, he excels
at descriptions of people, weather, rooms, and atmosphere, includ-

ing a strong evocation of Manhattan in a snowstorm. Lines of metaphorical prose establish the scene and the character's frame of mind simultaneously: "An icy wind was blowing off the East River and it bullied me along in its rush to Jersey." "A jaundiced sunset was seeping through the clouds as I drove into Tarrytown, and it tinted the Hudson in the colors of a faded bruise."

March's interaction with lawyers and cops doing their jobs rings true. The unlikelihood and inadvisability of a p.i. treading on police turf to investigate murder is motivated reasonably. The characters come to life, and the mystery is genuinely puzzling and satisfactorily resolved. The only thing missing is the fairly placed clues that Hammett or Macdonald would have provided to enable the canny reader to anticipate the surprise solution. Among the attributes that make Spiegelman worth recommending—style, characters, sense of time and place, specialized background, procedural details, mystery—thrills are well down the list.

Some crime novels show the reader how things work in a particular line of business or profession; how people live in another time or place. Serving both these informative functions is Kathryn Miller Haynes's first novel *The War Against Miss Winter*, which in current mystery parlance must be designated a cozy. After all, it has a cat for a character (albeit an unpleasant one), and it is told by a wisecracking female narrator whose romantic conflicts and longings are important to the narrative. In 1943 New York, unemployed actress Rosie Winter is working as a receptionist for a private eye. The discovery of her boss hanging in the office closet begins her involvement in a tantalizing mystery involving the rumored lost play of an admired experimental playwright. In order to stay a resident of a women's theatrical boarding house, recalling the setting of George S. Kaufman and Edna Ferber's play *Stage Door*, Rosie must get an acting job. She and her now-soldier boyfriend parted on bad terms, and various possible (if mostly unlikely) substitute romantic interests present themselves.

It may be that the most accurate period fiction takes place within the last half to three quarters of a century before it is written, a time within memory of (if not the author) living people: close enough to understand the mores and attitudes, easier to get the language and cultural details right (though more likely to be called out if you get them wrong), a sense of the reality without rose-colored-glasses nostalgia or sentimentality, a better chance at capturing how people talked, thought, and lived with a few years of perspective. Haines is nearly note perfect most of the way in capturing the home-front mood and lifestyle, but trips up on pronouns that are politically correct by current standards but off base historically. No proper writer of that time would have written "a participant places *their* ego" rather than "*his* ego," and I doubt a theatrical woman of the time would have said, "you don't drag an actor through hell without *her* ass getting singed." (All italics mine.)

Still, the prose is lively, the characters well drawn, and despite the general unbelievability of the plot and its payoff, the novel should have no trouble drawing readers to its projected sequel. The brief segments trying to generate thriller-type suspense are disposably perfunctory.

Australian Garry Disher's *Chain of Evidence* begins with a situation more in the thriller line than either of the novels above: a ten-year-old girl is abducted by the operator of a fake children's modeling agency scam. What one foresees—alternating chapters from the viewpoint of the villainous captor, the child in jeopardy, the worried parents, and the law—happily does not materialize. What we have instead is a Down Under equivalent of Ed McBain's 87th Precinct, with several cops, various in their personalities and relationships, working on numerous cases, some related but most not.

Male/female police teams are almost de rigueur in current procedural fiction, with real or potential sexual tension an optional add-on. Here the two leads are separated by circumstance but deal with the novel's two principal cases. In Waterloo on the Mornington Peninsula, Sergeant Ellen Destry is holding the fort for her boss, Inspector Hal Challis, who has traveled to his South Australia home to spend a month with his dying father. While Destry spearheads the investigation of the abduction, Challis unofficially looks into his brother-in-law's unsolved disappearance of five years before. Based on the back story provided, particularly regarding Challis's late wife, both are apparently among those series characters with excessively eventful and harrowing personal lives. Other cop activities touched on include a detective training course, the dubious police shooting of a career burglar, and the breaking in of a new private forensics lab. Disher is clearly an expert at this sort of book, and the distinctive setting is an added benefit.

These are three very good crime novels of three diverse types. Though they could have gone in the direction of elongated action scenes and overwrought anxiety generation, they are better books for choosing another direction.

SECTION FOUR

TRUE CRIME
REVISITED

FORENSIC FAILURE

(review of *Portrait of a Killer: Jack the Ripper Case Closed*
by Patricia Cornwell, Putnam, 2002)

The Weekly Standard, December 9, 2002

Trying to smoke out Jack the Ripper, who slaughtered at least five prostitutes in the Whitechapel District of London in 1888, has degenerated into a hobbyist pursuit, like bird watching or crossword puzzles or rotisserie football, and best-selling crime novelist Patricia Cornwell doesn't like it. In an interview promoting her book on the case, *Portrait of a Killer*, Cornwell says, "These were not cute little mysteries to be transformed into parlor games, or movies, or the subject of conventions of mystery buffs, but rather a series of horrible crimes that no one should get away with, even after death." She also deplores the posthumous character assassination of wrongly accused Ripper suspects: "I don't think you should ever theorize about someone being a criminal just because they're dead and you can get away with it. That's a terrible thing."

Cornwell's objections are well taken. Too often in ostensibly factual treatments of the Ripper case, the author picks a suspect (often outrageously unlikely and preferably famous—Lewis Carroll is an extreme example) and looks for evidence in support of the theory, ignoring evidence against. Writers who admit they are writing fiction can take even wilder flights of fancy, accusing everyone from Sherlock Holmes to Rasputin. The more honest nonfictional accounts consider the pros and cons of many suspects and usually conclude we will never know for sure.

Cornwell, though, is positive she has cracked the case once and for all. Unfortunately, her arrogant expressions of certainty despite the absence of compelling evidence put her in the same category as those reputation-destroying games players she holds in such contempt. Fans of her novels will loyally buy her book, and some of them will no doubt be convinced she is right. Anyone with concern for the rules of evidence will not be fooled.

Judging by the size of her name on the dustjacket, Cornwell may be the first commentator on the case to be bigger than Jack the Ripper. The Whitechapel killer has been a durable commercial commodity, the subject of websites, fanzines, motion pictures, television documentaries, and a stream of articles and book-length studies. Why does he (probably not she, though a "Jill the Ripper" theory has been floated) retain such a fascination well over a century after his crimes?

First, there's that chillingly colorful name, whether invented by the killer himself or an impostor. That Jack was never identified or caught is an indispensable factor. The visuals are sure fire: the image of a menacing figure creeping through the pea soup London fog, blade in hand. Then there's the more respectable sociological angle: the spotlight the killings put on the underside of hypocritical Victorian society. The cult of Jack was jumpstarted by the relative uniqueness of the crimes in their time and place. Serial murder, though not unknown, did not seem epidemic as it does today. Investigative methods in 19th-Century Britain were unlikely to connect a series of crimes unless (like the Ripper murders) they were confined to a relatively small area and had startling similarities in modus operandi.

Some of the Ripper suspects are known for nothing else, notably suicidal barrister Montague John Druitt, accused by Tom Cullen in *Autumn of Terror* (1965), and Russian agent Peduchenko, the candidate of Donald McCormick in *The Identity of Jack the Ripper* (1970). Of candidates known for other endeavors, the most popular, because of highest station, was Prince Albert Victor, Duke of Clarence, known as Prince Eddy. The rickety case against Queen Victoria's gormless grandson was first advanced in veiled and cautious fashion in a 1970 magazine article by the elderly Dr. Thomas Stowell, who died shortly after publication and whose notes were burned by his survivors. Frank Spiering's *Prince Jack* (1978) unconvincingly embroiders on Stowell's case. In *Clarence: Was He Jack the Ripper?* (1972), Michael Harrison answers in the negative and offers an entertaining but unpersuasive alternative: James Kenneth Stephen, the Prince's tutor, a cousin of Virginia Woolf, and a writer of misogynistic verse. David Abramsen's *Murder and Madness* (1992) posits a Leopold-and-Loeb-ish collaboration of Clarence and Stephen. The ostensible author of *The Diary of Jack the Ripper* (1993), a probable forgery, was James Maybrick, alleged victim of arsenic poisoning at the hands of his wife Florence in another notorious British murder case.

The most persistent theory was propounded by Stephen Knight in *Jack the Ripper: The Final Solution* (1976) and recycled fictionally in the Sherlock Holmes film *Murder by Decree* (1979) and Anne Perry's novel *The Whitechapel Conspiracy* (2001): an elaborate plot of Dr. William Gull, the Royal physician, other

Freemasons in the highest ranks of the British government, and even Queen Victoria herself to cover up Prince Eddy's secret marriage to a Roman Catholic. Among Knight's accused conspirators is British impressionist artist Walter Richard Sickert (1860-1942), a one-time assistant to James McNeill Whistler. Knight's argument is effectively presented and convincing on its face, but according to Ripper specialist Donald Rumbelow in *Jack the Ripper: The Complete Casebook* (1988), an independent look at Knight's evidence reveals enough extreme selectivity and distortion to discredit his theory.

Patricia Cornwell was introduced to the Jack the Ripper case while doing research in Great Britain for a new novel about her forensic pathologist detective Kay Scarpetta. Cornwell writes that as of May 2001, she "had never read a Ripper book in [her] life..., knew nothing about his homicides..., did not know his victims were prostitutes or how they died." However, by December 6, she was telling ABC *Frontline*'s Diane Sawyer she would stake her reputation on the claim that Walter Sickert was the Whitechapel killer. Cornwell reportedly spent millions of her own dollars pursuing the investigation, buying and sometimes destroying the suspect's paintings to the horror of the British art world, and sponsoring DNA analysis of old documents. Many Ripperologists have devoted decades of study to the mystery without claiming to have solved it, but a scant eighteen months after her introduction to the case, Cornwell's brief against Sickert has been published.

A Scotland Yard detective to whom Cornwell presented her evidence told her, "If we didn't get any more evidence than what we've now got,...we'd be happy to put the case before the crown prosecutor." Perhaps the detective was jollying a famous writer along. An obsequious review in *Publisher's Weekly* quoted on Amazon.com says, "Compassionate, intense, superbly argued, fluidly written and impossible to put down, this is the finest and most important true-crime book to date of the 21st century." Most of Amazon's volunteer reviewers are less gullible. It doesn't take a barrister or a Ripper expert, only a careful reader, to see that Cornwell's case against Sickert is all smoke and mirrors.

At no point does Cornwell offer any real evidence directly or even circumstantially linking Sickert to the Ripper murders. Instead, she devotes her energies to connecting Sickert to the supposed Ripper letters, of which hundreds were received by police and press. Some of the Ripper letters were found to have used artists' materials of the kind Sickert would have employed and to have watermarks similar to stationery used by Sickert. Likewise, some of the doodles with which Sickert decorated his own letters were similar to doodles on the alleged Ripper letters, as were some of the expressions used. (Cornwell believes the "Ha! Ha!" that recurs in Ripper letters is an Americanism Sickert picked up from his mentor Whistler.)

For all its trumpeting in publicity, the DNA evidence is admittedly inconclusive. "The best result," writes Cornwell, "came from a Ripper letter that yielded a single-donor mitochondrial DNA sequence, specific enough to eliminate 99% of the population as the person who licked and touched the adhesive backing of that stamp. This same DNA sequence profile turned up as a component of another Ripper letter, and two Walter Sickert letters." This sounds impressive at first, but diminishes on closer examination. For one thing, it does not take into account contamination by all the persons who might have handled the various letters in the century since they were written, or the possibility that Sickert did not lick his own stamps. Research continues, we are assured, but book deadlines do not wait on science.

Even one who finds these tenuous associations connecting Sickert to the Ripper letters convincing must follow Cornwell in a second mighty leap to the conclusion that the Ripper actually wrote the letters. Most writers on the case, in common with the police of the time, believe the Ripper letters were all or nearly all hoaxes. Sickert was a prolific author of articles on art and a compulsive writer of letters to the editor. It is possible (though hardly proven) he could have written some hoax Ripper letters, but that is a long stretch from concluding that he committed the Ripper murders.

Cornwell reports that she initially agreed with the conventional wisdom that the Ripper letters were fakes. She writes, "However, during my intensive research of Sickert and the way he expressed himself—and the way the Ripper expressed himself in so many of his alleged letters—my opinion changed. I now believe that the majority of the letters were written by the murderer." This is circular reasoning. The implication that she has somewhere presented other evidence Sickert was the Ripper is not borne out anywhere in the book.

Cornwell believes Sickert, who underwent a series of operations for a fistula in childhood, was genitally disfigured and that an inability to have sexual relations fueled a hatred of women. Her backing for this speculation is shaky, and according to some accounts, Sickert, though his three marriages were childless, had numerous illegitimate offspring. In making her point, Cornwell commits a textbook example of a reasoning fallacy that is unfortunately losing its meaning through popular misuse, begging the question, i.e., stating in argument as a fact the very contention which has to be proven, or in this case, using one unproven assertion to support another unproven assertion: "The lack of seminal fluid in the Ripper lust-murders is consistent with the supposition that Sickert was incapable of sex."

Cornwell includes much interesting if tangential information on British criminal justice history, contrasting the methods of British police in the 1880s with forensic detection as now practiced in the United States. The underlying theme is that Sickert would have been caught if modern scientific methods had been available and utilized. More begging the question. The Ripper might have been caught, true, but where is the proof that Sickert was the Ripper?

Cornwell notes that some of Sickert's paintings "bear a chilling resemblance to mortuary and scene photographs of Jack the Ripper's victims." The examples among Cornwell's illustrations do not bear this out as dramatically as she suggests, but even if the point is conceded, it proves nothing. Certainly Sickert had a fascination with the Ripper crimes and the sordid world in which they took place, but it is not necessary to believe he painted from a first-hand memory of the scene. He often painted from photographs, and photographs of the victims could have been available to him. Cornwell is never able to demonstrate that clincher of guilt in detective fiction: that Sickert had knowledge of the crimes that only the Ripper could have.

In her effort to put Sickert in as damning a light as possible, Cornwell asserts that as a teenager he "stalked" Ellen Terry and Henry Irving. The lack of notes prevents the reader from tracing where she got this idea, and despite loaded language that cries for more detail, she never expands on the accusation.

The most extensive website devoted to the Whitechapel killer, "Casebook: Jack the Ripper" (www.casebook.org), includes an excellent detailed analysis of Cornwell's central claims by a student of the case who convincingly refutes nearly all of them. Stephen P. Ryder's "Patricia Cornwell and Walter Sickert: A Primer," after exposing all of her inaccuracies, may be too generous in lauding Cornwell's efforts, including the identification of another possible Ripper hoaxer. A writer who is so dogmatic in making her accusation, after deploring earlier writers who made their cases on no more tenuous evidence, should not be let off the hook so easily.

At best, Sickert is an intriguing possible (albeit unlikely) suspect, and for all of Cornwell's authorial shell-and-pea, the case is emphatically not closed. In one interview Cornwell expresses the horror she would feel if anyone proved her wrong. She's probably safe. It's unlikely anyone at this late date can prove that Walter Sickert was not Jack the Ripper, or that anyone else was. But the burden of proof rests with the prosecution, not the defense. Stephen Knight presented a prima facie case that required a rebuttal from other writers to show its inadequacy. In contrast, if Cornwell's case went to court, the judge would dismiss it as without merit at the end of the prosecutor's evidence, sparing the defense the need to call any witnesses.

Cornwell's argument can be boiled down to a sentence: Walter Sickert was Jack the Ripper because I say so.

D𝘼DDY DID IT

(review of *The Black Dahlia Avenger: A Genius for Murder*
by Steve Hodel, Arcade, 2003)

The Weekly Standard, August 18, 2003

On January 15, 1947, the mutilated body of a young woman, neatly cut in half and drained of blood, was found in a Los Angeles vacant lot. She was identified as Elizabeth Short, a 22-year-old beauty from Massachusetts known to acquaintances as the Black Dahlia. Her murder would become the LAPD's most notorious unsolved case, and now a retired Los Angeles police detective named Steve Hodel believes he has cracked it: *His own father*, he concludes, was the Black Dahlia killer.

That may be true. Dr. George Hill Hodel may have been the murderer. But there's something odd whenever sons go hunting for evidence with which to attack their fathers, and in the course of writing *Black Dahlia Avenger*, he has handed hostile critics too many clubs with which to beat him.

Such hostile critics abound, of course, for every crime writer in the world has a theory about what happened in 1947. Beth Short, who had come to Hollywood with the customary dreams of show business success, was friendly and attractive. She enjoyed a good time, and she often lied or embroidered the truth, inventing love affairs and even a marriage to a pilot killed in action. Her aura of mystery, her black hair, and her preference for black clothing combined with the title of a current movie (*The Blue Dahlia*, a film noir classic written by Raymond Chandler) inspired her memorable nickname. With a beautiful young victim, weird circumstances, and that evocative ready-made tag, the murder became a media sensation, fueling the circulation wars of Los Angeles's then-numerous dailies. The aggressive reporters and the police competed for leads, depending on each other for vital information.

The murder of Elizabeth Short has joined Jack the Ripper, Lizzie Borden, the Princes in the Tower, and a few other historical mysteries as catnip to writers of fact and fiction. At least three major crime novels have been based on the case: John Gregory Dunne's highly fictionalized *True Confessions* (1977), James Ellroy's *The Black Dahlia* (1987), and Max Allan Collins's *Angel in*

Black (2001), the last two using real names and sticking closer to the documented facts. The theories advanced range from the plausible to the wildly fanciful. The most off-the-wall suspect to date is Orson Welles, accused by Mary Pacios in the nonfictional *Childhood Shadows: The Hidden Story of the Black Dahlia Murder* (1999).

The best-regarded book-length account of the case has been *Severed* (1994; revised ed. 1998) by true-crime specialist John Gilmore. The prime benefit of the book is its portrait of the victim, including extensive material on her early life. Its main drawback is that Gilmore asks the reader to take his word for too much of his information. His account is based primarily on personal interviews, including those with his declared suspect, Jack Anderson Wilson a.k.a. Grover Loving, Jr. a.k.a. Arnold Smith, who was burned to death in a 1982 hotel fire before he could be interviewed by the police. Though Gilmore's solution has many advocates, it is not completely convincing.

In *Black Dahlia Avenger*, Steve Hodel, who retired from the LAPD in 1986, has written an intensely readable account of the case. His literary knack should be no surprise, since he came from a family of writers. His mother wrote film and radio scripts and was the first wife of writer-director John Huston. His older brother, Los Angeles broadcaster Michael Hodel, wrote mystery and science fiction. And his father Dr. George Hill Hodel (1907-1999) counted among his accomplishments a teenage stint as a newspaper crime reporter with a knack for lurid prose.

The elder Hodel, a wealthy and socially prominent Los Angeles physician at the time of the Dahlia murder, was a child piano prodigy, a radio broadcaster, and a photographer, as well as a surgeon and psychiatrist. George Hodel, several times married and a frequent host of wild parties, clearly had a sinister side in contrast to his apparent respectability. Two years after the Dahlia murder, his teenage daughter Tamar, Steve's half sister, accused Dr. Hodel of incest. Though acquitted in a highly publicized trial, he fled the United States, leaving his family behind, to spend most of his remaining years in Asia as a successful marketing consultant. Though Dr. Hodel was never an easy man or a particularly good father, his often-estranged son felt enough filial love to reestablish their relationship in his last years.

After Dr. Hodel's death, a pair of photos Steve Hodel found in his father's album piqued his curiosity. Believing the young woman pictured was Elizabeth Short, he began to research the

Dahlia case, without access to police files but using newspaper accounts and personal contacts. His investigation led him to conclude that his father was not only the murderer of Elizabeth Short but a serial killer of several Los Angeles women in the 1940s. Furthermore, he connects his father's alleged partner in crime, Fred Sexton, with several other murders committed after Dr. Hodel left the country, including the 1958 killing of Geneva Hilliker Ellroy, mother of novelist James.

Serial killers were not as closely studied nor as well understood in the 1940s as they are today, and the lack of cooperation among law enforcement agencies made the connections between their crimes less likely to be detected. Still, police of the time believed the same killer might have been responsible for several slayings of young women, including the Black Dahlia. Finally, and somewhat inexplicably, the LAPD adopted the official position that the killing was an isolated crime.

As a police detective, Hodel knows how to build a case. Much of the circumstantial evidence he gathers is persuasive, especially the connection, bolstered by support from a graphology expert, between hand-printed messages to the police and press, ostensibly from the Black Dahlia killer, and his father's own life-long hand-printing style. Some of them were signed "Black Dahlia Avenger" or with the abbreviation "B.D.A." Like the Jack the Ripper letters, which they often resembled, these might have been hoaxes. But a message in the same style of printing, including the letters B.D., was found written in lipstick on the body of a subsequent female murder victim, Jeanne French, whose nude and mutilated body was found, in another vacant lot, on February 10, 1947.

According to Steve Hodel, the achievements of Chief William Parker and Chief of Detectives Thad Brown in turning the tarnished and corrupt LAPD into the exemplary big-city force celebrated on the radio and television program *Dragnet* were real—but on the way to that goal, they were party to one of the most infamous cover-ups in law enforcement history. Hodel contends that his father was known by Los Angeles police to be the Black Dahlia killer but escaped justice because he knew too much about local vice, including an abortion clinic run by two LAPD detectives, and police connections to organized crime.

Steve Hodel has made a solid prima facie case against his father, one that gets a stamp of approval from Los Angeles County's Head Deputy District Attorney Stephen Kay, quoted summarizing the evidence in a ten-page memo. Information revealed since the

publication of Hodel's book supports the claim that his father was
a prime Black Dahlia suspect. Los Angeles *Times* columnist Steve
Lopez quotes the following statement by Dr. Hodel from wiretaps
of his phone: "Supposin' I did kill the Black Dahlia. They couldn't
prove it now. They can't talk to my secretary, because she's dead."

But what about those clubs Hodel handed his critics?

The first of them was unavoidable. In accusing a parent of the
crime, Hodel joins a small and bizarre sub-genre already occupied
by the generally derided *Daddy Was the Black Dahlia Killer*
(1995), in which Janice Knowlton, assisted by writing pro Mike
Newton, accused her father of the crime based on repressed memory. Deservedly or not, some of the cynical ridicule vented on
Knowlton has spilled over onto Hodel.

Admittedly, the spectacle of a son pinning such heinous
crimes on his own father, who is both beyond earthly justice and
unable to defend himself, invites questions of morbid psychology,
familial disloyalty, exploitation, insensitivity, and greed. Many
readers will ask themselves if they could posthumously accuse a
close family member in the same situation. But a police detective's perspective is not the average person's. A murder investigator comes to identify with the victim, becoming her primary advocate. Hodel's respectful attitude to Elizabeth Short, seen in his refusal to depict her as a prostitute or to reproduce graphic post-
mortem photos, underlines his role as victim's surrogate, as does
his disgust at Will Fowler's trivializing of a torture murder as "an
unopened present" and "a wondrous thing" in his 1991 memoir
Reporters. In accusing his father, Steve Hodel is also salvaging the
reputation of his half-sister, who at the time of the incest trial was
excoriated by Dr. Hodel as a vicious pathological liar, a charge
believed even by her own family. Indeed, Tamar Hodel's apparently outrageous witness-stand statement that her father killed the
Black Dahlia was a factor in the jury's disbelief.

Hodel is more to blame for the second critical club. The opening chapter follows the thoughts of the victim, an effective dramatic device in fiction but a bad sign in a factual account. Fortunately, Hodel never does this again, approaching the case in the
fact-based fashion one would expect of a veteran police detective.
Though his penultimate chapter advances a possible timeline leading to the murder of Elizabeth Short, he draws a clear distinction
between fact and conjecture.

The third critical club is the heaviest and most damaging: the
first link in Hodel's chain of evidence is the weakest. The book's

critics have justifiably assailed his confident identification of those two photographs in his father's album. It's unclear that they both depict the same woman, let alone that the woman is Elizabeth Short. Hodel claims he reached his conclusion after examining numerous photos of Short on the Internet, but apart from the dust jacket, his book presents no bona fide images of Short for comparison. This one gaping hole in his reasoning is especially unfortunate since the circumstantial case he builds is otherwise so strong. Though the photos are what caused him to reconsider the Black Dahlia case and his father's possible involvement, his whole case does not depend upon their authenticity.

Apart from the glib photo identification, Hodel's most doubtful venture is his treatment of painter and photographer Man Ray, who lived in Los Angeles at the time of the crimes and reportedly was a close friend of Dr. Hodel. Steve Hodel contends that his father posed the body of the Black Dahlia in homage to some of Man Ray's artistic work and their shared enthusiasm for the Marquis de Sade. The claim is not fully convincing and has the unfortunate effect of making Man Ray appear almost a co-conspirator.

Hodel obviously is not required to make an iron clad case connecting his father and Fred Sexton to every crime mentioned in his book, and the connections understandably vary in persuasiveness. Still, reasoning that is far-fetched or obviously erroneous serves to cast further doubt on his main case. For example, Hodel compares one of his father's typewritten letters with one purportedly from the killer of Georgette Bauerdorf, victim of a 1944 bathtub murder. Hodel assumes that using a double hyphen to represent a dash is somehow unusual. On the contrary, it is standard. Word processing programs do it automatically.

Few of Hodel's most outspoken critics have been willing to look objectively at the evidence and admit that at least parts of his case are persuasive. Some of these critics owe allegiance to Gilmore, including novelist Gary Indiana, who reviewed Hodel's book dismissively for the *Los Angeles Times Book Review* after contributing a glowing cover blurb to *Severed*. Gilmore himself has been among those quoted as disputing Hodel's photo identification. His book has more pictures of Short for comparison, including a particularly gruesome post-mortem head shot—and no, Gilmore's selections look no more like the pictures in Dr. Hodel's album than does the shot of Short on Steve Hodel's dust jacket.

So what is the final verdict on *Black Dahlia Avenger*? Its accounts of cover-ups and civic corruption are all too believable, and much of the circumstantial evidence it presents against George Hodel is persuasive. Still, the more fanciful speculations along with that dubious first step taint its authority. Has Steve Hodel solved the case? I think so, but he has some tidying up to do for the paperback edition. Perhaps the next Dahlia book should be an objective assessment of all the competing theories by someone without a dramatic new suspect to advance. But that approach doesn't make for bestsellers.

Postscript 2008: Hodel did in fact include additional material to strengthen his case, along with pictures of Elizabeth Short, in the paperback edition. One writer who believes his solution is Orson Welles biographer Simon Callow, who examines the evidence against Welles with some admiration in Orson Welles: Hello Americans *(2006) before averring that Hodel's conclusion is definitive.*

INDEX

Abbot, Anthony, 197
Abraham, Henry, 255
Abramsen, David, 278
Ade, George, 255
Aird, Catherine, 113, 240
Akunin, Boris, 113
Albert, Susan Wittig, 9, 176
Aldrich, Ann, 88
Aleas, Richard, 113
Allen, Steve, 191
Allingham, Margery, 46, 67, 238, 239
Amanda Cross, 125
Ambler, Eric, 184, 241, 271
Anderson, Edward, 23
Anderson, James, 114
Ardai, Charles, 113
Armstrong, Charlotte, 182, 184
Asch, Penelope, 198
Astray, Millán de, 102
Austen, Jane, 146, 174, 184
Avallone, Michael, 83
Axton, David, 144
Bachman, Richard, 143
Bailey, H.C., 237
Bain, Donald, 9, 189, 192
Baker, Josephine, 59
Baldwin, James, 59
Ball, John, 4, 114, 216
Ballard, Todhunter, 252
Bandy, Franklin, 251
Barnard, Robert, 115, 240
Barnes, Linda, 217
Barnum, P.T., 175
Barr, Nevada, 199, 208
Barr, Robert, 235
Barratt, F.M., 31
Barzun, Jacques, 44, 108
Bauerdorf, Georgette, 287
Bechet, Sidney, 59
Beinhart, Larry, 229
Bell, Joseph, 174

Bentley, E.C., 195, 235
Berkeley, Anthony, 46, 195, 237, 241, 243
Bernhardt, William, 186, 195, 200
Biddle, Cordelia Frances, 186
Bierce, Ambrose, 176
Biggers, Earl Derr, 29, 218
Billheimer, John, 208
Blake, Nicholas, 67, 239, 244
Blanc, Nero, 9, 185, 186
Blatty, William Peter, 218
Block, Lawrence, 116, 197, 217, 229, 253
Bodkin, M. McDonnell, 234
Borden, Lizzie, 205, 283
Boswell, James, 173
Bottum, Joseph, 13, 61, 255
Boucher, Anthony, 12, 83, 87, 88, 90, 91, 94, 105, 109, 182, 200, 204, 261
Bowen, Michael, 116
Brackett, Leigh, 184, 190
Bramah, Ernest, 235
Brand, Eleanor Taylor, 218
Braun, Lilian Jackson, 204
Breen, Jon, 13
Breen, Rita, 13
Brett, Simon, 117, 127, 201
Brontë, Charlotte, 242
Brontë, Emily, 184
Brown, Dan, 271
Brown, Fredric, 114
Bruen, Ken, 117, 244
Buchanan, Edna, 198, 203
Bullett, Gerald, 243
Burger, Knox, 250
Burke, James Lee, 18, 118, 163
Burnett, W.R., 23
Burroughs, Edgar Rice, 177
Cadett, Herbert, 234

JON L. BREEN is the author of eight novels and around a hundred short stories, along with many critical articles and book reviews. He won Edgar Awards from Mystery Writers of America for *What About Murder: A Guide to Books about Mystery and Detective Fiction* (1981) and *Novel Verdicts: A Guide to Courtroom Fiction* (1984). His 1988 novel *Touch of the Past* was shortlisted for the Crime Writers Association's Dagger Awards. Breen's most recent short story collection is *Kill the Umpire: The Calls of Ed Gorgon* (Crippen & Landru, 2003). His most recent novels are *Eye of God* (Perseverance, 2006) and *Probable Claus* (Five Star, forthcoming in 2009). Proprietor of the "Jury Box" column in *Ellery Queen's Mystery Magazine,* he is also a frequent contributor to *Mystery Scene* and *The Weekly Standard.* Retired as a librarian and professor of English at Rio Hondo College, he lives in Fountain Valley, California, with his wife, Rita A. Breen, with whom he edited the 1986 anthology *American Murders.*

RAMBLE HOUSE's
HARRY STEPHEN KEELER WEBWORK MYSTERIES
(RH) indicates the title is available ONLY in the RAMBLE HOUSE edition

The Ace of Spades Murder
The Affair of the Bottled Deuce (RH)
The Amazing Web
The Barking Clock
Behind That Mask
The Book with the Orange Leaves
The Bottle with the Green Wax Seal
The Box from Japan
The Case of the Canny Killer
The Case of the Crazy Corpse (RH)
The Case of the Flying Hands (RH)
The Case of the Ivory Arrow
The Case of the Jeweled Ragpicker
The Case of the Lavender Gripsack
The Case of the Mysterious Moll
The Case of the 16 Beans
The Case of the Transparent Nude (RH)
The Case of the Transposed Legs
The Case of the Two-Headed Idiot (RH)
The Case of the Two Strange Ladies
The Circus Stealers (RH)
Cleopatra's Tears
A Copy of Beowulf (RH)
The Crimson Cube (RH)
The Face of the Man From Saturn
Find the Clock
The Five Silver Buddhas
The 4th King
The Gallows Waits, My Lord! (RH)
The Green Jade Hand
Finger! Finger!
Hangman's Nights (RH)
I, Chameleon (RH)
I Killed Lincoln at 10:13! (RH)
The Iron Ring
The Man Who Changed His Skin (RH)
The Man with the Crimson Box
The Man with the Magic Eardrums
The Man with the Wooden Spectacles
The Marceau Case
The Matilda Hunter Murder
The Monocled Monster

The Murder of London Lew
The Murdered Mathematician
The Mysterious Card (RH)
The Mysterious Ivory Ball of Wong Shing
   Li (RH)
The Mystery of the Fiddling Cracksman
The Peacock Fan
The Photo of Lady X (RH)
The Portrait of Jirjohn Cobb
Report on Vanessa Hewstone (RH)
Riddle of the Travelling Skull
Riddle of the Wooden Parrakeet (RH)
The Scarlet Mummy (RH)
The Search for X-Y-Z
The Sharkskin Book
Sing Sing Nights
The Six From Nowhere (RH)
The Skull of the Waltzing Clown
The Spectacles of Mr. Cagliostro
Stand By—London Calling!
The Steeltown Strangler
The Stolen Gravestone (RH)
Strange Journey (RH)
The Strange Will
The Straw Hat Murders (RH)
The Street of 1000 Eyes (RH)
Thieves' Nights
Three Novellos (RH)
The Tiger Snake
The Trap (RH)
Vagabond Nights (Defrauded Yeggman)
Vagabond Nights 2 (10 Hours)
The Vanishing Gold Truck
The Voice of the Seven Sparrows
The Washington Square Enigma
When Thief Meets Thief
The White Circle (RH)
The Wonderful Scheme of Mr. Christopher
   Thorne
X. Jones—of Scotland Yard
Y. Cheung, Business Detective

Keeler Related Works

A To Izzard: A Harry Stephen Keeler Companion by Fender Tucker — Articles and stories about Harry, by Harry, and in his style. Included is a compleat bibliography.

Wild About Harry: Reviews of Keeler Novels — Edited by Richard Polt & Fender Tucker — 22 reviews of works by Harry Stephen Keeler from *Keeler News*. A perfect introduction to the author.

The Keeler Keyhole Collection: Annotated newsletter rants from Harry Stephen Keeler, edited by Francis M. Nevins. Over 400 pages of incredibly personal Keeleriana.

Fakealoo — Pastiches of the style of Harry Stephen Keeler by selected demented members of the HSK Society. Updated every year with the new winner.

RAMBLE HOUSE's OTHER LOONS

Mysterious Martin, the Master of Murder — Two versions of a strange 1912 novel by Tod Robbins about a man who writes books that can kill.

The Master of Mysteries — 1912 novel of supernatural sleuthing by Gelett Burgess

Dago Red — 22 tales of dark suspense by Bill Pronzini

The Night Remembers — A 1991 Jack Walsh mystery from Ed Gorman

Rough Cut & New, Improved Murder — Ed Gorman's first two novels

Four Gelett Burgess Novels — *The Master of Mysteries, The White Cat, Two O'Clock Courage, Ladies in Boxes,* with more to come from Surinam Turtle Press

The Organ Reader — A huge compilation of just about everything published in the 1971-1972 radical bay-area newspaper, *THE ORGAN*.

A Clear Path to Cross — Sharon Knowles short mystery stories by Ed Lynskey

Old Times' Sake — Short stories by James Reasoner from Mike Shayne Magazine

Freaks and Fantasies — Eerie tales by Tod Robbins, collaborator of Tod Browning on the film FREAKS.

Four Jim Harmon Sleaze Double Novels — *Vixen Hollow/Celluloid Scandal, The Man Who Made Maniacs/Silent Siren, Ape Rape/Wanton Witch* and *Sex Burns Like Fire/Twist Session.* More doubles to come!

Marblehead: A Novel of H.P. Lovecraft — A long-lost masterpiece from Richard A. Lupoff. Published for the first time!

The Compleat Ova Hamlet — Parodies of SF authors by Richard A. Lupoff – New edition!

The Secret Adventures of Sherlock Holmes — Three Sherlockian pastiches by the Brooklyn author/publisher, Gary Lovisi.

The Universal Holmes — Richard A. Lupoff's 2007 collection of five Holmesian pastiches and a recipe for giant rat stew.

Four Joel Townsley Rogers Novels — By the author of *The Red Right Hand: Once In a Red Moon, Lady With the Dice, The Stopped Clock, Never Leave My Bed*

Two Joel Townsley Rogers Story Collections — Night of Horror and Killing Time

Twenty Norman Berrow Novels — *The Bishop's Sword, Ghost House, Don't Go Out After Dark, Claws of the Cougar, The Smokers of Hashish, The Secret Dancer, Don't Jump Mr. Boland!, The Footprints of Satan, Fingers for Ransom, The Three Tiers of Fantasy, The Spaniard's Thumb, The Eleventh Plague, Words Have Wings, One Thrilling Night, The Lady's in Danger, It Howls at Night, The Terror in the Fog, Oil Under the Window, Murder in the Melody, The Singing Room*

The N. R. De Mexico Novels — Robert Bragg presents *Marijuana Girl, Madman on a Drum, Private Chauffeur* in one volume.

Four Chelsea Quinn Yarbro Novels featuring Charlie Moon — *Ogilvie, Tallant and Moon, Music When the Sweet Voice Dies, Poisonous Fruit* and *Dead Mice*

The Green Toad — Impossible mysteries by Walter S. Masterman — More to come!

Two Hake Talbot Novels — *Rim of the Pit, The Hangman's Handyman.* Classic locked room mysteries.

Two Alexander Laing Novels — *The Motives of Nicholas Holtz* and *Dr. Scarlett,* stories of medical mayhem and intrigue from the 30s.

Four David Hume Novels — *Corpses Never Argue, Cemetery First Stop, Make Way for the Mourners, Eternity Here I Come,* and more to come.

Three Wade Wright Novels — *Echo of Fear, Death At Nostalgia Street* and *It Leads to Murder,* with more to come!

Four Rupert Penny Novels — *Policeman's Holiday, Policeman's Evidence, Lucky Policeman* and *Sealed Room Murder,* classic impossible mysteries.

Five Jack Mann Novels — Strange murder in the English countryside. *Gees' First Case, Nightmare Farm, Grey Shapes, The Ninth Life, The Glass Too Many.*

Six Max Afford Novels — *Owl of Darkness, Death's Mannikins, Blood on His Hands, The Dead Are Blind, The Sheep and the Wolves* and *Sinners in Paradise* by One of Australia's finest novelists.

Five Joseph Shallit Novels — *The Case of the Billion Dollar Body, Lady Don't Die on My Doorstep, Kiss the Killer, Yell Bloody Murder, Take Your Last Look.* One of America's best 50's authors.

Two Crimson Clown Novels — By Johnston McCulley, author of the Zorro novels, *The Crimson Clown* and *The Crimson Clown Again.*

The Best of 10-Story Book — edited by Chris Mikul, over 35 stories from the literary magazine Harry Stephen Keeler edited.

A Young Man's Heart — A forgotten early classic by Cornell Woolrich

The Anthony Boucher Chronicles — edited by Francis M. Nevins
Book reviews by Anthony Boucher written for the *San Francisco Chronicle,* 1942 – 1947. Essential and fascinating reading.

Muddled Mind: Complete Works of Ed Wood, Jr. — David Hayes and Hayden Davis deconstruct the life and works of a mad genius.

Gadsby — A lipogram (a novel without the letter E). Ernest Vincent Wright's last work, published in 1939 right before his death.

My First Time: The One Experience You Never Forget — Michael Birchwood — 64 true first-person narratives of how they lost it.

The Black Box — Stylish 1908 classic by M. P. Shiel. Very hard to find.

The Incredible Adventures of Rowland Hern — Rousing 1928 impossible crimes by Nicholas Olde.

Slammer Days — Two full-length prison memoirs: *Men into Beasts* (1952) by George Sylvester Viereck and *Home Away From Home* (1962) by Jack Woodford

Beat Books #1 — Two beatnik classics, *A Sea of Thighs* by Ray Kainen and *Village Hipster* by J.X. Williams

Ruled By Radio — 1925 futuristic novel by Robert L. Hadfield & Frank E. Farncombe

Murder in Silk — A 1937 Yellow Peril novel of the silk trade by Ralph Trevor

The Case of the Withered Hand — 1936 potboiler by John G. Brandon

Inclination to Murder — 1966 thriller by New Zealand's Harriet Hunter

Invaders from the Dark — Classic werewolf tale from Greye La Spina

Fatal Accident — Murder by automobile, a 1936 mystery by Cecil M. Wills

The Devil Drives — A prison and lost treasure novel by Virgil Markham

Dr. Odin — Douglas Newton's 1933 potboiler comes back to life.

The Chinese Jar Mystery — Murder in the manor by John Stephen Strange, 1934

The Julius Caesar Murder Case — A classic 1935 re-telling of the assassination by Wallace Irwin that's much more fun than the Shakespeare version

West Texas War and Other Western Stories — by Gary Lovisi

The Contested Earth and Other SF Stories — A never-before published space opera and seven short stories by Jim Harmon.

Tales of the Macabre and Ordinary — Modern twisted horror by Chris Mikul, author of the *Bizarrism* series.

The Gold Star Line — Seaboard adventure from L.T. Reade and Robert Eustace.

The Werewolf vs the Vampire Woman — Hard to believe ultraviolence by either Arthur M. Scarm or Arthur M. Scram.

Black Hogan Strikes Again — Australia's Peter Renwick pens a tale of the outback.

Don Diablo: Book of a Lost Film — Two-volume treatment of a western by Paul Landres, with diagrams. Intro by Francis M. Nevins.

The Charlie Chaplin Murder Mystery — Movie hijinks by Wes D. Gehring

The Koky Comics — A collection of all of the 1978-1981 Sunday and daily comic strips by Richard O'Brien and Mort Gerberg, in two volumes.

Suzy — Another collection of comic strips from Richard O'Brien and Bob Vojtko

Dime Novels: Ramble House's 10-Cent Books — *Knife in the Dark* by Robert Leslie Bellem, *Hot Lead* and *Song of Death* by Ed Earl Repp, *A Hashish House in New York* by H.H. Kane, and five more.

Blood in a Snap — The *Finnegan's Wake* of the 21st century, by Jim Weiler and Al Gorithm

Stakeout on Millennium Drive — Award-winning Indianapolis Noir — Ian Woollen.

Dope Tales #1 — Two dope-riddled classics; *Dope Runners* by Gerald Grantham and *Death Takes the Joystick* by Phillip Condé.

Dope Tales #2 — Two more narco-classics; *The Invisible Hand* by Rex Dark and *The Smokers of Hashish* by Norman Berrow.

Dope Tales #3 — Two enchanting novels of opium by the master, Sax Rohmer. *Dope* and *The Yellow Claw.*

Tenebrae — Ernest G. Henham's 1898 horror tale brought back.

The Singular Problem of the Stygian House-Boat — Two classic tales by John Kendrick Bangs about the denizens of Hades.

Tiresias — Psychotic modern horror novel by Jonathan M. Sweet.

The One After Snelling — Kickass modern noir from Richard O'Brien.

The Sign of the Scorpion — 1935 Edmund Snell tale of oriental evil.

The House of the Vampire — 1907 poetic thriller by George S. Viereck.

An Angel in the Street — Modern hardboiled noir by Peter Genovese.

The Devil's Mistress — Scottish gothic tale by J. W. Brodie-Innes.

The Lord of Terror — 1925 mystery with master-criminal, Fantômas.

The Lady of the Terraces — 1925 adventure by E. Charles Vivian.

My Deadly Angel — 1955 Cold War drama by John Chelton

Prose Bowl — Futuristic satire — Bill Pronzini & Barry N. Malzberg .

Satan's Den Exposed — True crime in Truth or Consequences New Mexico — Award-winning journalism by the *Desert Journal*.

The Amorous Intrigues & Adventures of Aaron Burr — by Anonymous — Hot historical action.

I Stole $16,000,000 — A true story by cracksman Herbert E. Wilson.

The Black Dark Murders — Vintage 50s college murder yarn by Milt Ozaki, writing as Robert O. Saber.

Sex Slave — Potboiler of lust in the days of Cleopatra — Dion Leclerq.

You'll Die Laughing — Bruce Elliott's 1945 novel of murder at a practical joker's English countryside manor.

The Private Journal & Diary of John H. Surratt — The memoirs of the man who conspired to assassinate President Lincoln.

Dead Man Talks Too Much — Hollywood boozer by Weed Dickenson

Red Light — History of legal prostitution in Shreveport Louisiana by Eric Brock. Includes wonderful photos of the houses and the ladies.

A Snark Selection — Lewis Carroll's *The Hunting of the Snark* with two Snarkian chapters by Harry Stephen Keeler — Illustrated by Gavin L. O'Keefe.

Ripped from the Headlines! — The Jack the Ripper story as told in the newspaper articles in the *New York* and *London Times*.

Geronimo — S. M. Barrett's 1905 autobiography of a noble American.

The White Peril in the Far East — Sidney Lewis Gulick's 1905 indictment of the West and assurance that Japan would never attack the U.S.

The Compleat Calhoon — All of Fender Tucker's works: Includes *The Totah Trilogy, Weed, Women and Song* and *Tales from the Tower,* plus a CD of all of his songs.

RAMBLE HOUSE
Fender Tucker, Prop.
www.ramblehouse.com   fender@ramblehouse.com
318-455-6847   10325 Sheepshead Drive, Vancleave MS 39565